D0642636

THE OUTSIDER

THE OUTSIDER

PREJUDICE AND POLITICS IN ITALY

Paul M. Sniderman

Pierangelo Peri

Rui J. P. de Figueiredo, Jr.

Thomas Piazza

WITHDRAWN

UTSA LIBRARIES

PRINCETON UNIVERSITY PRESS   PRINCETON AND OXFORD

Copyright © 2000 by Princeton University Press
Published by Princeton University Press, 41 William Street,
Princeton, New Jersey 08540
In the United Kingdom: Princeton University Press,
3 Market Place, Woodstock, Oxfordshire OX20 1SY
All Rights Reserved

Second printing, and first paperback printing, 2002
Paperback ISBN 0-691-09497-7

The Library of Congress has cataloged the cloth edition of this book as follows

The outsider : prejudice and politics in Italy / Paul M. Sniderman, et al.
p.   cm.
Includes bibliographical references and index.
ISBN 0-691-04839-8 (CL : alk. paper)
1. Italy—Race relations. 2. Italy—Ethnic relations. 3. Racism—Italy.
4. Italy—Emigration and immigration. 5. Culture conflict—Italy.
6. Italy—Social conditions—1976–1994. 7. Italy—Social
conditions—1994– I. Sniderman, Paul M.
DG455.O96 2000
303.3′8751—dc21   99-089723

British Library Cataloging-in-Publication Data is available

This book has been composed in Galliard

Printed on acid-free paper. ∞

www.pupress.princeton.edu

Printed in the United States of America

3   5   7   9   10   8   6   4   2

Library
University of Texas
at San Antonio

To Madame Isabelle de Vienne

Contents

Acknowledgments

IN THE BEGINNING our orientation was critical. Contemporary theories of prejudice were too "social," we were persuaded. They left out the individual. Our objective was correspondingly modest—to strike a fairer balance and show that individual factors as well as social ones played a role. But the more we read of contemporary approaches—above all, the more we reflected on the contribution of Henri Tajfel—the more persuaded we were that he, not we, was right. He was not right on every point—certainly not about the irrelevance of personality, as an abundance of statistical analyses will show—but right nonetheless about the heart of the matter. This, then, is the story of a discovery stamped with ironies: on our side, that in setting out to show Tajfel and his colleagues to be wrong, we found that prejudice could be understood best through the lens of their work; on their side, that the very mechanism that they thought crucially underpins the social basis of prejudice, "categorization" as they have labeled it, in fact makes intelligible the impact of the factor that they insisted was irrelevant, namely, personality. And if we reject the idea of sides, a theoretical perspective emerges, integrating a whole medley of approaches—theirs, ours, and others besides.

Carrying out a national survey, and doing so with a multinational team of investigators, requires many helping—and generous—hands. Our largest debt is to the University of Trento and, more particularly, to the following people: Fulvio Zuelli, who, as rector of the University of Trento, encouraged and funded the principal portion of our study; Antonio Schizzerotto who, as dean of the Sociology Faculty, strongly supported the project and, as research colleague, got this project off the ground; Carlo Buzzi, Francesca Sartori, Barbara Ongari, and Renato Porro, our colleagues at Trento, whose ideas contributed to the development of the research instrument and whose encouragement helped in the completion of the work; Mario Callegaro, whose energy, patience, and hard work as supervisor of interviewing was indispensable; and the Department of Sociology and Social Research of the University of Trento, which provided both financial support and a hospitable environment for the project. Finally, we very gratefully thank the Fondazione Caritro and its president, Giovanni Pegoretti, for their financial contribution to our International Conference in 1995.

We are indebted as well to Stanford University and more particularly to the Institute for International Studies, which made it possible for us to teach as well as do research on Italian politics; to the Center for European Studies, which supported our International Conference; and, above all, to Walter Falcon who, as director of the Institute of International Studies, stood behind both. We also want to thank Norman Nie, director of the Stanford Institute of Quantitative Studies of Society, for support and encouragement in completion of the manuscript. Our partners in this study, as in its predecessors, were the Computer-assisted Survey Methods Program (CSM) at the University of California at Berkeley, under the leadership of J. Merrill Shanks, and the Survey Research Center (SRC) at Berkeley, under the leadership of Michael Hout. The SRC assisted in the design of the instrument, and all of the special features of the interview schedules were made possible by the CASES program developed by CSM. Finally, we owe a special debt to the Institute of Personality and Social Research at the University of California. The expertise of those at the institute, together with a unique archive of validational studies of personality, has been indispensable.

Our debts to individuals are as large as those to institutions. For counsel on issues of measurement and estimation we want to thank Brian Gaines, Paul Gertler, and James Wiley and, for going well beyond the duties of collegiality, Henry Brady, Douglas Rivers and Peer Scheepers. Zach Elkins was indispensable in the last lap, replicating our model over a whole medley of measurement assumptions. Above all, we are in debt to Louk Hagendoorn of the University of Utrecht and Philip Tetlock of the Ohio State University for a stream of suggestions, both critical and constructive; indeed, we have so often taken their advice that we are fully prepared to email any criticisms straight on to them. We are grateful to our families for both their generous and unstinting assistance on this study (some even going so far as to accompany us on the fieldwork) and, not less important, their gracious but unyielding insistence that we bring this work to a finish. In particular, we should like to acknowledge and thank Teresa Peri, Rui and Isabel de Figueiredo, Mary Crosby, and Susan Sniderman.

It may seem inappropriate to single out for appreciation one person in particular, since we are obliged to many for so much. But were it not for the way that she spontaneously and ingeniously marshaled the resources of the Institut d'Études Politiques de Paris, this book would not have been written. To mark our gratitude for the generosity that makes possible an international community of scholars, we gratefully dedicate this book to Madame Isabelle de Vienne.

THE OUTSIDER

CHAPTER 1

Introduction

TWO STORIES, both reported in a Milan newspaper, the *Corriere Della Sera*:[1] The first comes from Genoa and the latter from Rome:

> [A]t 3 o'clock in the morning, Samlal Ali, a 24-year-old Moroccan, was selling cigarettes to passers-by. A car with four youths inside stopped in front of him. The man sitting next to the driver leaned out and said something to the Moroccan. He then grabbed him by the neck and pulled his head into the car. Then, at 80 kph, the Moroccan was dragged along the asphalt for a kilometer, hanging onto the car, his head trapped in the window, crashing into parked cars, rubbish bins, and lamp-posts. The men in the car hit him repeatedly. The nightmare was only ended when the car was stopped by a police patrol. The four men, Massimiliano Bordonaro and Constantino Carta, both 23, Davide Cavallaro, 18, and Giovanni Mariani, 30, have been arrested for attempted murder.

> [T]wo Egyptians were attacked by a group of seven skinheads. One of them, Phami Sbavvio, 33, was treated at the Grassi hospital for cuts and grazes on his arms and legs. This assault happened at just after one o'clock in Viale delle Repubbliche Marinare as the two foreigners were on their way home. The gang was probably waiting in ambush like the one sprung on the young leftists the other week, when the former secretary of the WWF Fabio Converto was left bleeding on the ground in the front of the station. With his fair hair he had been mistaken for a Pole. And yesterday, once again in front of the Ostia station, a group of skinheads wearing bomber jackets casually told a TV crew, 'They did well to whack that Tunisian. They come over here, take our jobs and steal our women.'
> Yesterday evening, the mayor Francesco Rutelli appealed to all Romans not 'to tolerate this brutal and mindless violence.' Also because between now and the elections the Wild West of Ostia-Fiumicino is liable to explode. Standing for the Right is the ex-fascist Teodoro Buontempo . . . who has never concealed his sympathies for the skinhead Nazis.

Only two stories in a newspaper, but they drive home the depth of the problem. It is again a time of refugees in Western Europe. They are making their way from former colonies of the West in Africa and Asia and of Russia in Eastern Europe, attempting to escape poverty or find asylum, sometimes intending to return, sometimes not. Many have found refuge, contributing to the countries that have given them sanctuary. But a storm has been gathering around them. Its force is felt, most conspicuously, in acts of violence committed by individuals clumped at the periphery of contemporary European societies. Less visibly but no less consequentially, political institutions at their center show the stress. These strains of intolerance—their strength, their deeper-lying sources, their impact on the politics of the society as a whole—deserve exploration.

STARTING POINTS

Two problems provided the point of departure for our study. The first concerns the distinctive status of race in marking others as outsiders. Even people who are diligently unreflective have shown themselves capable of impressive powers of imagination in finding, or formulating, lines to mark off those who belong to their group and those who do not. Over a range of historical conflicts, however, a limited number of cleavages have been particularly prominent—among them, class, religion, ethnicity, and nationality, and last, but hardly least, race.

Whatever was true of other eras, it seemed to us that differences of race now cut deeper. In taking this view, we did not doubt the divisiveness of other cleavages, particularly ethnicity and nationality. With the myriad clashes from Yugoslavia through Rwanda, it would call for a special measure of obtuseness to overlook the murderous variety of group differences. Yet, differences of race, we reasoned, can be stigmatizing in a way that other differences need not be. However long African immigrants live in their new country, however well they learn its language, with however much self-restraint and dignity they bear the blows that fall on them, they are marked off by their color. Just so far as they are visibly different, they cannot escape notice of their difference. And the visible sign of their difference, the color of their skin, is indiscriminately connected to a complex of associations—emotional, symbolic, historical, even psychosexual—so much so as to make blacks specially vulnerable to the prejudices of others. All who have come from outside a society aiming to make their way within it labor under a burden of prejudice. But blacks, we feared, bear a heavier burden.

The second problem has to do with the roots of prejudice. It once was common to conceive of prejudice as an intrinsically—and narrowly—psychological phenomenon. So conceived, prejudice was not connected to the actual world, to the frictions, abrasions, and conflicts for the limited goods on offer, whether material or symbolic. Prejudice was psychological in the specific sense of being irrational, and both psychological and irrational in the still narrower sense of being principally rooted in the interior lives of individuals, in the inner conflicts and emotional wounds that they suffered in the course of their early development rather than in the stream of their experiences as adults in the larger society and economy.

But fashions in explanation come and go. Psychological analyses in general, and personality-centered ones in particular, have fallen out of style. Once familiar chords of explanation—of authoritarian submission and dominance, of overcontrolling fathers and overwhelmed children, of dogmatism and intolerance of ambiguity—now have a recognizable quality of quaintness, where they are recognized at all. No form of explanation, it is true, disappears entirely from the market of ideas, and it is part and parcel of the ordinary commerce of social science for those versed in one form of analytic transaction to think little of those who practice another. It is therefore all the more striking that it is psychologists themselves who have undertaken root-and-branch critiques of personality-based analyses of prejudice[2] and that even their canonical reviews of prejudice research now pay only perfunctory attention to personality-centered explanations, summarizing the work, it almost seems, out of historical courtesy.[3] The explanatory parade has marched on, with considerations of group identity and group interest, the social, the cognitive, and the economic, taking the lead and personality factors lagging far behind. Yet the new perspectives, illuminating as they are, nonetheless seemed to us to miss the distinctively irrational, emotional, and expressive character of prejudice highlighted by the classical personality-centered perspective. So we took as one of our principal objectives the aim of demonstrating that prejudice is rooted less in the actual interplay of social and economic life than in the deep-lying folds of individuals' psychological makeup.

This book is a record of how, under the pressure of our own results, we have been required, if not to reject then fundamentally rethink both of the major ideas we held at the start.

FORMS OF PREJUDICE: THE "SWITCH" EXPERIMENT

There is, regrettably, no shortage of sites for a study of prejudice and politics. France, for example, is an obvious possibility. The National Front, under Jean LePen, openly campaigns on a plank of returning France to the French, working to incite hostility toward immigrants, not to mention taking pride in a succession of anti-Semitic thrusts. The Front, moreover, has continued to increase its margin of popular support, now approaching one out of every six or seven votes, in the process acquiring sufficient electoral strength to splinter the traditional right in the most recent regional elections. Germany is an equally obvious site.

The German People's Union, a party on the far right running on an antiforeigner and anti-European platform, made a striking breakthrough in the German state of Saxony-Anhalt; and Eastern Germany generally, not to mention a swath of Western Germany, has been pockmarked by skinhead violence and public agitation against immigrants. For that matter, Austria, with its thick history of anti-Semitism and the transformation of the traditionally conservative Freedom Party, in the 1980s, to a party of the extreme right, surely has much to recommend it as a site for the study of prejudice and politics. Then, too, Belgium, with its deepening internal divisions and the ballooning of support for the "Flemish Block," appears nearer crisis than any of the others.

All of these countries illustrate two crucial conditions for the study of prejudice and politics. The first is a deep strain of intolerance, in Western Europe now characteristically focused on immigrants or foreigners. The second is the emergence of at least one political party publicly committed to mobilizing public resentment against immigrants or foreigners. The second condition matters as much as the first. To realize the full potential of the politics of prejudice and group conflict, private grievances need a public vehicle.

Italy satisfies the first condition, and not merely because of the rash of hate acts against immigrants. Charges that immigrants are sopping up public benefits have become routine; so, too, have claims that immigrants promote crime, spread disease, and increase unemployment. Italy satisfies the second condition, too. Intolerance has visibly leached from the margins of the political system to very near its center. In the mid-1990s at least three of the political parties—Alleanza Nazionale, the Lega Nord, and Forza Italia—bid for public support by campaigning against the new immigrants. In a way inconceivable in the United States for all the nativism of the American tradition, political argumentation in Italy can be xenophobic and chauvinistic; and it is difficult to believe that the wave of prejudice against immigrants has crested.

But to understand the forces responsible for this eruption of intolerance, it first is necessary to fix what constitutes prejudice. How should it be defined? Can prejudice be pinned down? And what distinguishes a person who is prejudiced from one who is not? On the face of it, the answers to these questions are straightforward. There may be problems at a practical level. Perhaps because of the pressure to say the socially acceptable thing, perhaps because of the lack of time, it may not be possible to pin down the level of prejudice toward a particular group in a standard public opinion interview. And out of a concern for theoretical fastidiousness, some definitional crossing of t's and dotting of i's no doubt is in order. But a consensus has been reached on the core meaning of prejudice.

This consensus summarizes what thoughtful people have come to believe constitutes the heart of prejudice and it includes such obvious features as sterotyping, thinking ill of others without justification, and rigidity. But how to think about prejudice is, we have become persuaded, a question that should be thought through again. Speaking in the abstract, it sounds reasonable to say that prejudice involves characterizations of others that are stereotypical. Yet who is to say which characterizations are stereotypical? Are there truly objective standards to determine which assertions about groups, apart from the indisputably pathological, are true and which are false? And if there are not, is the definition of prejudice only a matter of convention, of political correctness if you will?

Our concern is not about the meaning of words. Our concern is to clarify the meaning of prejudice so that we can pick it out in the actual world and catch hold of that in which it truly consists. And the view that we take of prejudice, which we detail in the next chapter, has turned out to have potentially profound implications about the nature of prejudice that we did not see at all at the start.

We started with the presumption that for all the varieties of group conflict, the cleavage over race—the cleavage between black and white, above all—has defined the most fundamental terms in which we approach issues of bigotry and discrimination at the end of the century. Saying this may give the impression of being ethnocentric about ethnocentrism itself, implying that the problem of intolerance cannot rightly be understood outside of an American context. All that we can say is that in our research project in Italy, all who took part, Italians as much as Americans, believed that blacks must bear a special burden by virtue of being black.

Indeed, our shared conviction that differences of race are specially stigmatizing was our common reason for selecting Italy as a site for the study of prejudice and politics. For there are two distinct streams of immigration, one from Africa—from Morocco, Tunisia, Algeria, Senegal, and Somalia—the other from Eastern Europe—from Poland, Albania, and the former Yugoslavia. The first stream of immigrants is thus very largely (though not completely) black; the second, white. Here, then, is a natural experiment. Immigrants, whether from Africa or Eastern Europe, bear a burden of intolerance by virtue of being immigrants. But if we show that immigrants to Italy who are black bear a heavier burden by virtue of being black, then we should demonstrate that differences of race cut deeper than differences of ethnicity or nationality.

This idea of the special burden of blacks was one of the animating hypotheses of our study, though to speak of it as a hypothesis does not capture our certainty of its truth at the start of the study. All of us were sure it was so, and we only went about the business of conducting an experiment to demonstrate it was so because knowing something to be the case is not a substitute for showing it to be the case. So we took advantage of computer-assisted interviewing to conduct a specially designed experiment, the "Switch" experiment, in order to drive home the distinctiveness of race.

There is a standard litany of praises for genuinely randomized experiments, and no doubt we would have recited it just as others have but for the "Switch" experiment. So, before seeing the results of this experiment, we would have said that experiments have the power to persuade because they have the power to surprise—the power, that is, to demonstrate convincingly that the world is not as it has habitually been taken to be. But in speaking of the power of experiments to surprise we would tacitly have had in mind that it is others who would be caught up to find the world is not as they too confidently assumed it to be. In fact, it turned out that the results of the "Switch" experiment took us by surprise. Although it was designed to demonstrate that differences of race cut deeper than those of ethnicity and nationality, it instead showed that the wave of prejudice and group conflict now washing over Western Europe is more menacing than has been recognized because the readiness to categorize others as belonging to a group other than one's own is more indiscriminate than we had imagined.

This indiscriminateness throws a new light, we believe, on the nature of prejudice, exposing the fundamental sense in which prejudice truly is blind. For it is not, in the end, about the particular ways in which a group either is different or is said to be different; it is instead, at its core, about the fact that it is judged to be different. It is, we think, important to work toward a stronger grip on the nature of contemporary forms of intolerance. But we shall argue that prejudice, in addition to deserving attention in its own right, also merits attention because its consequences, when they spill over into politics, are not merely individual but societal.

THE VULNERABILITY OF THE LEFT: THE "RIGHT SHOCK" MODEL

It is the conviction of every informed observer that the eruption of anger and resentment over immigrants in Western Europe strengthens the hand of the political right there. Our results agree. But they go farther by exposing the basis of the vulnerability of the left.

The pivot point of our account is a cluster of values, including the importance of guaranteeing order, upholding authority, maintaining discipline, which we label "authority" values. This cluster of values is part of the core platform of the political right; and what is more, commentators on the right as well as the left would agree that they can provide a political base for opposition to immigrants and immigration. The rhetoric of immigrants' intruding their foreign customs and manners into daily life, of taking jobs away from native citizens, and of profiting from public assistance all resonate naturally and effectively with the right's emphasis on order, authority, and tradition. So very nearly everyone believes and so we shall show.

The core of our contribution consists of two further lines of argument. The first concerns the character of the causal connection between authority values and prejudice. It is standardly argued that the more firmly and consistently that citizens are committed to the values of authority, the more susceptible they are to the intolerance of others, very much including immigrants. The possibility that struck us as pivotal, however, is that the causal relation may run in both directions. Commitment to the values of order and authority can stoke hostility to immigrants. But hostility to immigrants also can stoke the appeal of the values of the right.

We draw out the implications of this hypothesis of reciprocal causation as we proceed, but we want to draw attention to one of the intuitions underlying it. The study of prejudice has emphasized, above all, the sources of hostility toward outgroups in the psychology and social circumstances of individuals: for example, those with the advantage of an extended education are, by virtue of their years of formal schooling, less susceptible to the strains of intolerance than those with comparatively little of it; or, again, those who live at the margins of society are more vulnerable to the appeals of prejudice than those situated at its center. But the level of intolerance in a society also can rise and fall along with the stream of changes within it. As pioneering studies have shown, a surge in the inflow of immigrants,[4] for example, can cause spikes in the aggregate levels of hostility toward immigrants; so, too, can a slump in the economy.[5]

The second line of argument is this. The more we have worked to specify the sources of prejudice, the more important it has seemed to us essential to acknowledge the embeddedness of the prejudice in the world of actual events, and although the design of our study does not permit us to get a direct grip on it, it has supplied the key intuition informing our formal account of the interplay of prejudice and politics, the "Right Shock" model. It is necessary, we suggest, to take account of a class of changes in the economy and society. Generalizing over the specific forms these changes can take, this set of societal changes can economically be represented as external shocks. Under the assumptions of the "Right Shock" model, hostility to immigrants is taken to be a function of the force of these shocks independent of the impact of the circumstances and makeup of individuals. The core idea is twofold: first, that the level of hostility to immigrants spikes in response to an external shock; second, that given the reciprocity of the causal connection between hostility to immigrants and authority values, insofar as prejudice increases in response to an external shock, the appeal of the values of the right will increase in response to the increase in prejudice.

Our third line of argument traces the strange filigree of political ideology in contemporary Italy and, we believe, Western Europe. For a study of the belief systems of ordinary citizens to focus on ideology may seem strange in itself. A half century into the systematic study of public opinion, it has been a wearying tale of minimal levels of attention and knowledge. If ordinary citizens often can barely make out the shapes of immediate and salient figures in politics, if they so frequently have not learned what goes together with what, let alone why, it cannot be surprising that their grip on the abstractions of political thought, and above all, of the complexities of political ideology has proven to be so conspicuously weak. Nonetheless we will suggest that a key to the politics of exclusion lies in the interplay between what citizens think that they think ideologically and what they actually think.

It is consensually agreed that the correspondence between the two—between ideological self-conceptions and actual ideological commitments—is imperfect. Many who think of themselves as being on the political left actually adhere to the beliefs of the right, and vice versa. But because it is perfectly obvious that ordinary citizens will make mistakes about ideological matters, the nature of the mistakes they will make has seemed so obvious as to be taken for granted. Just so far as mismatches between citizens' ideological self-conceptions and their actual ideological commitments follow from a failure to understand, in Philip Converse's classic phrase, "what goes together with what," the political consequences should wash out. It should be approximately as likely that those who think they are on the political left hold the values of the right as that those who see themselves as on the right hold the values of the left.

And there undoubtedly is a spray of random error. But there is also a pattern of systematic error. As we shall show, the cluster of authority values—the importance of guaranteeing order, securing respect for authority, maintaining discipline—has nearly as potent an appeal to those on the political left as to those on the right, their natural constituency. It is not, it should be underlined, that the European left's conception of itself is deformed at its core. Those on the left who are best positioned to understand the values of the left reject sharply these values of the right, as we shall see. It is another matter for the rank and file of the left. Handicapped by their limited education and understanding of the principles of the left, they are open to persuasion. The result: on one of the most basic dimensions of partisan conflict, the right has the support of its own constituency plus a large part of the left's.

The politics of immigration represents, we fear, a point of deep vulnerability for the political left in Italy—and, we believe, in Western Europe generally. What has so far provided an electoral defense against it is the power of traditional political self-conceptions to dominate the voting calculus. There is a knot of ironies to untangle here, and not the least of these, our results suggest, concerns the value of tolerance. It is the cosmopolitan and enlightenment value par excellence, yet its future may hinge on the tenacity of tradition and habits of allegiance.

AN INTEGRATED THEORY: THE "TWO FLAVORS" MODEL

What makes people susceptible to prejudice? Our touchstone has been two classic theories of prejudice. The first locates the sources of prejudice inside individuals. More particularly, the roots of intolerance, whether toward Jews, blacks, or an array of outgroups, are said ultimately to be sunk in people's emotional needs and inner psychological conflicts. There are a number of different ways in which these psychological processes may be conceived, and it certainly is conceded that a variety of societal and economic factors may aggravate or mitigate the problem of intolerance. But in this first approach the key premise is that prejudice is ultimately rooted in personality factors.

The second classic theory of prejudice and group conflict flies under the banner of "realistic conflict." It locates the sources of prejudice not in the interior needs of individuals, but in the objective conditions of social life. More particularly, it contends that the key mechanism generating prejudice is competition for scarce resources. The competition may be over economic well-being or social standing. Either way, those who belong to one group fear that they will be less well-off if those who belong to another group are better-off. The result: prejudice and group conflict.

Both of these classic theories, many will recognize, represent versions of more generic approaches to the explanation of human choice. The first views the choices that people make as an expression of their enduring emotions and attitudes toward others and themselves, their core beliefs about the way that the world is and how it should be understood, and their deep-rooted sense of what is meaningful, fulfilling, and valuable in their lives. The second approach treats the choices that people make as the product of a more objective, often material, and usually self-interested calculus. The first kind of explanation thus tends to have an expressive, psychological flavor; the second, an instrumental, rational choice flavor.

These two explanatory flavors seem naturally to clash. Though each can be variously formulated, psychologically oriented accounts (even when social in their orientation) have lent themselves to an interest in the inner needs and cognitive processes of individuals, while instrumentally oriented accounts have been contrastingly tough-minded, uninterested in the subjective, the irrational, or the emotional, and centered instead on the realistic calculus of advantage and disadvantage. Certainly judging by the record of current research, those with a taste for the first have an aversion to the second; those with a taste for the second, an aversion to the first.[6]

We were tempted to enter the fray. The arguments against personality-based accounts of prejudice, though cogent, are not hat-doffing, and we saw a way around the problems of measurement that have frustrated inquiry for so long. For that matter, at the start we were skeptics not about the validity but rather of the relevance of realistic conflict analyses applied to the particular problem of immigrants in Italy. No doubt a belief that Italians were worse-off just so far as immigrants were better-off lay behind some of the hostility directed at them. But it seemed to us a good bet that it would prove epiphenomenal, or at any rate marginal, to the main forces at work. In the interests of parsimony we therefore began by doing our level best to see if considerations of economic well-being (variously conceived) could either be eliminated or relegated to peripheral status. But whatever tack we took, the impact of considerations of economic well-being could not be ignored.

Our initial results thus required us to rethink our objectives. Rather than arguing on behalf of one explanatory approach and against another, our aim should be to show how each, if viewed from a larger perspective, could be fitted together with the other to form a larger, encompassing account of prejudice. But how could these two very different explanatory approaches, one expressive, psychological in flavor, the other instrumental, rational choice in flavor, possibly be blended together?

Mechanisms are the key to explanation. To understand is to grasp the means by which one thing leads to another, at any rate at the level that the social sciences are capable of yielding understanding.[7] What we were in search of, accordingly, was a common mechanism, a way of explaining *in the very same terms* how very different kinds of factors could lead people to be susceptible to prejudice. Only after wrestling with the problem of conflicting explanations of prejudice for several years did we suddenly see that the work of Henri Tajfel supplied a key. In the argument and analysis that follow in later chapters, we spell out Tajfel's insight into the centrality of categorization for the understanding of prejudice and group conflict. Here we wish to underline our debt to his work. For it suggested a pivotal mechanism to account for the impact of a wide variety of ostensibly quite different kinds of causal factors, running from social class at one explanatory pole to personality at the other.

Once we saw the opening, we had to follow it up and develop a causal model—we have dubbed it the "Two Flavors" model since its objective is to integrate explanations that are expressive or psychological in flavor and those that are instrumental and more rational choice in flavor. The model offers a comprehensive account of an array of explanatory factors—comprehensive but not complete. Given the design of our study, it focuses on factors at the level of individuals and—ironically, given that it is rooted in the work of Tajfel and his students—passes over factors at the level of groups. But integrating different explanations, even if the integration inevitably is incomplete, seems to us a worthwhile objective. Much of the intellectual energy in the study of prejudice has gone into the clash of competing explanations. It is now appropriate for more effort to go to pulling them together, to showing that instead of conflicting necessarily one with another, they may complement one another. And by pulling them together, we do not mean ritualistically acknowledging that each captures a part of the phenomenon of prejudice; we mean, rather, genuinely integrating them by showing how they can be brought together under a common explanatory framework.

It is the object of science to show that initially dissimilar phenomena, more deeply understood, can be understood as aspects of an overarching theoretical framework. It should similarly be the goal of the social sciences, imperfect as they are as sciences. And just for this reason, it has seemed to us a good idea to test the reach of the "Two Flavors" model, to see if it could account for not just what it was designed to account for, but also what it would, at first sight, not even apply to. Italy notoriously is split by a cleavage between North and South. From its national formation, Northern Italians have shown a formidable measure of prejudice toward Southern Italians. We say prejudice, but not in the classical sense. There was never a presumption of biological inferiority, of an inherent and gross lack of intelligence or ability. Indeed, if anything, the suggestion has run the other way around—that Southerners, thanks to a special shrewdness, have managed to evade the responsibilities of life and yet enjoy the pleasures of the day. But, to sketch the familiar historical portrait of Southern Italians as painted by their Northern compatriots, they lack—indeed take pride in lacking—essential qualities of character: honesty, independence, the willingness to work.

Northern Italians' view of Southern Italians, though not necessarily unique in every aspect, is so sunk in the soil of Italy's national experience that it may seem fundamentally incomprehensible apart from it. And from many perspectives this surely is so. But both the results of the "Switch" experiment and the logic of the "Two Flavors" model suggested a different perspective. What is central, both suggested, is the highlighting of differences between one group and another; the particular points of difference highlighted, and the specific factors responsible for their being highlighted, are secondary. A truly demanding test of the value of this reasoning, it occurred to us, was to apply the "Two Flavors" model to the evaluations that Northern Italians make of Southern Italians. There surely are one hundred ways that Southern Italians are recognized to differ from immigrants to Italy from Eastern Europe and Africa. And the operational version of the model had been expressly constructed to account for the evaluations that Italians make of immigrants. If, using exactly the same explanatory measures, and making use of exactly the same estimation procedures, the "Two Flavors" model could account for the hostility of Northern Italians toward Southern Italians as well for the hostility of Italians from both the North and the South toward immigrants, we could take a genuine measure of confidence in our argument. And the detailed analysis suggests that we should.

Our analysis rests on a representative, national survey of Italians.[8] There naturally are limits to what can be learned from a public opinion interview, and some of the subjects we wish to explore, prejudice most obviously among them, are famously elusive. Yet if you wish to know what others think, whether about immigrants or a possible breakdown in social order or the appeal of a new direction in politics, there is no substitute for asking them. Our survey, the first of its kind in Italy, offers a portrait of the causes and consequences of intolerance—a portrait that is partial, one that is certainly not free of blemishes (particularly at the level of measurement), but, we believe, one that is illuminating nonetheless.[9]

We are aware of, and want to underline, the limits of our analysis. We have worked to put our arguments to the test, through cross-validation, by multiple forms of statistical analysis and by conjoining randomized experimentation and representative sampling. But, it seems to us, the more one enters into the spirit of inquiry, the clearer it becomes that the goal is less to establish what is true than, progressively, to expose what is false. There never is certainty, but there sometimes is progress, and the latter is possible just because the former is unattainable. As Hilary Putnam, citing Charles Pierce, has remarked: "It's as if we were walking on unfirm ground, on swampy grounds, and that was good because, if the ground were firm, there would be no reason to go anywhere."[10]

CHAPTER 2

The Nature of Prejudice:
Race and Nationality as Bases of Conflict

RACISM is arguably the most deeply entrenched—certainly the most readily evoked—form of intolerance in our time. In a country like Italy, blacks stand out, inescapably and immediately, merely by virtue of being black, which is exactly what recommends Italy as a site for the study of prejudice and group conflict. There, immigration flows in two quite distinct streams. One stream consists of immigrants from North and Central Africa—Senegalese, Somalians, Moroccans, Tunisians—the other is made up of immigrants from Eastern Europe—Poles, Albanians, Slavs. Here, then, is a natural experiment—Senegalese and Polish, Somalian and Albanian, all newcomers to Italy, raised in other cultures and speaking different languages. But some are black, others white. Surely this difference of race, of color, cuts deep. All, because they are immigrants, will bear a burden of intolerance, but those who are black, by virtue of being black, must bear a heavier burden still.

Race is specially stigmatizing, if only because differences of race are visible in a way that differences of ethnicity and nationality need not be. And the conspicuousness of physical markers of difference are caught up in a complex of conspicuous points of differences—of forms of dress, culture, family pattern, styles of self-presentation, and mannerisms in everyday interaction. Each point of difference—of belief, appearance, mannerism, dress—can serve as a basis of discrimination.[1] Collected together and stamped with the brand of race, they set blacks apart and make them a target of intolerance as others are not—and cannot grasp apart from an act of imagination and empathy.

So we hypothesized. But to speak of this as a hypothesis, though technically correct, does not capture the character of our thinking. There was no uncertainty in our minds. Differences of race, we all agreed, are more easily evoked, and once evoked, rouse more primordial responses than do differences of ethnicity and nationality. But knowing something to be true is not the same as having demonstrated it to be true. Accordingly, taking advantage of the power of computer-assisted interviewing to combine the strengths of genuinely randomized experimentation and properly representative samples of the population of a country, we designed our study to demonstrate the uniquely stigmatizing effects of race.

But our central hypothesis, self-evident as it seemed, turned out to miss the defining feature of the prevailing politics of exclusion in Western Europe. It is therefore the aim of this chapter to point the way to a better understanding of prejudice by demonstrating why what all of us were sure was right, is wrong.

CONCEPTIONS OF PREJUDICE

Our starting point is the concept of prejudice. What does it involve? How should it be defined? To propose that the answers to the questions are not evident may seem perverse, a study in scholasticism. The number of studies devoted to the examination of the meaning of prejudice and dissection of its many forms of expression is legion.[2] Surely prejudice is a concept that has been wrestled to the ground by now.

And there is indeed a consensus view. Figure 2.1 lists a number of definitions in order to make it immediately obvious what prejudice now is taken to mean.[3] Their specific vocabulary naturally differs, and differences, particularly of emphasis, also can be picked out. Yet at least four points of agreement stand out.

The first point of agreement concerns who (or what) can properly be said to be the target of prejudice. In everyday life, it makes sense to speak of one person being prejudiced against another—a father may be prejudiced against a prospective son-in-law, or a department store salesman against a fellow employee. Prejudice, in this usage, refers to a judgment about an individual's faults. The father believes his prospective son-in-law is unambitious; the salesman, that his co-worker is unreliable: both the prospective son-in-law and the co-worker are given black marks because of the failings they are perceived to have as individuals. By contrast, in the study of intolerance, prejudice is directed at groups, not individuals. More precisely, it is about individuals just so far as they are taken to be members of groups. Thus the definitions in figure 2.1[4] refer to a response to members of a group by virtue of their membership in a group. Milner, for example, speaks of "the attribution of . . . characteristics of the whole group to all its individual members";[5] Allport, of a response "based on . . . generalization . . . directed toward a group as whole, or toward an individual because he is a member of that group";[6] Jones, of "a . . . generalization from a group characterization (stereotype) to an individual member of the group."[7] Groups are thus implicated twice over: as the basis for and as the target of generalizations about their members.

The second point of agreement concerns the logical character of the "generalizations" caught up in prejudice. They characteristically are pre-

Prejudiced attitudes . . . are irrational, unjust, or intolerant dispositions towards others. They are often accompanied by stereotyping. This is the attribution of supposed characteristics of the whole group to all its individual members. (Milner, 1975, p. 9)

It seems most useful to us to define prejudice as a failure of rationality or a failure of justice or a failure of human-heartedness in an individual's attitude toward members of another ethnic group. (Harding et al., 1969, p. 6)

An emotional, rigid attitude, a predisposition to respond to a certain stimulus in a certain way toward a group of people. (Simpson and Yinger, 1985, p. 21)

Thinking ill of others without sufficient warrant. (Allport, 1954, p. 7)

Ethnic prejudice is an antipathy based upon a faulty and inflexible generalization. It may be felt or expressed. It may be directed toward a group as a whole or toward an individual because he is a member of that group. (Allport, 1954, p. 9)

An unsubstantiated prejudgment of an individual or group, favorable or unfavorable in character, tending to action in a consonant direction. (Klineberg, 1968, p. 439)

A pattern of hostility in interpersonal relations which is directed against an entire group, or against its individual members; it fulfills a specific irrational function for its bearer. (Ackerman and Jahoda, 1950, pp. 2–3)

Hostility or aggression toward individuals on the basis of their group membership. (Buss, 1961, p. 245)

Group prejudice is now commonly viewed as having two components: hostility and misinformation. (Kelman and Pettigrew, 1959, p. 436)

A set of attitudes which causes, supports, or justifies discrimination. (Rose, 1951, p. 5)

An unfavorable attitude toward an object which tends to be highly stereotyped, emotionally charged, and not easily changed by contrary information. (Krech, Crutchfield, and Ballachey, 1962)

Fig. 2.1 Definitions of Prejudice

sented, in everyday exchanges, as factual. "I'm not telling you how I feel about blacks," says the bigot who believes blacks are inherently less intelligent than whites, "I'm telling you what they're really like." But although presented as descriptive, as merely a matter of fact, the generalization is evaluative, a judgment as to which groups are better and which are worse. In principle, these evaluations can be positive. One can be prejudiced in favor of, as well as against, a group. But a readiness to favor others because they belong to the same group as you do is not the mirror image of a readiness to punish others because they belong to a different group than you do.[8] And normatively the two are on a quite different footing. It sometimes is praiseworthy to respond especially positively to members of a group because they are members of your group; it is almost always inappropriate to respond especially negatively to members of a group merely because they are not members of your group. Hence the unvarying emphasis in all the definitions in figure 2.1 is not on responding favorably to members of your group, but on responding unfavorably to members of other groups. With his characteristic directness, Allport speaks of "thinking ill of others." Buss, more bristlingly, refers to "hostility or aggression toward individuals on the basis of their group membership"; Harding and colleagues, more judgmentally, to "a failure of human-heartedness." Prejudice, it thus is agreed, centers on the readiness to respond negatively to members of a group by virtue of their membership in the group.[9] We accordingly restrict the definition of prejudice to negative evaluations of group members by virtue of their membership in the group. Less antiseptically, prejudice centers on a swirl of mean-spirited ideas and feelings—among them, contempt, disdain, antipathy, dislike, distaste, and aversion—directed against those belonging to a group other than one's own.

The third point of agreement uniting the list of definitions detailed in figure 2.1 concerns veridicality. That an evaluation of a group is negative is a necessary but not a sufficient condition of prejudice. Imagine a Jew who describes Nazis as contemptible and barbaric. Her feelings incontestably are negative, but it would be a travesty to accuse her of prejudice. And the reason it would get things wrong to accuse her of bearing a prejudice against Nazis is perfectly obvious. Her view of them, negative though it is, represents the truth of the matter. Some negative evaluations of groups are warranted. Therefore, it is standardly stipulated that for a negative characterization of a group to qualify as prejudice, it must be, if not erroneous, at any rate unwarranted. So Milner speaks of "the attribution of *supposed* characteristics"; Jones of "a *faulty* generalization"; Kelman and Pettigrew of "*misinformation*"; and Allport of "thinking ill of others *without sufficient warrant*" and of "faulty and inflexible generalization."

Finally, a fourth point of agreement emerges from examination of the definitions summarized in figure 2.1. We all make mistakes about what others are like. We suppose them to have failings that they do not have, or to fail to have good qualities that they do have. But it is not making a mistake that counts; it is persisting in it in the face of evidence to the contrary. Fixity of belief, in short, is a defining feature of prejudice. Just so far as people cleave to their mistaken judgments about others, just so far as they are unwilling to surrender or correct them, they properly may be said to be prejudiced.

Indeed, prejudice represents a type of error that is costly because it is not corrigible. False characterizations of a group, once accepted, become entrenched, and once entrenched, persist because of their fixity. Simpson and Yinger, for example, speak of a "rigid" attitude; Allport of an "inflexible" generalization; Krech, Crutchfield, and Ballachey, of an attitude that tends to be "highly stereotyped, emotionally charged, and not easily changed by contrary information." The dissimilarity of their specific characterizations notwithstanding, the point of agreement among them is unmistakable. Bigots are bad Bayesians: they do not update when they should; they stand by their priors when they should not.

In sum, it is standardly agreed that prejudice consists in attributions about groups or members of groups, by virtue of their membership in the group, that are disparaging and hostile, false, or at least without warrant, and rigidly held.

A CLOSER LOOK

Definitions are tools. In gauging their value, the crucial question to ask is not about their validity but their utility—and their utility assessed not in the abstract but for the immediate task at hand.

Consider, for example, one of the standardly stipulated features of prejudice: inaccuracy. As a matter of common sense it is straightforwardly obvious that prejudice involves judgments about members of another group that are wrong as matters of fact, often egregiously so. Blacks are not inherently inferior; Jews are not intrinsically unscrupulous. But obvious and incontestable as these mistakes are at one level, the use of error as a criterion of prejudice turns out to be frustratingly elusive. In what sense, exactly, is an error involved? Must one, to disprove a characterization of a group, show only that there is at least one member of the group of whom it is not true? What if the descriptions fit most of the group, even if not all? Or, taking a harder case, what if the characterization, even if not true of most of the members of the group, is nonetheless more likely to be true of them than of members of other groups? Moreover, there often is a gulf between a mistake being made and being able to demonstrate that a mistake has been made. Much of the time the evidence to impeach a negative characterization of a group is not in hand; indeed, part of the time, extreme cases aside, it could not conceivably be gathered, even if it were clear what standard of proof had to be met.[10] And usually it is not.

It is tempting to say that a prejudice about a group gets things wrong because in concentrating on the central tendency of a group, it underestimates the variability within it. Prejudice, so viewed, goes wrong by simplifying. But as Roger Brown has argued, simplification cannot in itself be a sign of getting things wrong because it is a necessary condition of getting them right.[11] Experience is complex; distinctions must be drawn. Attending primarily to the mean and only incidentally to the variance is not only unavoidable but often invaluable. Stereotyping, in the sense of simplifying, is thus a necessary condition of getting judgments right, certainly as a first approximation.

Other criteria consensually taken to define prejudice prove similarly slippery. For example, the claim that prejudice consists in a negative evaluation of a group would seem obviously correct, indeed, nearly tautologically so. But what do we actually know if we know that a person has characterized blacks, for example, as "more aggressive and violent than whites?" In a great many cases, we know that he dislikes blacks and views them with a potent mixture of contempt and fear. But in other cases, it turns out on closer examination that the underlying sentiment is quite different: that in characterizing blacks as more aggressive and violent, people wish to condemn, not blacks, whom they see as victimized by their circumstances, but rather the brutalization and exploitation of blacks, which they believe lies behind the propensity of blacks to violence.[12] Here then is an evaluation that appears negative toward blacks in its manifest content, but is positive in its underlying orientation.

Consider another consensually agreed feature of prejudice. Prejudice, we are told, consists in persevering in a belief in the face of contrary evidence. But how exactly is rigid inflexibility to be distinguished from principled constancy? Why is it praiseworthy to continue to believe in the redeeming qualities of a friend in the face of a stretch of destructive self-indulgence, yet a form of obduracy to continue to believe in the failings of others over a similar stretch of time and where evidence of their qualities of character characteristically is indeterminate, ambiguous, inherently susceptible to conflicting interpretations. And even if the truth of the matter is ascertainable, it may be ascertainable only in the long run. And if the truth of the matter cannot be settled in the short run, who is to say how long the long run must be in order to settle the issue?

These questions about the standard conception of prejudice do not go equally deep. But they spring from a common root. Each, in its individual way, is grounded in the taken-for-granted presumption that prejudice is bound up with stereotypes and stereotyping. And it is this presumption that now we want to examine.

STEREOTYPES AND PREJUDICE

In working to untangle the knot of connections between prejudice and stereotypes, it is useful to distinguish two phases of research.[13] The first, inspired by the classic study of Katz and Braly, concentrated on the content of stereotypes. The second phase, inspired by the breakthrough work of Hamilton and his colleagues, focused on the process of stereotyping.[14] We take up the first phase of content before the second of process.

It may seem self-evident that prejudice consists in the attribution of specific characteristics, or stereotypes, to specific groups, as when blacks are said to be lazy and lacking in intelligence, or when Jews are said to believe they are better than other people or to be more willing to use shady practices to get ahead in life. But valuable as it may be for many reasons to investigate the content of stereotypes, it cannot be right to define prejudice on the basis of the attribution of trait characteristics considered most typical of a social group.[15] It cannot be right, for one thing, because it presumes that groups in fact do not differ whereas in reality they often do. For another, if it is the attribution of distinctive trait characteristics in the form of stereotypes that constitutes prejudice, then the content of measures of prejudice toward each group necessarily is unique just so far as the stereotypes taken either one at a time or as a whole truly are considered to be distinctive of a particular group. But if the measure of prejudice for each group is unique, then they are not comparable, and it seems a pity to take the position that purely as matter of definition, it never can be established that one group bears a heavier burden of enmity than any other. Then, too, just so far as the assessment of prejudice is tied to a set of particular stereotypes presumed to be distinctive of a group, it will not be possible to get a fix on the meaning of any changes that are observed over time, however large the changes happen to be. Consider the problem. In a classic series of studies of stereotypes of social groups in 1933, 84 percent of test subjects[16] described most blacks as "superstitious" and 75 percent described them as "lazy." By 1951, only 41 percent described most blacks as superstitious and only 31 percent as lazy. By 1967, the numbers had fallen still further, to 13 and 26 percent, respectively. What, exactly, is the conclusion to draw? Is it a fair inference, from this change alone, that racial prejudice has decreased approximately in proportion to the size of the change

observed? Possibly, but it is perfectly obvious that specific characterizations of particular groups—and indeed, whole styles of characterizing
groups (for example, as genetically inferior)—can go out of fashion for
exactly the same reasons that styles of dress (for example, short skirts) go
out of fashion. But just so far as the usage of particular stereotypes waxes
and wanes for reasons other than a change in the actual level of prejudice
toward a group, there is an incorrigible indeterminacy to the interpretation of change. We say indeterminacy, because the uncertainty often is
not whether a change in prejudice has occurred—professional cynics
aside—but rather what order of magnitude of change has occurred. In
America, for example, there is ample reason to believe that there is less
racial prejudice now than sixty years ago. The real difficulty is estimating, from change observed at the level of particular stereotypes, the
magnitude of change at the level of underlying evaluations. The Princeton studies suggest a transformation in racial attitudes has taken place.
But granting that there now is less prejudice than there was, we know of
no reason to believe that changes in the endorsement of specific stereotypes are a valid indicator of how much change in white feelings of aversion and contempt for blacks has taken place. As Glock and his colleagues hammered home, it is fallacious to infer from changes in levels
of agreement with specific stereotypes, which may reflect changes merely
in verbal fashion to an unknown degree, changes in the level of prejudice
toward a minority group.[17]

More broadly, there seems to be something causally wrong-footed
about pinning everything to consensus on certain specific traits characteristic of certain social groups. Suppose (contrary to fact) that a majority of whites no longer agrees on a set of trait characteristics they consider typical of blacks. Would it logically follow that blacks no longer
suffer from prejudice on the part of whites? Surely not, because there is
no reason to believe that consensus on the social image of a group is a
necessary condition for there to be prejudice against it. It is quite possible to be prejudiced against a group about which you have only the
vaguest idea. And similarly, it is also possible for two individuals to hold
the same degree of prejudice toward a group, even if they attribute different characteristics to it.

For all these reasons, it does not seem helpful to tie prejudice to particular stereotypes. But if particular stereotypes are not the key to prejudice, what about the process of stereotyping?

A generation of research has demonstrated that the process of stereotyping has a shower of cognitive effects. For example, individuals judged
to belong to another group tend to be viewed as more similar to one
another while those believed to belong to the same group as oneself
tend to be viewed not only as more diverse but also as more complex.[18]

It is an important insight that prejudice involves the minimization of differences of others judged to belong to a group other than one's own and to exaggerate their points of similarity and to minimize their distinguishing characteristics as individuals. Yet as important an insight as this is, concentrating on prejudice as a cognitive process constrains an account of prejudice and politics twice over. It is constraining, first, with respect to consequences. The swells of prejudice in the contemporary politics of Europe command attention both in their own right, with numbers of citizens wanting immigrants to be catalogued, detained, discharged from their jobs, and shipped back to whatever country they originally came from, and because of their potential political spillover, with parties of the far right striving to tap the deep pools of resentment and anger toward immigrants. It is not obvious how a strictly cognitive account can reach to give an explanation of either. And a cognitive account also is constraining—not disabling but *restricting*—with respect to the causes of prejudice. Clearly citizens who favor a campaign of exclusion underestimate points of difference among immigrants, perceiving immigrants in stereotypical terms. Putting things this way picks out a telling feature of the process of prejudice but does not capture *why* the native born want immigrants picked up and shipped out. A powerful mix of sentiments and assumptions—of anger, resentment, anxiety, and contempt, of fears of economic costs and burdens to both individuals and the country as a whole—fuels the desire to expel immigrants. It is the factors—social, economic, and personal—that are responsible for this highly charged mixture that need to be identified, and the approach to stereotyping as a cognitive process, for all its value, is not the right vehicle for doing so.[19]

EVALUATIVE CONSISTENCY

How, then, should we conceive of prejudice? If stereotyping or endorsing stereotypes is not a hallmark of it, what is?

Suppose, setting aside the problem of prejudice for a moment, we wanted to assess people's political orientation. In judging whether a person is liberal, it is not very helpful to learn that on one particular occasion, he took a liberal position on one particular issue. It is necessary instead to get a fuller sense of his political views, to learn the positions he takes over a range of issues, to see whether he systematically lines up on one side of the ideological divide. For we should say that he is liberal only if he predictably and reliably takes the liberal side; indeed, the more consistently and systematically he takes the liberal side, the more liberal we would say that he is.

In saying this, we are not suggesting that unless a person is liberal on every issue, he is not really a liberal. Being a liberal (or a conservative) is not an all-or-nothing proposition: it is a matter of degree. Even someone who is very liberal is unlikely to be liberal in every respect or on every occasion. But the consistency with which he supports liberal positions is the key to characterizing his political orientation. The more liberal he is, the more consistently he should take the liberal side of the ideological contest.

So, too, with prejudice: consistency is the key. But consistency with respect to what? Disliking and derogating others. An anti-Semite is one who dislikes and derogates Jews; the more he dislikes and derogates them, the more anti-Semitic he is. A racial bigot, correspondingly, is one who dislikes and derogates blacks; the more he dislikes and derogates them, the more racially bigoted he is. The endorsement of group stereotypes is telling, we are suggesting, because the sentiments being expressed are negative, disapproving, critical, not because they are inaccurate, though they often are.[20] On the other side, the larger the number of opportunities to express a negative judgment that are presented to an individual, and the larger the number of opportunities that he takes advantage of to express a negative judgment, the smaller the chance of classifying him inaccurately as intolerant. Negative stereotypes index prejudice toward a group just so far as endorsing them offers an opportunity to express aversion, contempt, rejection, or dislike toward the group. The consistency of evaluative judgments, not their specific content, is the key to prejudice.[21] Put most directly, then, by prejudice we mean a readiness to attribute negative characteristics or, correspondingly, to decline to attribute positive characteristics to a group.

Prejudice, as this definition underlines, revolves around a readiness to dislike and derogate others belonging to a group because of their membership in the group; and the more consistently and systematically people take advantage of opportunities to respond negatively to others, the more they rightly may be judged to dislike and derogate them. This is not at all to suggest that only those who on every occasion respond negatively respond consistently. On the contrary, many—perhaps even most—people will sometimes respond negatively to others, sometimes not. The point is, rather, that differences of degree can themselves be consistent. Consider two people, A and B. A dislikes blacks extremely; B, by comparison, dislikes them but less intensely. Because B does not as often exploit opportunities to respond negatively as does A is not, in itself, evidence that he is not prejudiced. On the contrary, you will systematically underestimate the force of prejudice if you count as prejudiced only those who are the most extreme in their dislike of others. Nor is the fact that responses are not always negative, in itself, evidence that

B is either uncertain about how he feels about blacks or caught in an internal conflict between positive and negative feelings toward them. Both uncertainty and ambivalence occur but both are expensive hypotheses, the former methodologically, the latter ontologically, since both entail nonlinearities.[22] The burden of proof is accordingly on those who wish to invoke them. What we wish to insist on is that the primary consideration should be the burden of animosity, resentment, and aversion that victims of prejudice must bear. And this entails, in turn, an appreciation that consistency of feeling does not confine itself to those at the extremes. It is perfectly possible to dislike blacks (or Jews or immigrants) sincerely, genuinely, and consistently even though someone else dislikes them even more strongly, intensely, and fervently. So we shall take the position that *the more consistently a person attributes negative characteristics or, alternatively, declines to attribute positive characteristics to a group, the more prejudiced he or she is.*

PREJUDICE AGAINST IMMIGRANTS:
AN INITIAL APPROACH

How much prejudice is there against immigrants? Is it confined to a comparatively small number of Italians at the margins of the larger society? Or has it made deeper inroads, winning a general following throughout the society? Is resentment and anger toward immigrants, so far as either have taken hold, focused on a limited—and, therefore, possibly a manageable—number of points of friction? Or is it more diffuse, more enveloping? And granting that differences of ethnicity and nationality matter, how much deeper do differences of race cut?

Prejudice, we have said, consists in a readiness to attribute negative characteristics or, correspondingly, to decline to attribute positive characteristics to a group. The most direct way to assess the extent to which Italians are prejudiced against immigrants, then, is to present them with a set of personal attributes, some positive, others negative, and ask which describe what immigrants are like. To be precise, we began with the following introduction: "Now we'll talk about different groups of people living in our country. For each of the characteristics that I mention, can you tell me whether you agree or not that it applies to the majority of persons belonging to that group."

The list of personal attributes runs the gamut of characteristics, unfavorable and favorable, by which all of us commonly register whether we have a good opinion of someone. Specifically, we asked Italians whether they believe that most immigrants are "honest—that is, behave honestly and properly toward others"; "selfish—that is, think only of themselves, without concerning themselves very much about others"; "law-abiding—behaving like good citizens, observing the regulations and laws of the government"; "intrusive—pressing themselves on you in an annoying and insistent way"; "slackers—trying to avoid working or at any rate doing tiring and heavy work"; "violent—willing to use physical force, or threatening to use it, in order to impose their will on others"; "complainers—trying to make others feel sorry for them"; and finally, "by nature inferior to Italians."

We do not claim that this list is exhaustive.[23] Selection is unavoidable. But it covers a considerable amount of territory. The characteristics canvassed run over different aspects of individual character and socially acceptable behavior—from honesty, for example, through intrusiveness, all the way to a propensity for violence—and run the gamut from mildly positive to expressly racist—from law-abiding, for example, through intrusive and lazy, all the way to inferior by nature. Everyone, it should also be noted, was asked not merely whether they agree or disagree with each evaluative characterization, but also whether they did so strongly or only somewhat.

What we wish to explore, making use of these materials, is the social construction of the concept of the outsider. Is everyone who has come from outside Italy, just because they have come from outside it, regarded as equally an outsider? Or are distinctions drawn based on race, at any rate of degree and perhaps even of kind?

This is the question we most want to answer, but there is an obvious stumbling block. Assume that race does indeed make a difference—that however much ill will Italians feel toward immigrants from Eastern Europe, they feel markedly more toward black immigrants from Africa. Assume, moreover, that we ask Italians first how they feel about immigrants from Eastern Europe, then about immigrants from Africa. A question mark will necessarily be attached to our results, as a moment's reflection will make plain. Suppose, for the sake of argument, that race is specially stigmatizing but that we nonetheless do *not* observe a difference between the evaluative characterization of East European and African immigrants. Should we then conclude that the hypothesis of racial hierarchy is wrong? Not necessarily, since the absence of differences may merely be an artifact of asking about the relatively more-liked group first. Having set a (relatively) positive baseline, respondents could not evaluate the second group more unfavorably than the first without making it evident they were prejudiced against it. But is the remedy to reverse the order in which we ask about African and Eastern European immigrants? Hardly, since if respondents are first asked about the group they dislike more, having established a lower baseline, they may be under pressure to be consistent with it in evaluating the second group, or risk revealing that they are prejudiced against the first. The quandary is thus symmetrical. Whether the white or the black immigrants are asked about first, finding that Italians respond similarly to immigrants whether white or black will be suspect methodologically.

In a standard public opinion survey, there is no way around this quandary. How people respond to the group they are asked about second may always be influenced by how they responded by the group they were asked about first; and since in a regular opinion survey groups can be asked about in only one order, it is impossible purely as a matter of logic to establish what difference, if any, the order makes. In a computer-assisted survey, by contrast, a remedy is at hand—simply randomize the order of the groups about which respondents are asked. Since each of the sets of respondents is assigned at random to make a judgment about either one or the other group, each of the groups is asked first for one half of the sample; and since the sample as a whole is randomly selected, then each randomly composed half of the sample constitutes a sample representative of the country as a whole as well, albeit one with larger standard errors. In short, by asking Italians about immigrants from either Eastern Europe or Africa on a random basis, we can learn what Italians think about each group without the judgment being contaminated by what they have said about the other group.

This is the logic of the strategy that we shall follow, but there is a critical detail to take care of. We have been speaking, in broad brush strokes, of white immigrants from Eastern Europe and black ones from Africa. Strictly speaking, this is not true. Some immigrants from Africa, particularly from regions in North Africa like Morocco, Tunisia, or Algeria, are not considered black by themselves or by Italians. As a precaution respondents were therefore randomly assigned to three independent conditions, not two. In the first they were asked about the characteristics of "North Africans, like Moroccans, Tunisians, or Algerians"; in the second, about "Africans from the regions of Central Africa, like Senegal and Somalia"; and in the third, about "Eastern Europeans, like Poles, Albanians, or Slavs." We thus can compare and contrast reactions to immigrants, some of whom are black, all of whom are black, and none of whom are black. Table 2.1 accordingly sets out the proportions of Italians who agree (or disagree) with the full battery of characterizations, positive as well as negative, and in addition the strength (strongly or only somewhat) of their agreement (or disagreement) with each.

If one begins by scrutinizing responses to the pair of positive qualities we asked about—whether immigrant groups are honest and law-abiding—one may first think that immigrants are reasonably well-

TABLE 2.1
Evaluative Reactions to Immigrants

Item	% SA	% A	% D	% SD	Unweighted N
Honest	20.7	55.3	16.3	7.7	1743
Selfish	6.9	25.5	35.8	31.8	1510
Law-abiding	12.5	44.4	28.5	14.6	1636
Intrusive	14.9	34.1	23.8	27.2	1705
Slackers	9.8	25.6	31.0	33.6	1667
Violent	7.5	26.5	32.0	34.0	1613
Complainers	17.4	39.9	19.1	23.6	1649
Inferior by nature	6.2	9.5	12.8	71.5	1794

Notes: SA = strongly agree, *A* = somewhat agree, *D* = somewhat disagree, *SD* = strongly disagree. Weighted frequencies

regarded.[24] An overwhelming majority of Italians—about three in every four—agree that most immigrants—whether North African, Central African, or Eastern European—behave honestly and properly toward others. A majority, moreover, also believe that immigrants, again whatever their country of origin, are law abiding and behave like good citizens, observing the regulations and laws of the government. As essential as it is to qualify these results, it is necessary not to minimize their importance, since it is not difficult to imagine circumstances in which far fewer Italians would perceive immigrants to have at least some good qualities. Yet, on closer examination, warning signs abound. A majority of Italians, it is true, believe that most immigrants are law-abiding. But it is a thin majority indeed. Moreover, if you think about this particular pair of positive characterizations—honest and law-abiding—neither requires that you think especially highly of someone in order to apply them. On the contrary, they are the kind of pocket-change compliments routinely exchanged in ordinary social intercourse. It is instructive, therefore, that so many Italians—one out of every two decline to agree with either or both—are nonetheless unwilling to pay even modest compliments to immigrants. It is doubly instructive, moreover, that so few of the ones who are willing to attribute these positive qualities to immigrants are willing to do so without qualification. Thus, at a rough approximation, of those Italians willing to agree that immigrants are honest, only about one in four are willing to do so strongly; and of those willing to agree that immigrants are law-abiding, between one in four and one in five are willing to do so strongly. The commendations that Italians pay immigrants, when they pay them at all, are tepid.

Let us turn from a reluctance to make positive remarks to a readiness to make negative ones. Examining responses to negative characterizations of immigrants, it is the extremes that catch one's eye first. On one side, close to six out of every ten Italians agree that immigrants are "complainers," trying to make others feel sorry for them, and nearly one in every three feel strongly that this is so. On the other side, strikingly fewer—only between one in six and one in seven—agree that immigrants are "by nature inferior to Italians."

Two rather different interpretations can be draped around these results. In one reading, they suggest a willingness of many Italians to offer mild criticism of immigrants but the readiness of only a few to make strong criticism. In an opposing reading, the "only" in "only a few" leaps out. The approximately 15 percent who agree that immigrants are "by nature inferior" are making a radical claim. They are expressly endorsing the quintessential dogma of traditional racism: the inherent inferiority of the outgroup. And in this day and age, given the uniformity of institutional and normative prohibitions on the explicit assertion of the inherent inferiority of any group, what surely is striking is not how few Italians but how many of them are willing to openly declare that immigrants are "by nature inferior."

Numbers in public opinion surveys do not have an absolute meaning, however. Modify the wording of a question, and the smallest number could be larger, the largest smaller. So what we should like to concentrate on is the central tendency of negative evaluations of immigrants, all in all.

Putting to one side the assertion of inherent inferiority, palpably the most extreme, what is striking is the height of the floor of negative evaluations of immigrants. Never fewer than one in every three Italians agree with a negative characterization of immigrants whatever the negative characterization. It is, perhaps, not surprising that so many would say that immigrants "try to avoid working, or at any rate to do tiring and heavy work" and "think only of themselves, without concerning themselves very much about others": these are the kind of (mildly) negative evaluations that tacitly imply a (mildly) positive evaluation of oneself. But it is another matter to characterize immigrants as "violent"—"willing often to use physical force, or to threaten to use it, in order to impose their will on others." And, as a glance at table 2.1 will show, sometimes a far larger number of Italians are prepared to find fault with immigrants. Thus, fully one out of every two perceive them "to press themselves on you in an annoying and insistent way"; and an even larger

TABLE 2.2
Evaluative Reactions to Immigrants Contingent on Region of Origin

Item	North Africans (minimum N = 398)				Central Africans (minimum N = 371)				East Europeans (minimum N = 759)			
	% SA	% A	% D	% SD	% SA	% A	% D	% SD	% SA	% A	% D	% SD
Honest[a]	21.6	53.5	16.3	8.6	25.7	53.8	13.4	7.1	17.8	57.0	17.7	7.5
Selfish[b]	7.3	24.4	39.7	28.6	5.3	22.4	34.5	37.8	7.6	27.6	34.4	30.4
Law-abiding[c]	12.0	39.1	34.7	14.2	13.7	49.5	24.3	12.5	12.2	44.5	27.3	16.0
Intrusive[d]	17.0	38.9	21.9	22.2	14.3	35.4	21.6	28.7	14.1	30.7	26.0	29.2
Slackers	9.9	23.2	31.4	35.5	6.8	29.8	27.8	35.6	11.4	24.9	32.3	31.4
Violent[e]	6.2	25.5	34.9	33.4	7.1	23.6	33.2	36.1	8.4	28.5	29.9	33.2
Complainers	15.3	44.8	18.7	21.2	16.9	38.6	19.6	24.9	18.8	37.8	19.0	24.4
Inferior by nature[f]	5.7	12.7	11.3	70.3	8.5	9.3	10.9	71.3	5.3	7.9	14.6	72.2

Notes: SA = strongly agree, A = somewhat agree, D = somewhat disagree, SD = strongly disagree. Weighted frequencies; unweighted N

[a] Central Africans are considered significantly more honest than North Africans and East Europeans (all significance is for one-tailed test at 0.05 significance level)

[b] Central Africans are considered significantly less selfish than North Africans and East Europeans

[c] Central Africans are considered significantly more law-abiding than North Africans and East Europeans

[d] North Africans are considered significantly more intrusive than Central Africans and East Europeans

[e] Central Africans are considered significantly less violent than East Europeans

[f] Central Africans are considered significantly more inferior by nature than East Europeans

number characterize them as "complainers, trying to make others feel sorry for them." As a first approximation, it therefore seems fair to say that a large body of Italians find fault with immigrants across a number of fronts.

There cannot be anything surprising in this. But what must be surprising—certainly it was to us—are the reactions of Italians to immigrants as a function of nationality and race. We had expected—we have been altogether candid on this—to demonstrate that race is specially stigmatizing, and hence to observe that Italians' evaluations of Central Africans, all of whom are black, are the most negative; that their evaluations of North Africans, a number of whom are black, are the next most negative; and that their evaluations of Eastern Europeans, all of whom are white, are the least negative. But that is *not* what the data show.

Consider responses to questions about Central Africans and Eastern Europeans in table 2.2. Instead of the former being evaluated more unfavorably than the latter, so far as the two are consistently evaluated differently, it is the other way around. Eastern Europeans are more likely to be described as violent and selfish and less likely to be described as either honest or law-abiding than are Central Africans.[25]

Why this reversal of our expectations for this cluster of traits? The contrast between Africans themselves, specifically between those from Central African countries like Senegal and Somalia and those from Northern African countries like Algeria and Morocco, offers a clue. Central Africans, as table 2.2 shows, are more likely to be described as honest or as law-abiding and, on the other side of the ledger, less likely to be described as selfish and as intrusive than are North Africans.[26] And the reason, observation suggests, is tied to social reality. Most of the public contact Italians have with Africans is with street merchants, most of whom are Central Africans. They are polite, quiet, respectful, and in no way menacing. They palpably are badly off, and from their first appearance on the streets hawking knockoffs, purchases from them have had an element of compassion and charity. By contrast, immigrants from North Africa and Eastern Europe have acquired a reputation for criminal behavior, and without of course implying that this is true of all or most of them, it is generally agreed this reputation has a basis in reality. These results are a nonobvious demonstration of the fallacy of stereotypical judgments about racial stereotypes.

There is, having said this, one aspect of the results in table 2.2 that fits exactly our presumption that race is specially stigmatizing. The traditional cornerstone of racism is the presumption of biological inferiority, and as table 2.2 shows, Italians are indeed more likely to judge Africans as "inferior by nature."[27] In judging the figures, it is worth underlining again the extremity of this characterization. Yet, the proportion of Italians who characterize immigrants as inherently inferior approaches one out of every five. We take this finding to be a salutary reminder that even when grounds for contempt go out of fashion they still maintain their hold on a sizeable portion of the public.

Responses to immigrants, then, can hinge on differences of nationality and race, though in ways both more complex and more interesting than we had initially supposed. Yet, acknowledging these points of difference, the dominant feature of the results is the similarity, not the dissimilarity, of Italians' response to immigrants wherever they happen to come from and whatever they characteristically look like. A sizeable segment of the Italian public denies that immigrants, whether white or black, whether from North Africa or Central Africa, act honestly and properly toward others, behave like good citizens, and observe the regulations and laws of the government. They perceive immigrants as intrusive, pressing themselves on others, as lazy, trying to avoid honest work but complaining about being badly treated, and not infrequently using or threatening to use physical force.

A MULTIFORMAT MULTITRAIT APPROACH

Differences of detail notwithstanding, the prototypical approach to the measurement of prejudice against social groups has consisted in the attribution of negative characteristics to them. But just because this approach is indispensable, it does not follow that it is sufficient.

Every approach to measurement has its vulnerabilities. The optimal strategy, as Campbell and Fiske argued in a classic paper,[28] is triangulation—obtaining a more reliable assessment through converging estimates of independent measurement approaches. Variation in method falls on a continuum, the differences between some being dramatic, between others more modest. Given our reliance on a public opinion interview, necessary (it should be remembered) to assure the generalizability of our findings, the alternatives in triangulation between different methods fall much closer to the latter pole than to the former. Yet even if what is done is limited, it is worth doing all that can be done since triangulation has often been the text of sermons on measurement—and like other subjects of sermons, honored in the breach rather than the observance. So we committed ourselves at the outset of this study to the first effort to assess prejudice in a public opinion survey making use of multiple measurement formats.

Measuring prejudice through the assessment of personal characteristics is one approach. What form should a second take? Logically, it must meet a pair of conditions. First, it must differ in substantive content from the first. Second, since so much of the vulnerability of error of questions is tied to the specific manner in which people are asked to respond to them—for example, by agreeing or disagreeing—it must also differ in response format. Italians' beliefs about the responsibility of immigrants for societal problems meets both requirements.

Broadly, then, our second strategy is to explore how ready Italians are to lay responsibility for the ills of the day at the doorstep of immigrants. Two points deserve attention, however. First, the notion of "responsibility" needs specification. Consider the problem of crime. It would make no sense to ask whether immigrants are responsible for the problem of crime, in the sense that there otherwise would not be one. Crime had been a problem in Italy long before immigration got underway in the 1960s, indeed, long before Italy was even established as a state. It is necessary, therefore, to distinguish between responsibility for creating a problem and for aggravating it. Second, in defining prejudice, we took as its hallmark consistency of evaluative response: the more consistently a person responds negatively to a group, the more prejudiced he or she is. What is telling is not whether a person perceives immigrants to have

TABLE 2.3
Attribution of Social Problems to Immigrants

Item	Africans	East Europeans	Total	Unweighted N
Crime*	47.5	53.4	50.4	1808
Unemployment*	31.1	40.8	35.9	1916
Housing*	29.8	37.6	33.7	1890
Health	38.0	38.1	38.1	1779
Taxes*	35.8	46.8	41.3	1719

Notes: Cell quantity is percentage of respondents saying that group has made the problem worse. Weighted frequencies
* Africans significantly lower (at significance level 0.05)

aggravated this or that particular problem, but whether he or she tends, consistently and systematically, to hold immigrants responsible for making worse the ills of contemporary society.

Therefore, we began by saying:

Some people think that the presence of [a group of immigrants] has made worse some problems that already existed.

Do you think that the presence of [the group of immigrants] in our country has made crime rates go up?[29]

In addition to asking about crime, we also asked whether immigrants were responsible for "increased unemployment for Italians"; for making it "even more difficult for Italians to find a place to live"; for "creating health problems, in the sense that they carry new diseases"; and finally, whether their presence "will involve an increase in taxes, inasmuch as the demand for public services will increase."

We thus canvassed the principal concerns commonly expressed about the presence of immigrants. This second approach to exploring current sentiments and feelings of Italians toward immigrants naturally offers another venue in which to explore social representations of "the outsider" and, in particular, to establish whether or not race is specially stigmatizing. But this time we took a slightly simpler approach in testing the impact of race. Instead of distinguishing between Northern and Central Africans, as we had in assessing the evaluative characteristics of immigrants, this time we asked one (randomly selected) half of the sample about Africans and the other half about Eastern Europeans.

Table 2.3 summarizes the readiness of Italians to attribute responsibility to immigrants for an array of societal problems becoming worse. The results deserve examination, for it is striking how they corroborate the previous results. Again it is the size of the segment of the public, even judged in absolute terms, willing to express negative judgments that stands out. At least about one-third of the Italian public is always ready to blame immigrants for having aggravated a problem regardless of the nature of the problem. And for some social problems, even more Italians are ready to blame immigrants. Thus, four out of every ten declare that because immigrants require more public services, taxes will increase. And still more—one out of every two—say that crime rates have gone up because of the presence of immigrants in Italy. In the face of the range of public problems we have canvassed, running from issues of public health to problems of unemployment and crime, and the real diversity of these societal problems, the regularity with which a sizable number of Italians lay responsibility at the doorstep of immigrants for making societal problems worse is striking.

The sheer frequency with which Italians are ready to blame immigrants, of whatever color, for social problems, of whatever kind, is the principal lesson to draw from table 2.3. But a second feature of the findings is also of interest. Just as before, there is a tendency to differentiate between types of immigrants. And just as before, so far as a distinction is drawn, it is to the disadvantage of immigrants from Eastern Europe and to the advantage of those from Africa. Italians, when they hold immigrants responsible for societal problems, are more likely to blame Eastern European immigrants than African ones for increasing problems of crime, unemployment, housing shortage, and taxes. The regularity, not the size, of the differential response to black and white immigrants is the interesting feature of the results and it points to what will become one of the principal themes of our larger argument. For the pattern of differential responses to immigrants from Eastern Europe and Africa broadly fits the differences in their ties to the economy and society, suggesting that responses to immigrants have a basis in the specific conflict of interests between outsiders and insiders. [30]

ATTRIBUTION OF PERSONAL CHARACTERISTICS AS A MEASURE OF PREJUDICE

Two questions need consideration. The first is this: What do the variety of specific judgments that Italians make about immigrants represent when they are considered not one at a time but together? At one extreme, it is possible that each represents a unique judgment; at the other extreme, it is possible that they represent semantically different ways of saying essentially the same thing. The truth no doubt lies between the two, but it matters greatly whether it lies closer to the former pole or the latter. Prejudice, we have said, consists in the readiness to respond negatively (or to refuse to respond positively) to a social group. It is a necessary condition, it follows, that if either the survey questions on evaluative characteristics or on the attribution of responsibility for social problems measure prejudice, then either or both must collectively tap an underlying generalized evaluative orientation toward immigrants.

The first question, then, is whether the individual items of each set of measures capture, in addition to a component unique to each, a common element. The second question is nested within the first. Suppose that at least some of these questions reflect a generalized disposition to respond positively (or negatively) to immigrants. Since we have asked them about two quite different groups of immigrants, the question that next must be asked is obvious. Do these questions, whatever they measure, measure the same thing when asked about black immigrants as about white ones?

To get a grip on both questions, we take advantage of factor analysis. Factor analysis, particularly of the confirmatory variety, is a handy technique for estimating the degree to which a set of indicators, though diverse in their manifest content, share one or more elements in common. Analytically, the objective is to rotate a "cloud of data" in a k-dimensional space to locate the underlying dimensions best reproducing the pattern of intercorrelations among the specific indicators.

Our strategy, then, is to determine how many underlying dimensions there are and how they capture the information conveyed by the full run of answers to the specific questions. Having announced the strategy we shall follow, we want at once to add that factor analysis is of limited value. The factor solution inevitably requires *ex post* interpretation. So it inescapably has an ad hoc character. But factor analysis, although no substitute for causal analysis, can be a useful prelude to one,[31] particularly when, confronted with any set of indicators, it is necessary to gauge whether they measure one thing or more than one thing and, if more than one, what those different things may be.

To answer these questions, figure 2.2 offers a set of scree plots of the eigenvalues of the correlation matrix of the eight items in the attribute series in descending order. The term "scree" standardly refers to rocky debris at the base of a hill. Applied by analogy to factor analysis, the idea is to contrast genuine factors and the comparative shards alongside them. Thus a scree plot starts at the highest point, identifying the most prominent factor. The point of interest is to see how quickly the plot drops, indicating that all that remains is, so to speak, statistical debris. Separate scree plots have been calculated for African and Eastern European immigrants to assure that any observed interitem homogeneity does not mask intergroup heterogeneity.

Figure 2.2 makes clear that there is only one primary, underlying characteristic that the series of attributes measures. Notice the abruptness of the fall of the slope, whether it is evaluations of African or

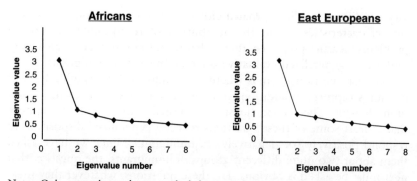

Notes: Only respondents who were asked about one group on both attribute and problem series were included; N = 291 for Africans, 274 for East Europeans

Fig. 2.2 Scree Plot of Eigenvalues of Attribute Series

Eastern European immigrants, between the first and the second eigenvalues, then the relative flatness of the curves thereafter. The steepness of the initial drop underlines the radical difference in prominence of the first factor, which accounts for almost 40 percent of the total variance in the series for both Africans and Eastern Europeans, and all the others, while the subsequent flatness of indicates that each additional dimension contributes roughly the same (small) amount to the variance.[32]

Having determined that the eight items do, in fact, measure a single primary characteristic—in this case, prejudice—factor analysis proceeds on the assumption that just so far as things are bound up with each other, they are bound up with something in common. Not the least strength of factor analysis, however, is that it does not pose the issue of commonality categorically, in all-or-nothing terms. Instead, it translates the issue into quantitative terms, treating the issue of commonality as a matter of degree, with the factor loadings indicating the degree to which each specific indicator is correlated with a latent factor.[33]

Table 2.4 summarizes a factor solution to the "personal attribute" series. There are eight descriptors in all, two favorable, the remainder unfavorable. What should we expect to see?

It is periodically suggested that in keeping track of how we feel about other things, including other people, we keep track of their positive and negative qualities separately.[34] The idea is an intriguing one, and part of its attraction, as with most forms of dualism, is its underscoring of our potential for complexity of judgment. But the form of judgment that it concerns is bounded. Our aim is to get a grip on the nature of prejudice. Thus fenced off, the idea of independent dimensions of evaluative judgment, one summarizing positive responses and the other negative ones,

TABLE 2.4
Factor Loadings for Attribute Items:
One-Factor Model

	Africans	Eastern Europeans
Honest	−0.473	−0.431
Selfish	0.536	0.537
Law-abiding	−0.455	−0.523
Intrusive	0.516	0.555
Slackers	0.543	0.566
Violent	0.594	0.602
Complainers	0.529	0.471
Inferior	0.332	0.340
% Variance explained	36.7	41.4
N	767	759

Note: Method is maximum likelihood estimation; N is minimum pairwise.

is not intuitively the right way to frame the problem. Would you really expect that a person who believes that African immigrants are lazy, violent, and inferior by nature is just as likely to find them honest and trustworthy as one who rejects these contemptuous characterizations of immigrants? Notice that the question is not whether if a person perceives immigrants to have a number of favorable characteristics he or she may not perceive them also to have some unfavorable ones, or the other way around. Many, or even most, people may perceive immigrants, African or otherwise, to have both favorable and unfavorable qualities, and form, in this sense, a differentiated view of them, even though it is broadly true that the more likely they are to believe that immigrants have unfavorable qualities, the less likely they are to believe that they have positive ones. By contrast, the hypothesis that we keep track of others' positive and negative qualities separately imposes a far more restrictive condition. It holds if, but only if, our views of others' positive and negative characteristics are independent of one another. This condition of independence means that people must have two completely separate counters, as it were, one registering how much they like immigrants, the other how much they dislike them, and that a reading of one would give us no idea at all of the reading on the other. It seems to us, on the contrary, that part of the reason that prejudice can have the force it does is precisely that it consists in the conjunction of disposition both to accentuate the unfavorable characteristics *and* to minimize the favorable characteristics of members of a group by virtue of their membership in a group.

Table 2.4 offers a test of the two alternatives—consistency or independence of positive and negative judgments. The outcome is clear-cut.[35] The signs of the factor loadings of the positive and negative characterizations are opposite in direction. But this is merely an arithmetic difference. Substantively, it means that Italians tend to be consistent in the evaluations they make of immigrants. If they perceive immigrants to have negative characteristics, they are disinclined to perceive them as having positive ones, and vice versa.[36]

No less instructively, rough similarity in the size of the factor loadings is the rule of the day, with one exception only. The one exception, the same for both Africans and Eastern Europeans, is the "inferior by nature" item, which loads less strongly on the latent factor than the other personal attributes. This may seem odd at first. The latent factor captures a disposition systematically to respond negatively or to decline to respond positively to immigrants, which matches our conception of prejudice as evaluative consistency. But since the belief that a group is inherently inferior is a quintessential expression of prejudice, shouldn't it be the item that loads the most strongly on the latent factor, whereas in fact it is the one that loads the most weakly? The appearance of paradox, however, is a statistical artifact. The size of factor loadings, like that of correlation coefficients generally, is constrained by the marginal distributions of measures. When distributions are highly skewed, as responses to the "inferior by nature" item are, an artificial ceiling is imposed on the size of the factor loading.

But granted that these eight questions do measure the same thing when asked about a particular group, do they measure the same thing when asked about different groups? It is not hard to imagine that the characterization "intrusive," for example, means something different when applied to immigrants from Eastern Europe—something, perhaps, more menacing—than when applied to immigrants from Africa. But if this is so—and so far as it is so—then the factor loadings of the same characterization will differ in magnitude for black and white immigrants. In fact, as a close examination of table 2.4 will disclose, the factor loadings for the same characterization of different groups parallel each other with impressive fidelity and, indeed, do not differ from one another more than is to be expected due to chance alone.[37]

The situation, then, comes to this. First, attribution of these characteristics to immigrants is dominated by a single factor. This factor, as examination of the loadings makes plain, reflects a tendency to consistently evaluate immigrants negatively (or positively), matching our conception of prejudice. Second, given the virtual interchangeability of different characterizations of the same group and of the same characterization of different groups, represented by the similarity in factor loadings, each may be taken as approximately as good an indicator of prejudice as any other. To say that all are equivalently good indicators of prejudice is not to say that any are perfect. Each is fairly noisy, considered on its own. But that is exactly the rationale for weighting them equally and then combining them in a single measure. By averaging them together, the noise specific to each item tends to be averaged out.[38] We accordingly have constructed the Index of Personal Attributes, adding responses to all eight personal attributes, counting them equally, and combining them so that a high score indicates a consistently negative characterization of immigrants, a low score a consistently positive one.[39]

This index manifestly is a candidate measure for prejudice, since it expressly measures the defining characteristic of prejudice: the systematic readiness to respond negatively to members of a group on the basis of their membership in the group. But what use, if any, should we make of the questions attributing responsibility for social problems to immigrants?

ATTRIBUTION OF RESPONSIBILITY FOR SOCIAL PROBLEMS AS AN INDICATOR OF PREJUDICE

Triangulation is our strategy. Therefore, we want to see if the beliefs that Italians hold about immigrant responsibility for societal ills may serve as a supplemental approach to assessing hostility toward immigrants. As we did with the attribution of personal characteristics, we employ factor analysis to understand the underlying similarity of responses to items concerning Italian social problems and immigrants' roles in creating, sustaining, and encouraging them.

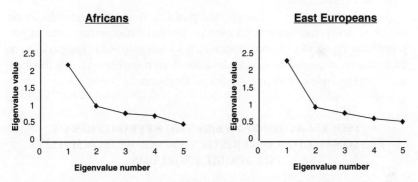

Notes: Only respondents who were asked about one group on both attribute and problem series were included; N = 383 for Africans; 350 for East Europeans

Fig. 2.3 Scree Plot of Eigenvalues of Problem Series

TABLE 2.5

Factor Loadings for Problem Items:
One-Factor Model

	Africans	Eastern Europeans
Crime	0.330	0.393
Unemployment	0.483	0.489
Housing	0.469	0.504
Disease	0.404	0.460
Taxes	0.385	0.462
% Variance explained	43.0	46.6
N	867	863

Note: Method is maximum likelihood estimation; N is minimum pairwise.

Figure 2.3 presents scree plots of the responsibility for social problems. As with the personal attributes items, the plots level off after a single, dominant dimension, indicating that a one-factor solution is a reasonable characterization of the data. And again, a large portion—over two-fifths—of the variance can be explained by this dimension.

Table 2.5 presents the results of a factor analysis of the social problem items, separately for Africans and Eastern Europeans as targets. The picture is familiar. As with the attribute items, the analysis of the factor loadings shows two additional things. First, across items, the factor loadings are all roughly the same, although the loadings for responses to Africans do have a larger range. Second, comparing responses to immigrants from Africa and Eastern Europe, no substantive difference in the loadings reveals itself.[40]

As with the attribution items, the problem items can individually be taken as noisy indicators of attitudes toward immigrants. And again, given that one and only one major factor emerges, the noise peculiar to each can be averaged out by adding them all together. We call this new measure the Index of Blame for Social Problems.[41]

THE RELATION BETWEEN THE ATTRIBUTION OF PERSONAL CHARACTERISTICS AND OF RESPONSIBILITY FOR SOCIAL PROBLEMS

An unwieldy number of specific indicators can now be reduced to two summary measures—the Index of Personal Attributes and the Index of Blame for Social Problems. We know, thanks to the factor analyses, that

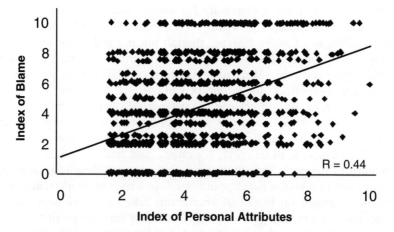

Note: Observations contain small, random deviations in order to observe densities.

Fig. 2.4 Index of Personal Attributes vs. Index of Blame
for Social Problems

each is of a piece. What we do not yet know is how each is related to the other.

In terms of their manifest content, they are obviously about quite different things: one centers on the personal characteristics of immigrants—whether they are honest, lazy, or violent—the other, on their responsibility for social problems—whether problems of crime, unemployment, or public health are worse because of them. But although the two types of attributions are distinct conceptually, it should be obvious that they will be related empirically. The more problems that Italians hold immigrants responsible for, the more negatively they will evaluate them. To drive the empirical connection between the two home, figure 2.4 graphically portrays the relationship between blaming immigrants for social problems and attributing unfavorable personal characteristics to them: the more tightly packed the cloud of points around the regression line, the stronger the covariation between the two. Attributing responsibility for social problems to immigrants and finding fault with them, as the angle of the line shooting up in figure 2.4 makes plain, are closely tied up together wherever immigrants come from.

Although it is obvious that the two should be related, why they are related is not quite so obvious. One possibility, a realistic conflict interpretation, focuses on competition for resources between immigrants and native-born Italians. A key consideration, in this view, is the competition over job opportunities. The economy is partitioned, from the perspective of split-market labor theory, into two segments, one marked by low wages and poor opportunity for advancement, the other by high wages and abundant opportunity (cf. Bonacich, 1972). Immigrants from Africa and Eastern Europe, though not integral to the core economy, can be pivotal for the peripheral economy, competing for entry-level, low-wage jobs. Moreover, the argument also runs, immigrants represent competition for public benefits as well as private jobs. Since they are new to the country and characteristically bring with them minimal resources both materially and in terms of human capital, they require expensive public services, including job-training programs, housing, language instruction, education, and health services. The expenditures for each, though not massive, are considerable in absolute terms, not to mention heavily publicized. In a time of financial austerity, public programs on behalf of immigrants take on a zero-sum quality. The more money that goes to "them," the less that can go to "us."

But isn't this exactly what the Index of Blame taps? The core of the index, after all, consists of questions about whether the presence of immigrants has increased unemployment for Italians; made it more difficult for Italians to find a place to live; and, by increasing the demand for public services, increased taxes. What could be more relevant to assessing a concern that immigrants now compete for, and to a significant degree benefit from, scarce resources in the form of private advantages and public services? To be sure, two of the questions—that immigrants have brought about an increase in crime and problems of public health—do not conform to a strictly "materialistic" definition of group interests. But surely having to live in circumstances that are more dangerous, whether because of more crime or reduced public health, counts as a loss of actual goods. And the high factor loadings of the items dealing with unemployment and housing only reinforce a suggestion that the thrust of the underlying concern has to do with apprehension about being worse-off because of immigrants.

If this interpretation is right, then it is obvious that we ought to look to realistic conflict theory for the meaning of the relation between the Index of Blame and the Index of Personal Attributes. So viewed, Italians dislike immigrants because they are, or believe they are, worse-off because of them. No doubt other factors also are at work. But if this interpretation is right, the sheer strength of the relation between the two indexes (figure 2.4) shows that a principal engine of prejudice and group hostility is the clash of group interests.

This certainly is a possibility. But as a moment's thought will make plain, there is a second possibility. We have two sets of indicators to work with—first, the readiness of Italians to ascribe negative personal characteristics to immigrants ("lazy," "intrusive," "violent," etc.) and second, their readiness to attribute responsibility to immigrants for so-

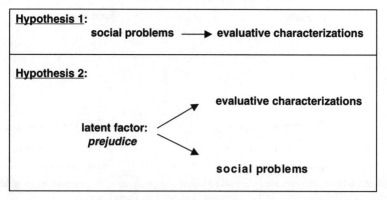

Fig. 2.5 Possible Paths of Causality

cial problems (crime, unemployment, etc.). What if both sets of indicators, though no doubt each tapping something distinctive, in the largest measure tap the same thing? Surely it is reasonable to suppose that the reason Italians perceive immigrants as "lazy," "intrusive," "violent," and the like is because they dislike them. And it is just as reasonable to suppose that the reason they perceive them as contributing to problems of crime, unemployment, and the like also is because they dislike them. But just so far as the reason underlying the way they answer both sets of questions—on personal characteristics and on responsibility for social problems—is the same, then the two sets of questions do not measure different things: they measure the same thing.

Two possibilities are depicted in figure 2.5. According to the first interpretation, the reason why Italians attribute negative characteristics to immigrants is because they blame them for Italy's social problems and thus for making Italians worse-off. In this view, the readiness to blame is the cause, the attribution of negative characteristics the effect. But to say that one is cause and the other is effect is to say that there are two things that can be distinguished. In the second interpretation, by contrast, disliking immigrants is the cause of both the readiness to blame and to attribute negative personal characteristics. But so far as this is right, then both blaming immigrants and attributing negative characteristics spring from the same source. And to say this is to say that there are not two things, one distinguishable from the other as cause and the other effect, but only one thing.

Whether there is more than one thing tapped by both sets of questions can be established by an analysis of the ordered eigenvalues.[42] Figure 2.6 shows scree plots for the correlation matrices of responses to both the blame and attribute questions, again looking separately at re-

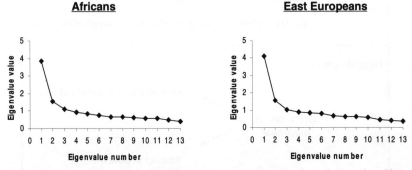

Notes: Only respondents who were asked about one group on both attribute and problem series were included; N = 240 for Africans; 206 for East Europeans

Fig. 2.6 Scree Plot of Eigenvalues of Blame and Attribute Series

sponses to questions about African and Eastern European immigrants. By contrast with previous analyses, instead of there being only one factor of prominence and the rest of the factors being (statistical) debris, two show up. The two are by no means equally prominent. The first is easily dominant, at least two and one half times as large as any other in terms of variance explained. But the second factor, although not nearly as large as the first, is distinctly larger than the others. Indeed, following the first two factors, the eigenvalues lose their distinctiveness, with the curve of eigenvalues significantly "flatter" after the second.

There are thus two factors derived from an exploratory analysis. But does this result confirm the realistic conflict interpretation, which holds that Italians evaluate immigrants negatively because they think they are worse-off because of immigrants? To see directly what is going on, we fit a two-factor model to the negative attribution and the social problems questions.[43]

As examination of table 2.6 shows, every question from both series loads positively (or negatively in the case of the positive attributes "honesty" and "lawfulness") on the first factor. It is notable that while on the fundamental factor the attribute items load more heavily in all but one case, there is a significant contribution from the problem items as well. The second factor loads in an almost opposite fashion: the problem items weigh more heavily here.

We began by setting out two possibilities. Italians may attribute negative characteristics to immigrants because Italians believe they are worse-off because of them, or because they may both attribute negative characteristics to them and blame them for social problems because they dislike them. The exploratory factor analytic results provide mixed results in navigating between the two. Table 2.6 indicates that there is a dominant

TABLE 2.6
Factor Loadings for Problem and Attribute Items:
Two-Factor Model

	Africans		East Europeans	
	Factor 1	Factor 2	Factor 1	Factor 2
Problems				
Crime	0.262	0.266	0.323	0.324
Unemployment	0.071	0.531	0.154	0.461
Housing	0.222	0.488	0.112	0.540
Disease	0.329	0.336	0.424	0.401
Taxes	0.044	0.369	0.117	0.417
Attributes				
Honest	−0.502	−0.082	−0.413	−0.077
Selfish	0.392	0.133	0.496	0.297
Law-abiding	−0.474	−0.112	−0.455	−0.178
Intrusive	0.509	0.178	0.515	0.118
Slackers	0.530	0.144	0.547	0.172
Violent	0.542	0.235	0.584	0.257
Complainers	0.459	0.138	0.417	0.128
Inferior by nature	0.212	0.317	0.305	0.235
% Variance	29.9	11.8	31.8	11.7
N	382		383	

Notes: "Africans" includes only those respondents who were asked about Africans for both the attribute and problem items. "East Europeans" includes only those respondents who were asked about East Europeans for both the attribute and problem items.

Method is maximum likelihood estimation with varimax rotation; N is minimum pairwise.

factor, one that taps the attribute series most heavily but also attracts a significant contribution from the problem series. The second factor measures something that taps the problems more heavily, and less so the attributions. Following the confirmatory method outlined by Bollen (1993), we estimate a model in which each indicator loads on two factors, one common to all, and another that is unique to the measurement approach—personal attributes or responsibility for social problems. This allows us to describe any common factor of prejudice while more precisely filtering out effects, whether they be correlated measurement error or causal constructs, unique to each approach.

Table 2.7 provides the results of this analysis. As in the exploratory analysis, all the items contribute significantly to the first factor, although the problem items generally have lower point loadings. The second factor for each item series behaves slightly differently: although there is

TABLE 2.7
Confirmatory Factor Analysis for Problem and Attribute Items:
Method Effects

	Prejudice Factor	Problem Factor	Attribute Factor
Problems			
Crime	0.178**	0.150**	
Unemployment	0.125**	0.278**	
Housing	0.111**	0.277**	
Disease	0.185**	0.240**	
Taxes	0.123**	0.230**	
Attributes			
Honest	−0.482**		0.130
Selfish	0.506**		0.164
Law-abiding	−0.592**		0.209
Intrusive	0.625**		0.100
Slackers	0.567**		0.306
Violent	0.578**		0.253
Complainers	0.547**		0.220
Inferior by nature	0.278**		0.267
N	1326		

Notes: Method is maximum likelihood estimation with varimax rotation;
N is minimum pairwise.
** significant at 0.05 level

little else in the attribute items, there is definitely a second factor for the social problem items.

What, then, are we to make of these results? A number of conclusions are forthcoming. First, the hallmark of prejudice, as we saw earlier, is a readiness to respond negatively to members of a group by virtue of their membership in a group. It follows that the more consistently a person responds negatively to a member of a group, the more prejudiced he or she is. Both sets of questions, whether about personal characteristics of immigrants or about their responsibility for social problems, provide comparable opportunities to respond negatively to immigrants. It follows that the more unfavorable characteristics that Italians ascribe to immigrants (or favorable ones they refuse to ascribe) *or* the more societal problems they hold them responsible for, the more prejudiced they are. Since the questions in both sets cover a wide variety of attributes and within each set share a common assessment format, cumulating responses to them yields a multitrait, multiformat measure of prejudice.[44] Indeed, the correlation between an index constructed using the factor scores and an average score loses little in explanatory accuracy in exchange for its great parsimony: the two are correlated at .91 for African and .93 for Eastern European target groups. In addition, the second factor we found in our exploratory analysis is confirmed in our later analysis to be a unique component to the method employed. Whether this second aspect is a method error component or, alternatively, a causal component such as realistic conflict, is impossible to judge based solely on this analysis. Using the results from this discussion, it is precisely that question we turn to in the next chapter.

THE IDEA OF THE OUTSIDER: THE "SWITCH" EXPERIMENT

Consistency of evaluation, of systematically taking advantage of opportunities to express negative views and feelings about a group, is the hallmark of prejudice. So far we have examined consistency across different forms of expressing negative feelings toward a group. But what about consistency across different groups of immigrants?

We began with the intuition that differences of race are different in kind, more intractable and deeply rooted, than those of nationality or ethnicity. Some of our findings are consistent with this intuition—above all, the greater readiness of Italians to declare that immigrants from Africa are "inferior by nature." Other results, however, appear to cut the other way—for example, the greater readiness of Italians to blame immigrants from Eastern Europe for shortages in housing and jobs. The two sets of results are not logically contradictory. The first set may reflect a disposition to draw primordial distinctions on the basis of race; the second, a tendency to stigmatize groups as a function of particular circumstances of the moment, especially economic. But the two sets of results, taken together, suggest a need to think through more precisely how the categories of race and nationality are actually engaged in the social construction of the concept of the outsider.

A thought experiment may be useful. Imagine a small knot of Italians on a street corner late one night. They are talking about immigrants from Africa, some expressing criticism after criticism, others disagreeing. Down the street and across the corner is another group of Italians. They, too, are talking about immigrants from Africa, some complaining, others not. But then, after fifteen minutes or so, this second group of Italians switches the topic of conversation. Instead of continuing to debate about immigrants from Africa, they start discussing those from Eastern Europe. Imagine also that you were on the same block, midway between the two groups of Italians, close enough to both to be able to make out the tenor of the two conversations, but far enough away from both to be unable to hear precisely *who* was the subject of discussion in either. Imagining all of this, our thought experiment turns on one question. Could you tell that, part way through their conversation, the second group had switched which immigrants they were talking about but the first had not?

If differences of race cut deeper than differences of ethnicity, then the answer necessarily must be yes. Even though you were too far away to hear clearly the change in the name of the group of immigrants in the second conversation, you were close enough to hear distinctly the evaluative tone of both conversations. Since the evaluative tone of responses to a group is the hallmark of prejudice, if differences of race in fact cut deeper than differences of nationality, it necessarily must be the case that you could distinguish the first conversation, which centered on Africans throughout, and the second, which began with Africans and then switched to Eastern Europeans.

How can our thought experiment be translated into a real experiment? We have on hand two methods of measuring prejudice, the factor analyses have established, one focusing on the attribution of personal characteristics to members of a group, the other on the attribution of responsibility for societal problems to the group. Each, you will recall, was asked about immigrants from *either* Africa *or* Eastern Europe, with the choice made on an entirely random basis. This means that the sample was divided into four approximately equal-sized parts: (1) those who were asked about Eastern Europeans for both the series of questions on responsibility for social problems and personal characteristics; (2) those who were asked about Africans for both; (3) those who were asked about Eastern Europeans for the first but about Africans for the second; and (4) those who were asked about Africans for the first but about Eastern Europeans for the second. We have, as it were, created four conversations. In two, Italians talk about the same group of immigrants throughout; in two, they switch halfway through. Is it possible to tell the difference among them?

How exactly should the four differ if differences of race matter more than differences of nationality? Prejudice, we have seen, consists in a readiness *consistently* to respond negatively to members of a group. If differences of race do cut deeper, it follows that the evaluative consistency of responses should be greater when Italians are discussing Africans throughout both series of measures than when they begin by discussing Eastern Europeans and switch to Africans or begin by discussing Africans and switch to Eastern Europeans.

There are two quite different possibilities to consider. On one side, if the view we held at the start is right, differences of race matter more than differences of nationality; on the other, if the view we hold now is closer to the mark, what matters most is not the particular ways that outgroups differ but the judgment that they differ. So far as the first view is right, Italians should be more consistent if they are evaluating the same group throughout. So far as the second view is right, they should be just as consistent even if they switch the groups they are evaluating halfway through.

Consistency of evaluation can be calculated in terms of the odds of a negative personal characterization being made of a group as a function of the likelihood of attributing responsibility for societal problems to a group.[45] Simply put, the more problems that you believe a group causes, the more negative characteristics you are likely to think that they have. The crucial question, though, is whether it actually matters whether you have in mind the same outgroup when it comes to stereotyping their characteristics as you have in attributing responsibility for societal problems.

The "Switch" experiment is expressly designed to give an answer, for the first time, to this question. Figure 2.7a accordingly plots the average percentage of negative attributions a respondent will make, given the percentage of social problems he or she has claimed that African immigrants make worse. Does it make a difference whether, after discussing the problems that African immigrants may cause, the subject is switched to the personal qualities that Eastern European immigrants have? The solid line in figure 2.7a plots the likelihood of a negative evaluation for those referring to black immigrants all the way through; the dotted line, the likelihood of negative characterization for those who, halfway through, are suddenly switched to evaluating white immigrants. The results are dramatic: the odds of responding negatively on the personal attribute series, given a negative response on the social problems series, is virtually identical for those who, halfway through, switched to talking about Eastern Europeans as for those who, all the way through, talked about Africans. The chances of ascribing a negative characterization to Eastern Europeans, given that a person believes Africans have aggravated social problems, are statistically the same as the chances of ascribing a negative characterization to Africans themselves.

Yet this similarity, it could be argued, is an artifact of the fact that respondents were asked about Africans first. If differences of race do cut deeper than those of nationality, then, possibly, starting off by evaluating Africans over a series of items created a mental set that respondents then carried over to their evaluations of Eastern Europeans. The "Switch" experiment, however, was designed to test for the possibility of an order effect. There are two experimental conditions in which respondents switch the group of immigrants they are evaluating: in one

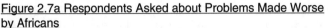
Figure 2.7a Respondents Asked about Problems Made Worse by Africans

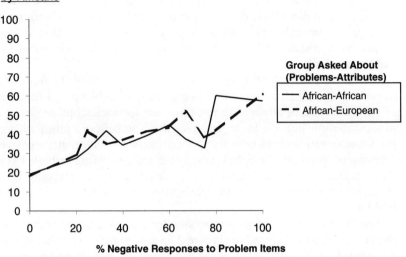

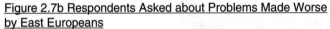
Figure 2.7b Respondents Asked about Problems Made Worse by East Europeans

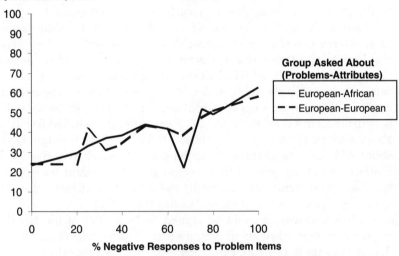

Fig. 2.7 Mean % Negative Responses to Attribute Items as a Function of % Negative Responses to Problem Items

TABLE 2.8
Regression of % Negative Responses to Attribute Series on
% Negative Responses to Problem Series

Target Combination:	African-African	African-European	European-African	European-European	Combined
% Negative responses to problems	0.386** (11.34)	0.365** (11.33)	0.376** (9.92)	0.350** (9.30)	0.370** (29.55)
Constant	19.8	22.8	20.5	22.1	21.2
n	480	492	470	467	1909
R-squared	0.204	0.208	0.174	0.157	0.187

Note: t-statistics appear in parentheses below parameter estimates

they begin by evaluating Africans, then turn to evaluating Eastern Europeans; but in the other, they begin by evaluating Eastern Europeans, then turn to evaluating Africans. If asking about Africans first is responsible for the similarity of response to Eastern Europeans, then we should see a dissimilarity of response to Africans when Eastern Europeans are asked about first. Figure 2.7b accordingly plots the equivalent odds of attributing negative characteristics given an attribution of responsibility for societal problems for those who evaluate Eastern Europeans throughout and for those who, halfway through, switch to Africans. Again the results are arresting. The chances of ascribing a negative characterization to Africans, given that a person believes Eastern Europeans have aggravated social problems, are statistically the same as ascribing a negative characterization to Eastern Europeans themselves.

Finally, comparing figures 2.7a and 2.7b, one can see by inspection, whether your eye is on the slope or intercept,[46] that the lines plotted in either can be laid right on top of those in the other. The counterhypothesis of an order effect can thus be rejected.

Table 2.8 presents an alternative method to underwrite this conclusion. The first four columns of table 2.8 report, for each combination of target groups, the results of regressions of the percentage of negative responses to the attribution of personal characteristics series on the percentage of negative responses to the blame for social problems series. The final column reports the same regression, ignoring the identities of the target group. Simply by inspection it is possible to see that the relationship between the dependent and independent variables in the various regressions are virtually identical. Indeed, a formal test of this observation—a Chow test for parameter stability—does not reject the null hypothesis that the coefficients are identical in all the regressions

(F = 0.328, p = 0.96). This implies that *it makes no difference* which group is being asked about.

The question that we asked in our thought experiment was the following: Could you tell the difference between a conversation in which Italians were talking about the same group of immigrants throughout and another in which, midway through, they switched and began to talk about an entirely different group of immigrants? The results of the "Switch" experiment suggest that the answer is no. If you know how many problems Italians blame on Eastern Europeans you can tell just as well how many unfavorable characteristics they will ascribe to African immigrants as if you know how many problems they blame on Africans themselves.

This is a result genuinely worth consideration because it throws new light on the nature of prejudice, both in general and in the contemporary politics of Europe. If people who are prejudiced against a certain group are asked, in the course of a conversation, to explain why they believe the group has so many shortcomings, they will characteristically mention specific characteristics they believe to be distinctive of the group: blacks are lazy; Jews, unscrupulous in business; Eastern Europeans, violent and disposed to criminal extortion. It is natural, then, to think of prejudice as consisting in a set of social identities, all unfavorable, but each tailor-made to the actual attributes of specific groups just possibly because it captures a kernel of truth.[47]

Evaluations of outgroups are distinguishable. People will, if required, make distinctions among outgroups. As Hagendoorn has shown in a classic study,[48] presented with a set of outgroups, respondents will rate some as more desirable, others as less, and there is very nearly consensual agreement on these ethnic hierarchies. But because people can distinguish among outgroups with respect to social standing, it does not follow that they distinguish between them in their evaluative consistency. The "Switch" experiment reproduces, we believe, more faithfully the actual conditions of social life. On one side, it contains no specific directive to discriminate between outgroups; on the other side, respondents are free to discriminate between outgroups in the experiment *if they are ordinarily disposed to do so.* But they don't. As the "Switch" experiment shows, you can predict whether Italians will respond negatively to one outgroup just as well from knowing that they respond negatively to a quite different outgroup as from knowing that they respond negatively to the very same outgroup.

This interchangeability of outgroups exposes, we believe, a fundamental feature of prejudice. Nearly all of us, in our real lives, have noted a person who rejects a member of a different group out of blind prejudice. The "Switch" experiment results, however, throw a more revealing light on just what it means to say that prejudice is "blind." Superficially, prejudice appears to be bound up with the specific characteristics of the outgroup. Jews are castigated for being underhanded in business, blacks for lacking the initiative to get into business. But if you take the heart of prejudice to be the hostility that members of one group feel toward members of another group because they are members of another, the particular ways that hostility happens to be expressed at particular moments in time no longer becomes the defining feature of prejudice. Indeed, just so far as one can predict the odds of a negative response on the part of a member of one group to a member of a different group from knowing that there has been a negative response to a quite different group, then the rejection of either group cannot be evoked by the specific ways in which they differ from another. It instead is grounded in the fact of difference itself.

In saying this we are not at all proposing that race cannot matter on its own. Whether and how far it matters distinctively depends on the structure of the situation. If people's attention is directed specifically to race, whether by political entrepreneurs or by the mass media, it can be used distinctively to stigmatize blacks. Moreover, notwithstanding the interchangeability of groups dramatically illustrated by the "Switch" experiment, it is not helpful to pose the question of group characteristics in categorical terms. The claim is not that there are no differences whatever, under any conditions, in the consistency of evaluative reactions to African and Eastern European immigrants. It is, rather, that the differences are striking for their modesty when people are free to act as they are accustomed to act. It is the similarity, not the dissimilarity, of responses to African and Eastern European immigrants that stands out.

This similarity offers a clue to the heart of the problem of prejudice in contemporary Europe. The signature feature of prejudice in contemporary Europe, our findings suggest, is its enveloping character. An immigrant from Poland has many points of similarity, cultural and even physical, with Italians; an immigrant from Senegal, at least as many points of dissimilarity. Yet both, by virtue of being from somewhere else, are outsiders. The politics of exclusion, this suggests, has a potential for division in contemporary Europe even greater than the divisiveness of race in America. Understanding the forces behind this enveloping conception of the outsider is the task to which we now turn.

CHAPTER 3.

A Theory of Prejudice and
Group Conflict

WHAT IS responsible for the wave of hostility toward immigrants that has washed across not only Italy specifically but Western Europe generally?

Oddly, many of the explanatory factors are known, but the explanation is not—because every explanatory factor has generated a separate explanation. Discover that a clash of interests is involved, and a conflict of interest theory is advanced. Observe that ethnicity is implicated, and a theory of ethnic conflict is put forward. And each explanation is framed in its own terms; it is as though there are a dozen blueprints, all depicting the same building. But each presents a different elevation executed from a different perspective and drawn on a different scale. So the drawings seem not merely individualized but incomparable.

We want to push past the notion that every causal factor is the basis for a causal theory. Different factors can matter for the same reason, and the same factor can matter for different reasons. We therefore have devised a general framework. It is general in two senses. It offers, first, a common framework for understanding how an array of quite different factors, running from personality to social class, contribute to intolerance. But it also offers, second, a framework that highlights the commonality between seemingly different forms of prejudice. But if our framework is new, the intellectual materials out of which it has been assembled are not. On the contrary, we have sought to identify and preserve the vital insights of the principal previous approaches to the study of prejudice. If we have made a contribution, it is by illustrating how these different approaches can be brought together to reinforce rather than undercut one another.

Our plan is to proceed in several steps. Given the tendency to reify the problem of prejudice, we shall first put flesh on the bones of the intuitions that lie behind the principal approaches to the study of prejudice; then deduce from these intuitions specific hypotheses about the sources of prejudice; then derive from these hypotheses an overall explanatory model; and, finally, present evidence from the Italian study establishing the strengths—and the weaknesses—of our model.

THREE INTUITIONS

Our starting point is a summer camp for twelve-year-old boys, set up a half century ago as part of an historic series of experiments on realistic group conflict.[1] In order to be picked for the camp, the boys had to come from stable social backgrounds to ensure that they were themselves well adjusted. They also had to be unknown to each other to guarantee that how they behaved toward each other at camp could not be a function of prior friendships or conflicts.

Immediately on arriving at the camp, the boys were divided into two groups, more or less equal in size, each as nearly like the other as possible.[2] In the first phase, the two groups were kept apart. Each operated independently, developing its own patterns of activities, norms, sense and symbols of identity, and leadership. In the second phase tournaments were conducted. The two groups vied against each other in competitive games (e.g., baseball), with the winning group receiving a trophy for the group as a whole, and each of its members pocketing a valued prize (e.g., a penknife) for themselves. Finally, in the third phase, the boys undertook cooperative rather than competitive activities. They found themselves, for example, stranded, far from camp, a stalled truck nearby. But the truck was heavy and to give it a jump start and get back to camp, they had to join forces in pushing.

The results of the summer camp studies were striking. When the two groups moved from being independent of one another to competing with one another, hostility between them immediately flared up. Members of each group frequently denigrated, and sometimes even attacked, members of the other group. But then, even in the face of this hostility, when the two groups moved from competing against each other to cooperating with each other, the tension between them relaxed.

There are two propositions packed into this result, not usually distinguished, but analytically distinct. One specifies the role of common interests in the definition of groups; the other specifies the role of interests in promoting group conflict depending on whether they are common or conflictual. Each is subject to challenge. Sharing a common interest may be a sufficient reason for people to recognize that they belong to the same group, but it is not obviously a necessary reason for categorizing others as belonging either to the same or a different group. Nor is it obvious that when members of different groups share a common interest they have as unequivocal an incentive to cooperate as they do to compete when their interests converge.[3] But granting that there are questions to consider, it is clear that the finding on competing interests and group conflict goes deep. The summer camp studies demonstrated that no history of enmity is required to provoke group conflict. Nor is it necessary that the leadership of either group has an urge to dominate. Nor need the conflict between the groups in any important sense be the product of a misunderstanding, which could have been either avoided or ameliorated by more accurate information. To understand the hostility that broke out at the summer camp, it is necessary to know only that for one group of boys to get what it wants the other cannot get what it wants. Group conflict is rooted in the clash of group interests.

To go from the summer camp studies to the tangle of European hostilities obviously represents a giant step in scale and complexity. Analytically, however, it need be only a small step. Many motives may incline individuals to leave their country of birth—for example, to escape political persecution. In the largest degree, however, immigration is an economic phenomenon.[4] Immigrants immigrate to be better-off: to earn more, to enjoy better conditions of life, to ensure better lives for their children. But a growing number of Western Europeans, the argument runs, have concluded that a better life for immigrants means a worse one for them. More jobs for immigrants means fewer jobs for Italians, or, given the downward pressure on wages, less money. More immigrants also means more money must be spent on public services and benefits, housing and job training for them, which in turn means that native-born citizens must pay more in taxes to support expanded services to immigrants, or receive fewer benefits as immigrants get more, or both. Details to one side, more for immigrants means—or is understood to mean—less for Italians. And the result of the clash of economic interests between immigrants and native born, the argument runs, is the hostility now so conspicuously directed against outsiders.

So viewed, prejudice, which may seem the paradigm of irrationality, follows from a rational calculus of advantage.[5] To suggest that prejudice can be a rational economic response is not to approve of it, but to recognize that group conflict is rooted in the actual clash of interests and cannot be dismissed as an unfortunate misunderstanding that could be cleared up if people simply were better informed. Nor is it the product of individual irrationality that should be treated by therapeutic attention. Instead, hostility toward outsiders is tied to people's actual circumstances, above all, to the real conflict between the interests of immigrants and of native born. It is, after all, more than a coincidence that the wave of hostility toward immigrants surged in Germany, France, and Italy as economic growth faltered and mass unemployment mounted.[6]

The first intuition, then, is that Italians are hostile toward immigrants because just so far as immigrants are better-off, they fear that they will be worse-off. The second intuition is less familiar and focuses on the group basis of bias.

Imagine a U-shaped table in a small classroom. Seated around the table are half a dozen experimental subjects, each visible and audible to every other. At the head of the table is the experimenter. He shows all the subjects a line of a certain length and then asks each, in turn, which of the three other lines matches it, beginning with the "experimental subject" on his left. Figure 3.1 gives a stylized version of the task, displaying three lines, A, B, C, of which A manifestly matches the test line while B and C conspicuously do not. But what the real experimental subject, who will answer last, does not know is that all of his fellow "subjects" in reality are accomplices of the experimenter. When asked which line matches, they have been instructed that instead of picking A, which is the correct answer, they should answer C, even though it manifestly is the wrong answer. And so, one by one, they pick C, as the real experimental subject, in growing confusion and consternation, watches, powerless to intervene, waiting his turn. And when, finally, his turn comes, rather than say A, he may well answer C.

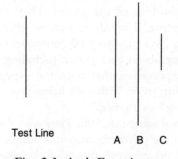

Test Line

A B C

Fig. 3.1 Asch Experiment

This stylized sketch describes a classic experiment, devised by Solomon Asch,[7] taken to demonstrate the power of social groups.[8] In the Asch experiment, however, it is not hard to understand how a group can wield power over an individual. Everyone else in the group agrees with each other. No one agrees with him. He stands alone. And he cannot escape. He must give an answer when his turn comes and he knows exactly what answer to give to conform to the group. Consider, by contrast, the "minimal group" experiment pioneered by Henri Tajfel.[9]

Imagine a set of experimental subjects, each unknown to all the others, none of whom will ever meet each other. All are taken, one at a time, into a room where, by means of a tachistoscope, they are shown a cloud of dots. They see the dots for only a fraction of second, too brief a time for them possibly to count them accurately, but nonetheless they are asked how many dots there are. So far everything is the same for all experimental subjects. Then, on a purely random basis, the experimenter forms two groups, telling one half of the subjects that they counted more dots than there actually are, and the other half, that they counted fewer dots than there actually are. Finally, at the end of the experiment, each is asked to decide how a strictly limited set of valuable goods should be distributed to the other experimental subjects. Since they have never met them, they know nothing about them except what the experimenter tells them. And all the experimenter tells them about each of the other experimental subjects is that they are either an "overcounter" or an "undercounter" of dots. And, remarkably, it turns out that if the experimental subjects believe that they themselves counted more dots than there actually were, they will assign more of the goods to their fellow experimental subjects who are said to be "overcounters," while if they believe that they themselves counted fewer dots, they will assign more to their fellow "undercounters." In short, even minimal groups can be the basis of discrimination in favor of the ingroup at the expense of the outgroup.

In the "minimal group" experiment, experimental subjects do not see or hear the other members of the group. They may never have done anything together before. They do not come from the same place nor, so far as they know, have anything of consequence in common. They know next to nothing about each other, including each other's names, and they have no expectation that once the experiment is concluded, they will have anything to do with each other ever again. In what sense, then, do they "belong" to a group?

In the most minimal sense possible. They are told they share a characteristic with some of the other experimental subjects. The characteristic that they supposedly share—over- or undercounting dots (or, in another experiment, preferring paintings by Kandinsky to those by Klee or the other way around)—is one that they have never connected to themselves. And the characteristic they are told that they share with some others (apart from being false) involves something of no importance to them. They cannot possibly attach importance to whether they go wrong by counting too many dots or too few, nor can they possibly have any experientially grounded reason for valuing others more highly if they, too, are "dot overcounters" or, conversely, thinking less of them if they are "dot undercounters." Although the idea of categorizing themselves (or anyone else) as an under- or overcounter of dots had never occurred to them before they were told that they were one or the other, once they are categorized as one or the other, they show a bias in favor of members of their group, the ingroup, and against members of the other, the outgroup.

Contrasts clarify. In the Asch experiment, what is striking is the power of a group to induce individual members to deny the clear evidence of their own eyes: but the whole point of the experimental design is to strip the experimental subject of protection against the power of a group, unified in its point of view, meeting face to face, bent on extracting conformity to its norms. By contrast, what is striking in the Tajfel experiment is the flimsiness of the group. Members of a group share no past experiences; no commonalities of social or economic circumstance; no cultural values; no similarities in belief, background, or prior experience—nothing to bind and, equally, nothing to divide. Yet merely by virtue of supposedly sharing a characteristic that is itself of no value to them, they display a bias in favor of the ingroup at the expense of the outgroup.

It seems to us essential to take account of the "minimal group" studies in developing a theory of prejudice and group conflict. They show that people have a remarkable readiness to accept categorizations of themselves as belonging to one group rather than another. Still more important, these studies demonstrate that even when the characteristics they supposedly share with others are of minimal importance, they nonetheless suffice to produce a bias in favor of the ingroup, at the expense of the outgroup. If groups so minimal as these can make a difference, one can only imagine the power of real groups—of ethnic, national, status, and class groups, each with their thick and closely interwoven strands of socialization, self-interest, and symbolic identification—to create a deep identification with the ingroup, very much at the expense of the outgroup.

The "minimal group" experiments thus supply a second intuition potentially of use in developing an account of prejudice and group conflict. What lies directly behind prejudice and discrimination is the potency of lines—even lines of minimal significance—that distinguish those who belong to a group from those who do not.

For a third intuition we turn to a celebrated study of prejudice, *The Authoritarian Personality*, by Adorno and his colleagues. There is a formidable, even baroque, complexity to the view of *The Authoritarian Personality* considered in detail. Its central premise, however, is straightforward. Individuals, for whatever complex of reasons, develop distinctive psychological profiles. One especially telling facet of their psychological profiles, for understanding prejudice, is authoritarianism. In its various conceptions,[10] authoritarianism is marked by an overly zealous insistence on conformity to conventional, middle-class values; by an idealized conception of established authorities and an uncritical insistence on unqualified compliance with their decisions and precepts; and by an overreadiness to respond aggressively and punitively to others, particularly if they are lower in status. Many of these elements are evident in many people, but the authoritarian personality is distinguished by the uncommon degree of their development. The crucial claim, then, is that although no doubt people are more susceptible to prejudice in some circumstances than others, it also is true that in the same circumstances some are more susceptible than others because of their psychological makeup. They have, as it were, an inner readiness to dislike and to derogate others, particularly groups of lower status. They need not be specially provoked, and it is not necessary for the economy to be in a tailspin or for their lives to be going badly for them to respond with hostility, for example, to immigrants. They are inherently susceptible to prejudice by virtue of their basic psychological makeup.

To give a more palpable feeling for the emotional tone and qualities of the mind of the authoritarian personality, consider some elements of an interview with a young man named Mack.[11] Mack, at the time of the interview, was a twenty-four-year-old freshman aiming at law school. When asked whether there are groups of people he dislikes, Mack begins by saying, "Principally those I don't understand very well." Then, without any prompting, and indeed barely pausing, he begins, "Austrians, the Japanese I never cared for; Filipinos—I don't know—I'd just as soon leave them as have them. Up home there were Austrians and Poles, though, I find the Poles interesting. I have a little dislike for Jewish people." The list lengthens, in a self-stimulating way, as though the mention of one group Mack dislikes calls to mind another, then another, then yet another.

Having worked his way through to Jews, though, Mack does not find himself short of things to say. His preliminary characterization is unflattering, but restrained—and, in retrospect it seems safe to say, deliberately so: "I have a little dislike for Jewish people. I don't think they are as courteous or as interested in humanity as they ought to be. And I resent that, though I have had few dealings with them." Then, as though now he has the bit between his teeth, Mack talks at length about how Jews "accent the clannish and the material"; how their "attention is directed very greatly toward wealth"; "how they won't mingle"; how, thinking of a Jewish classmate, "I would marry her if she had thrown off her Jewishness, but I wouldn't be able to associate with her class."

Mack, then, illustrates in a prototypical way the third of our intuitions: that some individuals are predisposed to prejudice, not because of their social circumstances or on account of the pressure of economic need, but by virtue of the deeper-lying and enduring makeup of their personalities.[12]

FROM INTUITIONS TO A MODEL

Each of our intuitions has something to recommend it. A properly rounded account of prejudice ought to take account of the group basis of invidious distinctions between "us" and "them"; of the power of common interests to induce cooperation and of a clash of interests to evoke conflict; of the role of people's basic psychological makeup and inner conflicts in stoking angry responses to those who stand out by virtue of their religion or race or simply because they are unfamiliar.

It might seem that developing a properly rounded account of prejudice is therefore straightforward. Simply recognize that each of these various intuitions has some validity and work to see how they fit together. But it only seems so when this assembly of ideas enjoys the natural vagueness of intuitions. When the precision of hypotheses is imposed on them, it becomes apparent that each in its standard version is at odds with the others. We have already seen one facet of this conflict. Both the realistic conflict and the social categorization approaches, as we have observed, were designed to obviate a personality-centered explanation. But the alliance of the first two approaches is primarily tactical, confined to their mutual rejection of a personality-oriented approach. Once one pushes past this point of agreement that unites the two, one is struck by the points of disagreement that divide them. A social categorization approach construes prejudice and group hostility as contextual and situational, with people rejecting others depending on whether their own social identity happens to be at the center of their attention or not. According to a realistic conflict approach, by contrast, Italians reject immigrants because if immigrants are better-off, native Italians fear they will be worse-off. The issue is thus not one of a person's identity, social or otherwise, but of their interests, especially material, and the calculus generating intolerance is not social-psychological but economic. There is, it needs to be appreciated, a chasm between an explanation of prejudice and group conflict centered on the importance of social identity and one organized around a calculus of gains to immigrants and losses to native Italians where the gains and losses, so far from being symbolic or merely psychological, are real and characteristically economic.

But grant that these intuitions represent rival hypotheses. What exactly follows from this? They surely are not logically contradictory. The truth of a social categorization hypothesis, supposing it is true, does not entail the falsity of a realistic conflict hypothesis. They both may be simultaneously true, and depending on the circumstance one may be more important than the other or both may matter equally. And although both have been surrounded by arguments against a personality-centered approach, these arguments are ancillary and can be stripped away without entailing the invalidity of either. Yet, supposing these different approaches are not mutually contradictory, in what sense, exactly, are they complementary? Is it in the weak sense that the truth of one supplements that of the others, the validity of each being freestanding of that of the others? Or are they possibly complementary in the stronger sense that each is a part of a common explanatory whole?

Our three intuitions, taken one at a time, seem self-evidently reasonable. Considered together, however, they are not obviously reconcilable. It is necessary, therefore, to work through the reasoning behind them in order to derive a systematic, explicit, and testable account of prejudice and group conflict. We proceed, therefore, in three steps: first, working out hypotheses, which define causal mechanisms of our model; next, ordering the mechanisms, which define its hierarchical structure; then, taking the model as defined, generating testable predictions.

HYPOTHESES AND DEDUCTIONS

Our starting point is Tajfel's classic "minimal group" experiments. Confronted with an opportunity to treat others differently or not depending on whether they are similar or not, people favor others that they believe are like themselves at the expense of those that they believe are different. They do so independent of their own personality profile or psychological makeup. They do so, moreover, even when the points of similarity they allegedly share with others are, on their face, of no importance, to themselves or to anyone else. These findings, replicated many times over, yield the analytical fulcrum for our model:

> H1: Whatever increases the likelihood of categorizing others as belonging to a group other than one's own increases the likelihood of hostility toward them.

Some implications of the categorization hypothesis are obvious. In the minimal group experiment, the meaning of a group is notional. Group "members" share no experience, identity, history, or symbolic attachment. Indeed, apart from knowing they have a common characteristic of minimal importance—the famously cited propensity to overcount the number of dots in a display, for example—they know nothing of each other. Yet if even so minimal a basis of commonality can serve as a basis of categorization, it obviously follows that categories of identity laid down by nationality, class, religion, and ethnicity can serve as fundamental bases of categorization into ingroup and outgroup.

But some of the implications of the categorization hypothesis are not obvious at all. The lesson seems to be that social categorization is hardwired into people: their propensity to categorize, and therefore to discriminate, is automatic or, at any rate, virtually unavoidable.[13] This, as straightforward an interpretation of the experimental results as it appears, is a misreading nonetheless. The readiness to categorize others, so far from being a constant, is contextual and social. The likelihood that people will see themselves as part of an ingroup or discriminate in its favor, as Tajfel and his colleagues have demonstrated, is contingent. It varies with, for example, the degree of people's identification with the ingroup; the salience of the characteristic that is the basis of categorization; the degree of similarity (or dissimilarity) of ingroup and outgroup; and the comparative status of in- and outgroup, among other factors.[14] Whether discrimination occurs at all and what form it takes, if it does occur, is contingent on specific social contexts and particular social meanings attributed to the differences between groups.

The need to take account of these differences in circumstances provides a bridge to the realistic conflict approach to explaining hostility and group conflict. It may be true, as a general proposition, that immigrants are a threat so far as they take away jobs, undercut wages, or compete for public resources in the form of housing or job-training programs. But they are not an equal threat to all Italians. Some are, precisely by virtue of their objective circumstances, more vulnerable than others. The person in need of housing assistance is more likely to see immigrants as taking away scare resources than the person who is well fixed; the one who has, or wishes to get, a low-skilled, low-wage job is more likely to see immigrants as underbidding wages and taking away jobs than is the well-paid professional. For that matter, it is easy to see why the same person might respond differently to immigrants at different points in time. In good times, when jobs are plentiful and prospects bright, he is less likely to see immigrants as a threat to either his current or future economic well-being; when jobs are in short supply and job security clouded, he is more likely to feel threatened by immigrants because, of course, they are more likely to *be* a threat in bad times.

We want a general way to express this without being tautological. It is necessary, it follows, to put in causal terms the relation between a concern about economic well-being and prejudice. Accordingly, our second hypothesis is:

H2: Whatever increases the likelihood of concerns about economic well-being increases the likelihood of categorizing immigrants as belonging to an outgroup, and given H1, increases the likelihood of hostility toward them.

One element in the argument remains. In Tajfel's view, a person who believes himself to be an "overcounter" of dots favors others that he believes to be "overcounters" at the expense of those whom he thinks are "undercounters" *because* he categorizes the former as like himself and the latter as different. The readiness to categorize others as different is not a constant, however. People are more likely to do it in some situations, less likely in others. But, we want to suggest, if it is true that people are predictably more ready to categorize others as different in some situations than in other situations, it is also true that some people are predictably more likely to do so than others.

More than one feature may mark those who are more ready to categorize others as different, but a major thread woven through psychologically oriented analyses of prejudice points to the importance of suspicion and hostility toward others.[15] Our third hypothesis is thus:

H3:   Whatever increases the likelihood of hostility and suspicion of people in general increases the likelihood of categorizing immigrants as an outgroup and, given H1, increases the likelihood of hostility toward them.

The pivot, again, is Tajfel's construct of categorization but viewed, we want to emphasize, from a perspective different than his. His commitment was to show how categorization was contingent on differences in people's circumstances; the third hypothesis treats it as contingent on differences between individuals independent of differences in their circumstances. We do not, at this point, claim that this is so: only that it is worth determining whether it is so.

From these three hypotheses we propose to derive a model of hostility and group conflict.

THE "TWO FLAVORS" MODEL

According to our first hypothesis, the more likely a person is to categorize others as belonging to a group other than his or her own, the more likely he or she is to be intolerant of them. By this we mean not only that if people categorize others as different they are more likely to be intolerant of them, but also that if they are intolerant of others, they are likely to be so by virtue of having categorized them as different. The validity of the first claim plainly does not guarantee the validity of the second. Categorization may be a sufficient condition to evoke prejudice without

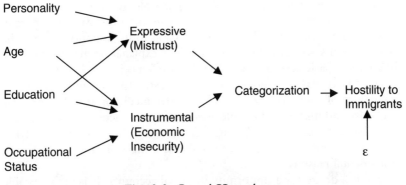

Fig. 3.2 Causal Hypotheses

being a necessary one. But part of the point of developing a model is to tie a rope around your hands, and so we shall claim to have supplied an explanation of prejudice toward immigrants so far as—but only so far as—the proximal source of hostility toward them is categorization.

If, in terms of our theory, categorization is the most proximate factor accounting for prejudice, then what accounts for categorization? Two explanatory mechanisms suggest themselves, one following from our second hypothesis, the other from our third. It follows, from H2, that the readiness to categorize others as belonging to an outgroup is sometimes the product of a calculus of (typically material but sometimes symbolic) gains and losses. That is, just so far as Italians believe themselves to be worse-off because of immigrants, they are more likely to classify them as an outgroup. But it also follows, from H3, that just so far as Italians are predisposed to view people in general with suspicion and hostility, they will be predisposed to categorize immigrants as an outgroup whether or not they perceive themselves to be economically worse-off because of them. Categorization, it follows, is a function, respectively, of economic insecurity and mistrust of people in general.

These hypotheses fix the shape of the basic model, shown in figure 3.2. Farthest to the right, since it is in the end what we wish to explain, is hostility to immigrants. Immediately adjacent to it, since it is what we believe to be most closely bound up with prejudice, is categorization.[16] Then, immediately to its left are economic insecurity and mistrust of people in general, since they are the two factors we hypothesize to be most directly responsible for a readiness to classify others as members of an outgroup. The model thus incorporates at its core two quite different explanatory mediators. One, economic insecurity, has the flavor of a rational choice account: it highlights the instrumental economic, self-interested calculus that lies behind hostility toward immigrants. By contrast, the other mediator, mistrust of people, has the flavor of a psychologically oriented account: it emphasizes the expressive, emotional, irrational sentiments that lie behind aversion to immigrants.[17] Since the two mediators so markedly differ in their explanatory flavor, we have dubbed our basic account the "Two Flavors" model.

The "Two Flavors" model derives its distinctive shape from the arrangement of categorization as a first-order mediator and of economic insecurity and mistrust of people as second-order mediators. This shape, if one has a sufficiently vivid imagination, resembles a martini glass lying on its side. And it must take the shape of a martini glass for a pair of fundamental reasons.

One is a desire for a uniformity in causal accounts. It is incontestable that a number of disparate factors can promote or inhibit hostility toward immigrants, such as education, social class, age, and personality factors. Each of these antecedent factors manifestly differs from the others. Some have to do with people's knowledge and reasoning abilities; others, with their emotions and sentiments. Some are social in character; others, psychological. And the natural temptation, given the variety of differences among these explanatory factors, is to develop a tailor-made explanation of how each contributes to intolerance. So the impact of education is attributed to "cognitive simplism": the poorly educated, the argument runs, lack the information and sophistication in reasoning necessary to recognize that sentiments of intolerance conflict with the established norms of the larger society.[18] By contrast, the impact of occupational status is explained in terms of "working-class authoritarianism": members of the working class, it is claimed, tend to be punitive and judgmental, susceptible to thinking in terms of short-term horizons, and overready to fixate on immediate economic risks and losses.[19] Yet again, when a connection is observed between people's age and their level of prejudice, the explanation often advanced is framed in terms of differences in the socialization of values between cohorts and, more particularly, to the central conflict between postmodern and materialist value orientations in contemporary developed societies.[20]

In this approach, each predictor becomes the basis of a distinctive theory. The most obvious result is a proliferation of "theories," each highlighting the role of a particular variable. The less obvious consequence is the establishment of a tacit presumption that each theory is at odds with the other, and since a choice must be made in favor of one at the expense of the others, and since each theory is pinned to a different variable, the practice has developed whereby statistical "horse races" are run, awarding explanatory honors to the variable accounting for the largest amount of variance.

To concentrate on the points at which alternative explanatory approaches conflict and to neglect the points at which they complement and round each other out is a mistake. It is surely true that a variety of antecedent factors—social class, education, possibly even personality—lie behind prejudice. But it does not follow that because each is discriminably different from the others, they all promote (or inhibit) prejudice for different reasons. Each of these antecedent factors, though different from the others, may matter for the same as well as different reasons. And just so far as different factors matter for the same reason, then rather than each undergirding a different explanation of prejudice, they underpin a common account.

It is worth putting the point more broadly, because it goes to the heart of the approach we have taken. There has been an effective presumption that given a set of alternative explanations of prejudice, it is necessary to choose among them. This presumption has given a notoriously adversarial character to research on intolerance. The emphasis has gone to accentuating the differences between alternative approaches, with one succeeding another as time and fashion go by. By contrast, the objective of the "Two Flavors" model is to illustrate how these approaches can be integrated.

A model, because it makes explicit reasoning about cause and effect, is a way of tying one's hands in advance. So we are drawing as explicitly as we can the boundaries of our account. Under the "Two Flavors" model, every antecedent factor, if it promotes prejudice, does so by virtue of increasing people's sense of economic insecurity or, alternatively, reinforcing their sense of the untrustworthiness of others, or both. Each mediator thus has a distinctive explanatory flavor, the first emphasizing the instrumental self-interested calculus that can lie behind hostility toward immigrants, the second, the expressive, emotional sentiments that also can lie behind aversion to immigrants.

Applying this scheme, every exogenous factor is itself "single" flavored or "double" flavored, depending on whether it affects one or both explanatory mediators. Personality and occupational status, as figure 3.2 makes plain, are both single flavored, though naturally opposite in taste. Personality is paradigmatically an expressive explanatory factor. It promotes prejudice toward immigrants, if the model is right, insofar as it shapes individuals' evaluative orientations toward other people in general and specifically predisposes them to be suspicious and mistrustful of people in general. Occupational status is a paradigmatically instrumental factor. It promotes a susceptibility to prejudice insofar as it is tied to people's insecurity about their economic well-being. By contrast, two of the other exogenous factors, education and age, can affect prejudice by affecting both the level of trust individuals have in other people in general and the level of their economic security. Thus, supposing that the model is correct, education and age are distinctively double-flavored explanatory factors.

It is, we think, useful to organize antecedent factors in terms of these two explanatory "flavors." The distinction between choices made according to an instrumental calculus and those made according to an expressive one picks out two naturally contrasting kinds of explanations. But it is, we think, a mistake to suppose that the difference in kinds of explanations must go all the way down. It encourages a tendency to bifurcate explanation, as though there are two altogether different logics of understanding, one instrumental and the other expressive, which do not intersect. It is far better to see if the two can offer converging, not contradictory, accounts of reasoning. And if instrumental and expressive calculuses are to be integrated, they must converge on a common factor. Hence the martini glass shape of the model.

Every explanatory factor, if the shape of the model is right, cashes out in the same causal terms: it increases people's hostility toward immigrants by increasing their readiness to categorize others as belonging to a group other than their own. It is thus the distinctive claim of the model that instrumental and expressive accounts of prejudice can be integrated by exploiting Henri Tajfel's insight on the centrality of categorization.

MEASUREMENT AND ESTIMATION

Before we are in a position to put the "Two Flavors" model to an empirical test, the first thing that needs to be done is to specify how the key elements in the model are to be measured. We will make clear why we have done all that we have done, but one element in the model, personality, manifestly merits special attention.

From the start, personality-oriented theories of prejudice excited controversy. Part of the concern has been over problems of measurement. As a practical matter, studies of prejudice and personality have amounted to studies of authoritarianism, and the actual measure of authoritarianism, the so-called F-scale, has been subjected to withering criticism.[21] The result has cut the ground from under personality-oriented explanations of prejudice. How ever many findings of a relationship between prejudice and the F-scale have been reported—and the number is enormous—there still is no proof that personality plays a role, since no one really knows whether what the F-scale actually measures has anything to do with personality.

But the problems, it is argued, go deeper than practical problems of measurement. On theoretical grounds a case is made for the marginality of personality-oriented explanations of prejudice. Essentially two principal lines of argument have been advanced. The first urges that it is, logically, a category error to attempt an explanation of prejudice and group conflict by reference to personality.[22] Consider Minard's classic study of West Virginia miners fifty years ago. In town, strict racial segregation was required. Blacks, white miners believed, were inferior. They should not mix with whites. They should eat, be educated, and be cared for separately, in their own restaurants, schools, and hospitals. In the mines, however, whites willingly followed a completely opposite set of norms. Rather than insisting on racial segregation, they accepted integration, working without complaint—or even comment—side by side with blacks.[23] Everything thus depended on specific circumstance. Above ground, whites insisted on strict racial segregation; below ground, under the discipline of a common and immediate danger, the very same whites accepted integration. How, then, could their behavior toward blacks be a product of their core personalities? Their personality structure was the same outside the mine as inside it. Yet their conduct on Main Street was altogether different from their behavior a thousand feet below the ground.

The same logical argument can be clothed differently depending on the conceptual level at which it is pitched. Thus, levels of prejudice and group conflict undeniably move up and down over time. Eruptions of prejudice have been triggered by an external threat—for example, the flaring up of anti-Japanese sentiments in the United States after the bombing of Pearl Harbor.[24] Eras of intolerance also have been provoked by an internal threat, for example, in the form of an economic downturn.[25] But, manifestly, historical peaks and valleys in prejudice cannot be explained in terms of fundamental personality factors, since people's basic psychological makeup can change only slowly and over a prolonged period of time, if indeed it can change at all. At both levels, the logical form of the argument is the same. Racially relevant behavior is variable, situationally and temporally. By contrast, a person's core personality is a constant by definition. And purely as a matter of logic, the argument runs, a variable cannot be explained by a constant.

The second line of argument turns on a contrast between individual-level and societal-level factors. It holds that the wellspring of prejudice cannot be primarily located in aberrations of personality and, indeed, that to attribute prejudice to dysfunctions of personality is, intentionally or not, to minimize the problem of bigotry, to reduce it to a "crackpot" phenomenon.[26] To appreciate the true dimensions of the problem of intolerance, this second line of argument contends, it is necessary to acknowledge that the roots of prejudice extend to the established structure of society itself, to its social norms, to the conflict of group interests integral to the very working of both the economy and society. Hence the classic line of debunking studies, contending that the ostensible influence of personality factors such as authoritarianism, correctly analyzed, reflects instead the impact of social institutions and processes such as class[27] or formal education.[28]

For the largest part of a generation of scholars, these two lines of conceptual argument have been hat-doffing. But it is not obvious, on examination, that either is conclusive. Thus, the first line of argument claims that variations in racial attitudes cannot be accounted for by personality factors, since purely as a matter of logic a variable cannot be accounted for by a constant. But the very same people who claim that differences in personality factors cannot be a central factor in the explanation of prejudice are perfectly willing to acknowledge that differences in educational level can. Yet variations between individuals in educational level are on exactly the same logical footing as variations between individuals in, say, authoritarianism. The weakness of the first line of argument is thus that it is too strong. It would, if valid, rule out the whole class of individual difference variables—and not simply individual differences in personality characteristics—as important sources of prejudice. Yet without exception studies of prejudice agree that some individual characteristics (education, for example, or social class) establish a susceptibility to prejudice. But if the argument from variability does not debar taking account of differences between individuals in their level of education to account (in part) for their levels of prejudice, then *pro tanto* it cannot debar taking account of differences between them in their psychological makeup.

There manifestly is a muddle here, and it follows from running together levels of variability. All of us are more likely to be, for example, more hostile in some situations than others. But it does not follow that in any given situation everyone is equally likely to be hostile. People's level of prejudice can be higher in some situations than in others and, relative to one another, the level of prejudice of some can be consistently higher than that of others.

Personality factors, in the second line of argument, may account for variation at the tails of the distribution of prejudice, explaining why some are, for example, pathological in their levels of intolerance. But it cannot account for the heart of the matter. There is a fairly obvious conceptual confusion clouding this second line of argument. When we speak of a personality factor—say, ego strength—we have in mind the whole range of variation on a continuum along which people can be ordered, not merely those who fall at an extreme, just as when we speak of, say, education, we have mind the whole range of variation along which people can be ordered, from those who have had only elementary schooling, to those who have attended high school, to those who have made their way into college, to those who have graduated from college or obtained an advanced degree. And the explanatory power of personality factors, so conceived, is an empirical, not a logical, question. There is no way to deduce *ex ante* whether they play an important or merely a marginal role. Empirical inquiry is necessary. And with the exception of studies of authoritarianism, which inherently lack the credibility to convince those who are not already convinced of the importance of personality, that is exactly what is lacking.

But how, as a practical matter, should we proceed? What aspect of personality is central to a study of prejudice, if authoritarianism is not? Is it actually possible to measure reliably a basic aspect of an individual's psychological makeup in a standard public opinion interview? And supposing it is, how exactly should it be done?

There are a number of attractive alternatives. George Marcus and his colleagues,[29] in their pioneering studies of political tolerance,[30] have surveyed a number of aspects of personality, including neuroticism, openness to experience, introversion/extraversion, and need for cognition. Another node, obviously enough, is the cluster of personal qualities caught up in the concept of self-esteem.[31] It is accordingly worth a moment to specify the considerations governing the choice we made.

Three were uppermost in our minds. The first was the problem of conceptual leverage. In our survey, given the array of political and social subjects that had to be canvassed, a comprehensive assessment of people's psychological makeup was not possible. We had to pick a discrete aspect of personality on which to focus. But given that we could measure only one aspect of personality, how could we tell how it fit in a larger network of psychological characteristics? The trick was to fix on an element of a comprehensive inventory on which a library of psychometric studies had been accumulated. By knowing in advance how a particular aspect of personality is embedded in a larger network of psychological characteristics, we could leverage our account, specifying in a way previously not possible just what this measure taps psychologically. The second consideration was comparative validity. Our study in Italy is one part of a larger research program in a number of different countries. It was thus minimally necessary to select a measure of personality whose validity had been established specifically in Italy, but it was manifestly desirable if its use could be shown to be warranted in a range of cultures and languages. The third consideration followed from our focus on prejudice. Given the pressures in the larger society to inhibit the expression of intolerance, it would be very attractive to have a measure of personality that could be administered in the course of a public opinion interview without respondents being able, by reflecting on the content of the questions they were being asked, to winkle out its objective.

All three of these considerations have led us to focus on the California Psychological Inventory (CPI). The CPI has been in use for more than thirty years; is one of the most widely used instruments for measuring normal personality; and has been translated and employed in a large number of countries including, as it happens, Italy.[32] Equally as important, an archive at the Institute of Personality and Social Research (IPSR) has been developed to house a library of validity studies on the CPI.[33] So far from being confined to standard self-report approaches, these studies include a range of assessment modes, with the sentiments and actual behavior of subjects being studied over extended observation periods by both expert observers and intimates, providing an exceptionally inclusive and tempered psychological portrait.[34] By taking advantage of this archive of studies, it is possible to leverage the assessment of a discrete facet of personality and locate it in a comprehensive network of psychological characteristics. Finally, one of the twenty constituent scales, Tolerance for inclusion (To), was specifically developed to assess the personological basis of prejudice.[35]

A short-form version of the Tolerance scale was developed for public opinion interviews.[36] Like the other basic CPI scales, the To scale was built by means of the criterion group method, with items selected not on the basis of their manifest content but solely with regard to their empirical power to discriminate between individuals who exemplify a high degree or a low degree of a target attribute. Table 3.1 lists the items selected for the short-form version of the To scale, indicating the proportion of respondents in the Italian survey who said that each is true.[37] It is worth taking a moment to examine the wording of the test items, not to dwell on what they say, but rather to drive home what they do not say. Consider two of them: "Most people make friends because friends are likely to be useful to them" and "I feel that I have often been punished without cause." Neither refers in *any way* to the question of prejudice or, indeed, to how people do, or should, feel toward members of other groups, whatever the nature of the group—ethnic, religious, or racial. And since there is no way to identify the objective of the To items from their wording, the problem of impression management is minimized, because people have no incentive to declare them as either true or false in order to appear open-minded and free of prejudice.

What aspects of personality does the To scale tap? Taking advantage of the IPSR archives and summarizing over a wide web of analyses,[38] our analyses show that *low* scorers are characterized by neuroticism, a lack of individual initiative and independence, and a comparative weakness of self-confidence, responsibility, and ego strength. They show discomfort

TABLE 3.1
Items Used to Measure Tolerant Personalities

Item	% Responding true	N
Most people are honest because they are afraid of getting caught	48	1932
Most people, deep down, do not like putting themselves out to help others	34	1922
Considering how things are going, it is very difficult to keep up hope of becoming someone in life	55	1895
Most people make friends in the hope that they may be useful	57	1938
I have the feeling that I have often been punished without cause	37	1964

Note: Weighted frequencies; unweighted N

with uncertainty and complexity and tend to be anxious, lacking in social poise and presence, and socially ill at ease. They are, moreover, self-defensive, with a tendency toward overcontrol of their needs, and characteristically are described as rigid, with narrow interests, and lacking in imagination, versatility, and cooperation. Finally, it should be observed that in the judgment of others, though not in their own, they tend to be described as resentful, bitter, and cold. By contrast, *high* scorers tend to be marked by self-assurance, openness, warmth, compassion, and a sense of responsibility, and more often are described by others as expressive and socially skilled, versatile, and fair-minded.

So much for the assessment of personality. What about the other variables that need to be tied down?

A number of them have standard treatments or nearly so. Age is one. So, too, is education, assessed here in terms of the highest school diploma received. Occupational status was initially scored through an open-ended inquiry into the person's present job, systematically recoded into the standard Italian eight-tier occupational status index developed by Schizerotto and his colleagues and described in appendix II.[39] By contrast, the assessment of the mediating variables, with one exception, has had to be tailor-made.

In our model, the pivotal variable is categorization. Every other factor—class, personality, age—increases prejudice just so far as it increases categorization. And by categorization we mean the comparative readiness of individuals to perceive others as different, as not like us, as belonging to another group. Categorization, so conceived, differs from Tajfel's conception. We differ, but it does not follow that we disagree.

Although we concentrate on differences among individuals in their readiness to mark off other people as different, as belonging to another group, we obviously agree that an individual's readiness to do so can vary with the situation. On the other side, although Tajfel certainly concentrated on the impact of context, he also agreed that some people are more ready than others to categorize other people as different.[40] This difference in emphasis notwithstanding, it is ideas that are pivotal in working out a theory, and the idea at the core of our account of prejudice is Tajfel's. If we are putting his emphasis on categorization to a different use than he did, it is because we think it has an even greater range of application than he explored.

But how as a practical matter shall we get a grip on differences among people in their readiness to engage in categorization? The key is to find a way to index the propensity to categorize other people, to perceive them as different, to classify them as not belonging to one's own group, to see them, as it were, as the Other. Our method of measurement necessarily is imperfect, capable of detecting only gross variations. But it is big differences among people, if those differences indeed exist, that we want to catch hold of. Education again offters an apt analogy. In taking account of differences in education in social analyses, it in not fine-grained differences between, say, those who have gone to an elite first-tier college and those who have gone to a second-level university that are mapped, important as those differences may be in other contexts. It is instead the gross contrasts—between those with a limited, a moderate, and a considerable amount of education—that are mapped. Similarly, we want to map *marked* differences among people in their readiness to categorize others as different, as not like us.

Operationally, we make use of two items, set out in table 3.2.[41] People who agree with the two items are more ready, we are suggesting, to draw a line and to put those who are like them on one side, and those who are not like them—or rather those whom they perceive to be not like them—on the other side. Three points about the two items should be underlined. The first item asks about distrust of those who act differently. The use of the word "distrust" raises the possibility of a spuriously inflated correlation with the Mistrust of People Index. But on examination this concern turns out to be groundless.[42] The second item captures a sense that immigrants specifically are different. We of course recognize that this makes for a close link between what we are attempting to explain and what we are introducing by way of an explanatory mechanism. At this point we will only say that this strengthens rather than weakens our account when the argument is generalized in the last section of this chapter. The final point applies to both items. For Tajfel, categorization

TABLE 3.2

Items Used in Measures of Categorization, Mistrust, and Economic Insecurity

Item	% Responding Affirmatively	N
Categorization Index		
One should distrust those who act differently from most people	42	1949
People who come to Italy should try to act like Italians	58	1959
Mistrust of People Index		
In your opinion, can most people be trusted, or do you have to be very cautious when it comes to dealing with people?	20	1995
Do you believe that most people are willing to help others, or do you think on the other hand that most people think only of themselves?	28	1995
Do you believe that most people would take advantage of you if they had the chance, or do you think on the other hand that they would do their best to act properly?	48	1996
Economic Insecurity Index		
If you had to decide, which do you believe is more important, liberty or economic security?	29	1977
If you had to decide, which do you believe is more important, equality or economic security?	39	1984

Notes: Quantity for economic insecurity index items are % responding "economic security" Weighted frequencies; Unweighted N

Frequencies for mistrust and economic insecurity items include responses of "don't know" as nonaffirmative.

is cognitive, involving assignment to categories with no prior valuations attached to them, for example, over- and undercounters of dots. What we are assessing, by contrast, is not mere categorization; there also is an evaluative attribution. It is accordingly essential to recognize that identification with the ingroup and dissociation from the outgroup are independent phenomena, sometimes related, but more often not.[43] And it is similarly necessary to appreciate that Tajfel's approach to categorization evokes an inclination to favor members of your own group, but not a readiness to discriminate against members of another group.[44] Useful as it has been for many purposes, Tajfel's approach to categorization is not the most useful for the study of prejudice and discrimination.

As for the concept of economic insecurity, ours was a frankly experimental approach. In our initial trial, we focused on two of the standard indicators from American surveys, one asking how satisfied individuals were with the economic situation of their family; the other, whether they think that five years from the time of the study their family's economic situation will be better, remain the same, or become worse.[45] Neither, as it happens, reveals much about how Italians respond to immigrants, whether considered by itself or combined with the other. Although disappointing, in retrospect this should not have been surprising, since the yield of both indicators has been disappointingly thin in American studies as well.

Fortunately, the Italian study had a new approach in reserve. Considerations of importance, though characteristically measured in absolute terms, seem naturally comparative. The importance that people attach to economic security is a potential indicator of apprehension about economic well-being, but economic security is of value to very nearly everyone, and very nearly everyone, accordingly, attaches importance to achieving it. Who wishes, the odd exception here and there aside, to be anxious about their economic well-being? The problem is of course a general one, by no means confined to considerations of economic well-being. The largest number of values are of value, considered by themselves, to the largest number of individuals. To get around this problem, the Italian survey experimented with a new approach to the assessment of values inspired by the notion of value pluralism.[46] Everyone may sincerely favor economic security as a value. But they inevitably favor a number of other values in addition to it, and these different values must, under some circumstances, conflict with one another. The trick in determining how important a particular value such as economic security is to them is to see whether, when they must choose between it and other values they hold, they choose that particular value or not. If this choice is to be telling, then the competing values must themselves be highly valued. So, as table 3.2 shows, we picked two of the most central to public affairs, liberty and equality. In short, our measure of the importance that people attach to economic security as a value relative to their other values is their readiness to choose it, if necessary, over liberty, equality, or both.[47]

Finally, to assess the remaining constituent of the analytical model, the expressive mediator, we make use of the Mistrust of People Index, originally developed by Rosenberg.[48] Its constituent items are also listed in table 3.2. As inspection of the text of the items will make plain, the Mistrust of People Index captures the readiness with which people are inclined to believe that caution is required in dealings with others, that most people are interested only in what is good for themselves, and that, given a chance, they will take advantage of other people. The index thus taps a disposition to cynicism and misanthropy.

Measurement disposed of, what about estimation? The basic causal model graphically presented in figure 3.2 can be translated into a system of four equations. The four, formally expressed, are:

(3.1) *Mistrust of People* $= \beta_{10} + \beta_{11}$ Personality $+ \beta_{12}$ Age
$+ \beta_{13}$ Education $+ \varepsilon_1$

(3.2) *Economic Insecurity* $= \beta_{20} + \beta_{21}$ Age $+ \beta_{22}$ Education
$+ \beta_{23}$ Occupational Status $+ \varepsilon_2$

(3.3) *Categorization* $= \beta_{30} + \beta_{31}$ Personality $+ \beta_{32}$ Age
$+ \gamma_{31}$ Mistrust of People $+ \gamma_{32}$ Economic Insecurity $+ \varepsilon_3$

(3.4) *Hostility toward Immigrants* $= \beta_{40} + \beta_{41}$ Personality
$+ \beta_{42}$ Education $+ \gamma_{41}$ Categorization $+ \varepsilon_4$

In this notation, variables are divided into those the model takes as given and those it is its purpose to explain. The parameters β are coefficients of the former, or exogenously determined variables; γ of the latter, or endogenously determined variables. The first subscript of both parameters indicates the equation they are associated with.

Equations 3.1 through 3.4 are a system of equations. If a moment is taken to read through them, the problem in estimation will be clear. Three of the variables—mistrust of people, economic security, and categorization—appear both on the left-hand side of one equation and the right-hand side of another. These variables thus are both what the system of equations is intended to explain and part of the explanation of hostility toward immigrants. If the errors in the equations are correlated, it follows that if the system of equations were estimated by ordinary least squares (OLS), the endogeneity of the variables on the right-hand side of equations 3.3 and 3.4 would yield inconsistent or asymptotically biased estimates of the parameters and their standard errors.[49] We therefore employ the two-stage least squares (2SLS) instrumental variables method.[50]

Instruments are necessary for equations 3.3 and 3.4 but not for 3.1 and 3.2, since in the latter equations (but not the former), mistrust of people and economic insecurity are solely functions of exogenous variables. The appendix on estimation of this model and its extension in the next chapter details the instrumental variables we employ (see appendix IV). Here we want to say a word about the requirements that instrumental variables must meet.

An instrument, to do its job, must be *correlated with the endogenous variable* it is meant to be an instrument for, yet *uncorrelated with the error terms* in the equation of interest. This condition, if met, means that the only correlation between the left-hand side variable and the instruments are from changes in the endogenous variable. For example, if we have an instrument for economic security, and it turns out that as the instrument increases so does categorization, this increase must be due entirely to the correlation between the instrument and economic security and not to any independent effect of the instrument. Instruments, as this suggests, are humble stand-ins: stand-ins in that they are substitutable for an endogenous variable; humble in that they contribute to the explanation of the variable on the left-hand side nothing above and beyond what they contribute by virtue of the variance they share with the endogenous variable.

Obviously enough, the quality of estimates in a 2SLS procedure is only as good as the instruments. But in selecting instruments, theory is the only guide. There is no way except on theoretical grounds to support a claim that an instrumental variable is correlated with the endogenous variable and, apart from this, uncorrelated with the left-hand-side variable of interest.

The difficulty is that the term "theory" is roughly synonymous with "warranted guess." We believe that the grounds on which we have selected our instruments are reasonable, and we have given some thought to assessing their adequacy. There are a series of tests we have done to help answer specific concerns about the instrumental variables we employ. First, as a check of the robustness of the model, we regressed (through ordinary least squares) the "left-hand-side" variables in equations 3.3 and 3.4 on all of the exogenous variables. In both cases, these "fully" reduced form equations yield results in which the coefficients are all significant.[51] This suggests the specification of the model is valid and robust. A second test is to determine the degree of bias in the estimates from the use of instrumental variables. As Staiger and Stock (1997) show, the bias is proportional to the inverse of the F-statistic from the regression of the dependent variable on the instruments used to estimate the equation. In this case, the F-statistics from these regressions corresponding to equations 3.3 and 3.4 are very large (145.2 and 161.8 respectively), indicating negligible bias in the estimates. Finally, a diagnostic for the quality of the instruments suggested by Bollen (1996) is the R^2 from the regression of the right-hand-side endogenous variables on all of the instruments for a particular equation. If the R^2 is too low (Bollen suggests less than 0.1) the instruments are of poor quality. In the context of our problem this means that we must regress mistrust and economic insecurity on all of the instruments for equation 3.3 and categorization on all of the instruments for equation 3.4. The R^2's from these regressions are .19, .13, and .25, indicating instruments of sufficient quality. Our instruments are not as good as we would like, but if a silver lining must be found in this cloud, it is this: so far as our instruments are theoretically valid but statistically inefficient, the biases in the estimates of our model will work against, rather than for, confirming our hypotheses and predictions.

THE "TWO FLAVORS" MODEL: EMPIRICAL RESULTS

It is necessary to test simultaneously all links in the "Two Flavors" model, in order to test whether a particular link holds or not. All four equations have accordingly been estimated as a system, but for the sake of clarity, they will be presented one at a time, beginning with the equation predicting the Index of Hostility toward Immigrants.

The question we begin with is the role of categorization. Tajfel's insight highlighted the connection between categorization and bias. We favor those we judge to be similar to us at the expense of those we believe to be different, even if the points of similarity and difference are of scarcely any importance whatever. It no doubt is true, as Tajfel and his colleagues have shown, that all of us are more likely to judge others as different in some situations than in others. But it also should be true that in many situations some people are systematically more likely to do so than others. What is more, it also is reasonable to hypothesize that the more insistent a person is that others make a greater effort to be the same as he is, the more likely he is to see them as different in ways that reflect badly on them.

On the theory of prejudice we are proposing, then, categorization is the choke point of intolerance: whatever leads people to be more ready to categorize leads them to be intolerant of immigrants. It would be a mistake, however, to reduce prejudice simply to a tendency to categorize. People are susceptible to prejudice for more than one reason. We have stressed, following Tajfel's insight, categorization as a pivotal process for prejudice. But even if categorization is a sufficient condition for prejudice, it surely is not a necessary one (and, even apart from this, the Categorization Index imperfectly measures a readiness to categorize others as different). The Categorization Index, therefore, will be one of the factors with a direct impact on prejudice against immigrants, but not necessarily the only one.

This is, indeed, what we see in the first two columns of table 3.3.[52] Education and personality have an impact quite apart from that of categorization, whereas age and status do not. Of course the heart of our account centers on the readiness to distinguish between people and table 3.3 also shows that it is at the heart of the matter. The more ready

TABLE 3.3
"Two Flavors" Model of Hostility Toward Immigrants (Part 1)

Independent Variable/ Dependent Variable	Hostility (1)	Hostility (2)	Hostility (3)
Personality	−1.309**	−1.146**	−0.489
	(−3.36)	(−5.25)	(−0.38)
Age	0.005		
	(0.49)		
Education	−0.123**	−0.107**	−0.066
	(−2.55)	(−3.86)	(−1.06)
Occupational status	0.032		
	(0.71)		
Categorization	0.961**	1.225**	1.712**
	(1.76)	(6.21)	(3.04)
Mistrust			0.620
			(0.52)
Economic insecurity			−0.527
			(−1.07)
Constant	3.871	3.236	0.322
n	1735	1735	1719

* $p < 0.1$ (one-tailed) ** $p < 0.05$ (one-tailed)
  Notes: t-statistics in parentheses
  Estimation technique is two-stage least squares.
  Ranges of variables: hostility—0 to 10; personality—1 to 2; education—1 to 12; categorization—1 to 4; mistrust—1 to 3; economic insecurity—1 to 3

that Italians are to categorize others as different, the more they are prejudiced against immigrants. (The zero-order correlation between the two is .44.)

More must be shown to be true, however, if the theory of prejudice we are proposing is to be shown to be credible. In claiming that categorization plays a pivotal role, we are claiming not merely that it is a principal predictor of prejudice but that a whole array of antecedent factors promote hostility to immigrants so far as—but only insofar as—each promotes categorization. Still more specifically, the "Two Flavors" model holds that two crucial mediators, one assessing instrumental calculations, the other expressive, affect prejudice by virtue of increasing categorization. It follows that if either economic insecurity or mistrust of people increases prejudice against immigrants—but not by virtue of increasing the readiness of Italians to distinguish between people—then that would count against the validity of our account. The last column of table 3.3 specifically tests this prediction, adding as predictors the measures of economic insecurity and mistrust of people. Neither has a signif-

TABLE 3.4
"Two-Flavors" Model of Hostility
Toward Immigrants (Part 2)

Independent Variable/ Dependent Variable	Categorization
Age	0.017**
	(7.89)
Education	−0.061**
	(−6.26)
Mistrust	0.508**
	(5.19)
Economic insecurity	0.507**
	(3.85)
Constant	−0.016
n	1700

* p < 0.1 (one-tailed)   ** p < 0.05 (one-tailed)
  Notes: t-statistics in parentheses
  Estimation technique is two-stage least squares
  Ranges of variables: categorization—1 to 4; person-
ality—1 to 2; age—18 to 69; mistrust—1 to 3; eco-
nomic insecurity—1 to 3

icant direct effect (although, incidentally, including these as control variables also washes out the effect of all but categorization).

This finding, welcome as it is, is only a partial validation of our account. For we mean our model to be a general one. If it cannot represent the whole reason why some people are more prone to prejudice
than others, and this surely is an unrealistic ambition, it should have
much to say about why a whole variety of factors contribute to prejudice. And this very much applies even to factors such as education or
personality. Even though they may contribute to prejudice for reasons
that our account does not touch, whether because of conceptual or operational limits, a good part of the reason they should matter, if our account is on the right track, is because they affect the readiness to distinguish between people. If this is so, we then must go back a step in the
explanatory process and ask what accounts for categorization. The answer, according to the "Two Flavors" model, is that it is a function of
two factors: one expressive, in the form of a readiness to suspect and
dislike other people in general; the other rational, in the form of a desire
to be better-off or a concern about being worse-off. And this answer
largely is right, as table 3.4 shows. The more likely that Italians are to
believe that other people cannot be trusted, the more likely they are to
categorize immigrants as the other. Similarly, the more importance that

TABLE 3.5
"Two-Flavors" Model of Hostility
Towards Immigrants (Part 3)

Independent Variable/ Dependent Variable	Mistrust	Economic Insecurity
Personality	−0.859**	
	(−18.10)	
Age	−0.006**	0.007**
	(−6.22)	(5.64)
Education	−0.020**	−0.047**
	(−4.03)	(−6.94)
Occupational status		0.025**
		(1.96)
Constant	3.992	1.629
n	1982	1969

* p < 0.1 (one-tailed)   ** p < 0.05 (one-tailed)
   Notes: t-statistics in parentheses
   Estimation technique is ordinary least squares.
   Ranges of variables: mistrust—1 to 3; economic insecurity—
1 to 3; personality—1 to 2; age—18 to 69; education—1 to
12; occupational status—1 to 7.

Italians attach to economic security as compared to either liberty or equality, the more prejudiced against immigrants they are. There is, to be sure, some explanatory leakiness. Categorization, in our two-stage estimates, is also influenced by age and education, independent of mistrust of people or economic insecurity. But the results in table 3.4 broadly underwrite the intuition behind the "Two Flavors" model that two explanatory mechanisms, one expressive and the other rational, lie behind categorization and thereby lie behind prejudice.

If so, this requires us to push the question still one step further back. If categorization lies behind prejudice, and mistrust of people and a concern for economic security lie behind categorization, what in turn lies behind them? Table 3.5 presents analyses of both Economic Insecurity and the Mistrust of People Indices.

The principal point of the architecture of the "Two Flavors" model is to recognize that two quite different kinds of explanation can be and have been given of hostility toward immigrants, one that presumes an instrumental calculus and favors realistic conflict and rational-choice type interpretations, the other that presupposes an expressive process and favors psychological and personality-oriented interpretations. How far do our results recommend this dualistic approach?

Consider first the role of the exogenous factors tied to either the expressive or the instrumental mediator. Personality, as measured by the

CPI Tolerance Index, is paradigmatically an expressive factor. It follows that so far as it has an effect on prejudice it should do so by having an effect on the expressive mediator in the model. And so table 3.5 shows that it does: the To scale is a very strong predictor of the Mistrust of People Index. This suggests that the principal route by which personality promotes hostility toward immigrants is by promoting suspicion and mistrust of people in general. It should not escape attention that this result fits hand in glove with Altemeyer's reconceptualization of the syndrome of authoritarianism, which specially stresses the elements of authoritarian aggression, authoritarian submission, and conventionality.[53]

Equivalently, evidence in favor of realistic conflict comes from the role of occupational status. In the standard view, the lower people's social and economic class, the more vulnerable they are to competition from immigrants in getting a job, earning a better wage from their jobs, or obtaining public services and benefits, such as a housing subsidy or access to a job-training program, which can directly improve their conditions of life. So viewed, to find that lower occupational status goes along with higher prejudice toward immigrants, as studies regularly do find, demonstrates that conflict between groups is driven by the clash of group interests. The results in table 3.5 match this line of argument. They show that feelings of economic security are rooted in part in people's objective economic circumstances: the lower their occupational status, the higher their feelings of economic insecurity. In considering this result, it is worth observing that the dice have been loaded against finding that status matters. Education and occupational status, naturally, go hand in hand, and indeed under some descriptions the former is a component of the latter.[54] Requiring status to make a contribution to the explanation of prejudice above and beyond the contribution of education thus imposes a high standard of proof—some might say unfairly high. Yet the results in table 3.5 show that, even so, it clearly plays an indirect role in promoting hostility to immigrants.[55]

And what about the two-flavored exogenous variables that we suggested in our model? We supposed age mattered because it simultaneously indexes changes in objective circumstances with time and patterns of values and interpersonal orientations acquired through the life cycle. Being older and being more prejudiced might go together, following the logic of our causal model, because older people are more likely to be concerned about whether they are sufficiently well-off economically. Alternatively, age and prejudice may go together because the process of aging inclines them to be more misanthropic and mistrustful of people in general. If the former, age should be a predictor of the Economic Insecurity Index; if the latter, of the Mistrust of People Index. As table 3.5 shows, one of our two arrows struck the target. Older Italians are more likely to be hostile to immigrants, because they are more concerned about economic security. This effect is countered in part by the fact that older people, contrary to our expectation, are more trusting.[56]

Education, we also suggested, was two-flavored; indeed, it was so integrally related to prejudice because it is bound up with both expressive and instrumental factors. Specifically, having more formal schooling is hypothesized to undercut the likelihood people will be prejudiced, in the first place, by undercutting the likelihood that they will be misanthropic in their view of other people and, in the second, by undercutting the likelihood that they will place economic security at the top of their hierarchy of concerns. In table 3.5, we see both predictions are confirmed, with education having a significant impact on both the Mistrust of People and Economic Insecurity Indices.

The limitations of the "Two Flavors" model need to be borne in mind. Yet it has, we think, its strengths. It offers an economical account of the impact of an array of exogenous factors, showing that they principally matter as sources of prejudice just so far as they have an expressive, psychological impact or an instrumental, economic one, or both.[57] No less important, it shows that expressive and instrumental factors not only have the same effect, but that they have the same effect for the same reason. Explanatory factors influence prejudice by promoting (or inhibiting) the readiness of people to categorize others as belonging to another group.

Here, then, is our basic account. But we want to undertake another test of its validity to give a stronger sense of its utility.

EVALUATING THE "TWO FLAVORS" MODEL: A SECOND TEST

Hostility toward immigrants is only one form of prejudice, and a comparatively recent one in the Italian experience. By contrast, another, to borrow a phrase of Eric Hobsbawm's, is part of the invention of the Italian tradition. It is the cleavage between North and South. The animus of the North against the South is deeply rooted in Italy's history. But it is a part of the past that is a part of the present. The contempt of the North for the South forms a thread woven through Italian politics, and it is tied as tightly to the clash of contemporary politics as to the cleavages of history.

The two phenomena—the attitude that the North of Italy strikes toward the South and the attitude that Italians, Northern or Southern, strike toward immigrants—manifestly differ. The latter has no historical past to speak of, and is, some would say deliberately, not part of the

debate over the character of the country; the former, because it is insep-
arable from the country's past, is integral to every argument over the
national experience. No less obviously, the latter is directed against
members of a group from the outside and justified because of their sepa-
rateness; the former, against members of a group on the inside and ra-
tionalized in terms of a common fate.

Far from wishing to minimize the differences between the two forms
of animus, we wish to underline them. Our objective has been to understand the sources of the wave of hostility toward immigrants that now
looms large in European politics. Our whole study was undertaken with
that objective in mind. It shaped the arguments that we worked
through, the questions that we asked, the measures that we built. The
result is the "Two Flavors" model. Analytically, it integrates a variety of
theoretical perspectives; empirically, it gives a good account of variations
in hostility toward immigrants. In the ordinary course of events, our job
would be done. But explanations and models come and go in the social
sciences, and a good part of the reason for their volatility is the narrow-
ness of the terms in which they are evaluated. Do they explain, those
who develop them ask, the phenomena that they were developed to explain? The answer, naturally, tends to be yes, since they otherwise would
not have seen the light of day. But then again, much that was done—the
framing of the question, the organization of the arguments, the construction of the measures—was done in order to give the model that was
developed its best chance of accounting for the phenomenon it was expressly built to account for. This suggested that we should take an extra
step and see whether the ideas underlying the "Two Flavors" model
could additionally throw light on phenomena it was not originally intended to illuminate.

So we want now to consider the animus that Northern Italians have
historically borne against Southern Italians.[58] The best place to start is
to consider how Northern Italians feel about Southern Italians, taking as
a benchmark how they feel about immigrants. Table 3.6 summarizes
their evaluations of the two.[59]

The comparison is striking. So far as there is a difference between
their judgments of Southern Italians and immigrants, it is the latter, not
the former, who are viewed more favorably. Consider, first, the readiness to acknowledge that either has positive qualities. Northern Italians
are more likely to judge that immigrants are law-abiding than they are to
say the same of Southern Italians, by a margin of 51 percent to 35 percent, and similarly they are more likely to declare that the former are
honest than they are to say the same of the latter, by a margin of 73
percent to 68 percent. Flipping the matter of evaluation around to unfavorable characteristics instead of favorable ones, Northern Italians are

TABLE 3.6

Evaluative Reactions by Northerners to
Southerners and Immigrants

Item	Southerners	Immigrants	Difference
Honest	68	73	−5*
Selfish	36	33	3
Law-abiding	35	51	−16*
Intrusive	61	55	6*
Slackers	57	37	20*
Violent	41	34	7*
Complainers	67	56	11*
Minimum N	1010	843	

* significantly different at $\alpha = 0.05$

   Notes: Cell quantity is percentage of respondents agreeing (strongly or
somewhat) with the description.

   Weighted frequencies; unweighted N

more likely to judge that Southern Italians are slackers than they are to
say the same of immigrants by a margin of 57 percent to 37 percent, and
in a consistent pattern but by a smaller margin, are more likely to say
that Southern Italians are violent, complainers, and intrusive. It is not
the size of the differences between the reactions to the two that is striking. On the contrary, the principal thrust is the same. Northern Italians,
in large numbers, think little of immigrants and they think little of
Southern Italians. But what is worth underlining is the consistency of
the direction of the differences in their evaluations of the two. Whenever
there is a (statistically) significant difference, whether in the form of a
reluctance to recognize that a group has a socially desirable characteristic or a readiness to contend that it has a socially undesirable one, it is
Southern Italians, not immigrants, who get the short end of the stick. In
a word, if Northern Italians do not think much of immigrants, they
think even less of their compatriots.

   One expression of the attitude of members of one group toward
members of another is a readiness to attribute unfavorable characteristics (or a reluctance to attribute favorable ones). But there is a need for
multiple approaches. Just as in gauging the attitudes of Italians toward
immigrants we took account of different expressions of sentiment, so in
gauging the attitudes of Northern Italians toward Southern Italians we
want to consult a diversity of indicators. Table 3.7 sets out three of
them. The first takes up the issue of commitment to work, asking respondents whether "People of the North have a greater commitment to
work than people of the South." Two-thirds of Northerners agree, one
half of them strongly. A second explores the commonly voiced com-

TABLE 3.7

Attribution of Social Problems to Southerners by Northeners

Item	% Responding Yes	N
People of the North have a greater commitment to work than people of the South	66	1100
A great part of the hostility of the North toward the South is due to the fact that most government jobs are filled by Southerners	59	1070
Too much government money has been spent and is still being spent for the South	68	1037

Notes: Weighted frequencies; unweighted N.

plaint that Southerners benefit unduly from public jobs, asking respondents whether "A great part of the hostility of the North toward the South is due to the fact that most government jobs are filled by Southerners." A third question takes yet another tack, asking respondents whether "Too much government money has been spent and is still being spent for the South." Again Northerners are quick to assent, with two-thirds of them agreeing, one half of them strongly.

Our aim is to see whether the explanatory model we developed to account for the hostility of Italians toward immigrants can also account for the hostility of Northern Italians toward Southern Italians. Our strategy is accordingly to duplicate the procedure for measuring the former in measuring the latter, so far as possible. In gauging animus against immigrants, a combination of measures was used. Some tapped personal characteristics attributed to members of the group; others tapped attributions of responsibility for societal problems. So in measuring animus against Southern Italians we similarly shall use a combination of indicators, some tapping personal characteristics, others attributions of responsibility.[60]

What must occur for it to be true that the same explanatory model holds for both hostility toward immigrants and hostility toward Southern Italians? The key is the Tajfel claim. An array of factors, including personality and social class, indirectly lie behind hostility toward immigrants, but they matter, if Tajfel's claim is correct, so far as they affect the readiness of individuals to categorize others as belonging to a different group. The readiness to insist that others need to be more similar to us, defined in exactly the same way for this analysis as for the last, is our indicator of readiness to perceive them as different from us. For that matter, all the other variables in the "Two Flavors" model are deployed for this analysis exactly as for the previous analysis, and the method of estimation, two-stage least squares, is applied just as before.[61] Everything is as it was except that we wish to understand the reasons for an animus against a group internal, not external, to Italian politics.

And the results, though not precisely the same, are strikingly similar, and on the central points, the results of the two analyses are interchangeable. Consider the direct predictors of the hostility of Northern Italians to Southern Italians. The crux, as the third column of table 3.8 makes plain, is categorization. The more importance that Northern Italians attach to others being the same, the more likely they are to categorize Southern Italians as being different and less admirable than Northern Italians. This result comes in *spite of*, not *because of*, the measures. One of the two indicators of categorization is "People who come to Italy should try to act like the Italians." It could have been suggested that the reason that readiness to distinguish between people appears to play a dominating role in triggering hostility toward immigrants is because explicans and explanandum overlap. It cannot be surprising that a person who believes that foreigners need to make more of an effort to assimilate dislikes foreigners. But in the case of Southern Italians there cannot be an illegitimate overlap here of what is being explained and what is doing the job of explanation. Southern Italians *are* Italians.

As before, there is some leakage. Psychological intolerance, as well as categorization, stimulates hostility toward Southern Italians directly. The explanation afforded by the "Two Flavors" model is thus partial. Moreover, unlike the analysis of the sample as a whole, there is no connection between occupational status and economic insecurity. (This follows from, further analysis suggests, the tighter linkage between education and occupational status in the North than in the South, with the former getting credit for its overlap with the latter in the prediction of hostility toward Southern Italians.) The dominant feature, however, is the points of similarity, not dissimilarity between the bases of hostility to Southern Italians and of hostility to immigrants. It is not merely a matter of the pivotal role of categorization in evoking intolerance of others, though this result offers an important measure of corroboration of Tajfel's insight into the nature of prejudice. It is also the larger framework of the "Two Flavors" model that is upheld. Categorization, which is a principal predictor of intolerance, is itself principally predicted by the two mediators, mistrust and economic security. Moreover, these two mediators are themselves anchored in sources that, occupational status aside, buttress a view of the first as reflecting psychologically centered, the latter instrumentally oriented, explanations of prejudice. This reanalysis, we want to emphasize, centers on the same individuals as before. But given the special demands of two-stage least squares analysis

TABLE 3.8
"Two Flavors" Model of Hostility Toward Southerners

Independent Variable/ Dependent Variable	Mistrust	Economic Insecurity	Categorization	Hostility
Personality	−0.878**			−0.627**
	(−13.67)			(−3.93)
Age	−0.005**	0.007**	0.017**	
	(−4.11)	(4.50)	(6.38)	
Education	−0.013**	−0.039**	−0.062**	−0.029*
	(−1.97)	(−4.00)	(−5.19)	(−1.51)
Occupational status		0.012		
		(0.70)		
Mistrust			0.057**	
			(4.69)	
Economic insecurity			0.446**	
			(2.70)	
Categorization				0.771**
				(5.59)
Constant	3.963	1.576	−0.060	4.598
n	1121	1105	971	1001

* $p < 0.1$ ** $p < 0.05$
   Notes: t-statistics in parentheses
   Estimation technique is two-stage least squares.
   Northern residents only respondents used in subsample.
   Ranges of variables: hostility—0 to 10; categorization—1 to 4; mistrust—1 to 3; economic insecurity—1 to 3; personality—1 to 2; age—18 to 69; education—1 to 12; occupational status—1 to 7

(and in particular the burdens on instrumental variables), it is by no means uninstructive that we can replicate our initial results using only a portion of the original sample.

A FINAL WORD

Very nearly a defining feature of research on prejudice has been the clash of competing perspectives. It is not clear why this is so. Certainly there is no logical necessity for conflict on this order. Gordon Allport, for one, blended the approaches of his era in his classic work on prejudice.[62] But, for whatever reason, it is only a slight exaggeration to suggest that in the work of the last three decades the truth of one approach is taken to entail the falsity of another.

   The clash of competing perspectives has not been without value. It has, for one thing, led to a sharpening of alternatives, bringing aspects into focus that otherwise would have escaped attention. It has, for another, been a stimulus to originality. But it also has exacted a price. It has, most obviously, strengthened a presumption that it is necessary to choose between alternative insights into prejudice. Less obviously, though no less importantly, it has obscured the possibility that these different approaches, so far from being at odds with one another, can buttress each other. Hence the objective of this chapter has been to throw new light on the nature of prejudice not by challenging the vital insights of the principal previous approaches, but by reconciling them.

CHAPTER 4

Prejudice and Politics

THE SWELLING of hostility against immigrants throughout Western Europe, including Italy, matters for many reasons. But the reason that matters most is its potential for reshaping European politics. The eruption of animosity and resentment offers a launching platform for the political right.

The parties of the established right of the postwar settlement have not sought to stanch the surge of hostility to immigrants. But the parties that principally have ridden this wave of animosity and frustration represent a right new to postwar European politics—the National Front in France, the Center Party in the Netherlands, the German People's Union in Germany. And this new right threatens, if not on its own then through its gravitational pull, a breakout from the larger ideological consensus that has defined—and contained—Western European politics since the end of the Second World War.

The irony of speaking of a new right in European politics is difficult to miss. For the fear is precisely that the emergence of a new right threatens a rebirth of an old right—the right of fascism. In summoning up the past, we are not invoking fascism in expressly ideological terms. There is a tangle of studies over whether fascism qualifies as an explicit ideology, and supposing that it does, how its canonical form should be distinguished from its derivative versions.[1] We have in mind, then, not a set of abstract categories but a strain of belief and sentiment. This strain is marked by an animosity toward "outsiders"—an animosity directed against immigrants but not confined to them; by an avowed identification with the "nation"—with common heritage advanced as a symbol of both individual purity and political citizenship and a resistance to the enlargement of individual rights, if not in the domain of economics, then in that of politics.

The new right does not declare itself a public enemy of democratic politics. On the contrary, it insists on its acceptance of both the institutions of democratic politics and its values, presenting itself as just another competitor in the political marketplace of liberal democracy. But there is a menacing quality to its avowals of national purity and identity. Diversity is its target. And although it is differences of ethnic and national origin that now are targeted, it is hard to miss the threat to diversity more broadly, including diversity of belief.

Without ignoring the multiplicity of aims of specific leaders of the new right, its animus against diversity is at the center of its popular appeal. Its institutionalization within the party system accordingly offers a new opening for the mobilization of bias. As E. E. Schaatschneider insisted a generation ago, citizens can only choose from the ideological alternatives on offer. The articulation of private grievances into political demands thus depends not simply on the intensity of individual resentments, but conjointly on the availability of a political vehicle that permits their public expression. Until the emergence of the parties of the new right, there was no vehicle purposely built to translate private resentments and grievances centered on prejudice into public claims and demands. Thanks to the emergence of the new right, individual prejudices and resentment can make their escape from the domain of private life and make their way into the play of public politics.

Yet it rarely pays to attend only to aspects of change and to ignore elements of continuity. There is, in different degrees in different political orders, a new right. But the politics of the right, new and old, are entangled. Part of our aim, therefore, is to explore the ironies of their entanglement.

Some of these ironies are obvious. The general election of 1994 in Italy put in power a national government based on the indirect partnership of a party of the right in the North, which is hostile to the national government itself, and a party of the right in the South, which is hostile to its partner in the North because of its partner's hostility to the nation-state. Moreover, the new right, by legitimizing the remains of fascism, has accomplished a revival of the old, while the politics of nationalism may yet prove to be the midwife of regional secession. But the ironies go deeper. At the level of electoral institutions, the defining feature of Italian politics in the 1990s is change. And with the end of the cold war also undermining the traditional ideological categories of left and right, it was declared that ideology itself had come to an end. Yet, as we shall see, continuity remains the constitutive feature of mass politics in Italy.

The complementarity of change and continuity is, we believe, integral to an understanding of the interplay of prejudice and politics in Italian politics. In this chapter we concentrate on how two strands of belief are interwoven: voters' ideological self-images, in the form of their sense of themselves as belonging to the political left or right, and their ideological commitments, in the form of their actual adherence to the values of the political left or right. To catch sight of the potential for change in the near future, however, it is necessary to have in view the changes of the recent past. Our account of the watershed election of 1994 thus begins with an overview of the structure of Italian politics.

THE ELECTORAL REGIME BEFORE 1994

The return of democracy to Italy after the fall of fascism and the end of the Second World War engendered a political and party system that dominated the political scene for more than forty years. As a result of the proportional electoral system, alongside the three main political parties—Democrazia Cristiana (DC), Partito Comunista Italiano (PCI) and Partito Socialista Italiano (PSI)—which to varying degrees enjoyed majority consensus, numerous small ones appeared: the Movimento Sociale Italia (MSI) on the right; in the center the Partito Liberale (PLI), which represented the interests of the more conservative entrepreneurial elite; the Partito Republicano Italiano (PRI), which drew its support from the more enlightened and progressive lay business class; on the left, the Partito Social Democratico Italiano (PSDI); and, since 1976, the Democrazia Proletaria (DP). The political picture was thus extremely fragmented, and through the course of the years the number of small political formations increased further. The DC, the largest party, dominated Italian politics until the 1990s by governing with coalitions that included most or all of the center parties and, after 1963, the PSI as well. The fragmentation of politics thus conferred important political weight, not only on the Socialist Party, but on the small center parties as well. Since the latter were indispensable for the governability of the country, they obtained ministries, and therefore visibility and power, although none of them could count on an electoral consensus amounting to more than 3 to 4 percent.

The constant attrition of unstable and quarrelsome majorities meant that for forty years the average duration of a government was less than one year. This feature gave Italy the image of a politically unstable country, which for many years penalized it in international politics. In fact, however, this instability was more apparent than real. Although it was true that the government changed frequently and that early elections were the norm rather than the exception from 1972 onward, the political situation remained substantially stable. The parties that made up the majority of governments always belonged to the same political area, and they were almost always the same. The turnover in personnel between one government and the next was minimal, and change consisted primarily in a partisan reshuffling of ministerial chairs, always, however, with the DC as a key participant.

Although it is arguably misleading to describe this situation as one of political stability, until the early 1990s Italy certainly displayed greater political continuity than the other European democracies. The reasons for this continuity were a set of factors that had to do with the international political situation and with the sociocultural features of the Italian electorate. It should not be forgotten that Italy had the strongest communist party in Western Europe, one that enjoyed electoral support reaching 34 per cent in the 1970s. Symptomatic of the ideological and social cleavage that has always characterized Italian society, the presence of a communist party poised to take power paralyzed the political system. The only alternative to the hegemony of the DC and the centrist parties was the PCI, which although it had shaken off the influence of the Soviet Union, had never achieved sufficient legitimacy to be accepted as a party of government. Among other things, the presence of the PCI upset the equilibrium established between the two geopolitical blocs at Yalta. There was consequently no lack of Western interference in Italian politics. Confined to opposition, and without concrete prospects of achieving government, the PCI performed its parliamentary role by avoiding isolation, and it sought to influence the legislative process by striking deals with the parties in government. When Italy was faced by a serious economic, social, and political emergency in 1976, the PCI gave its direct support to two governments of "national solidarity," from which it was excluded but whose policies it nevertheless influenced.

On the other side, the roots of the DC, the dominant party throughout the postwar period, were in the Partito Popolare, the Catholic party existing in Italy before the advent of fascism. Ideologically, its appeal was based on the translation into politics of Christian principles and on its "interclass" character. Having won the first postwar elections by virtue of its close links with the Catholic Church, and benefiting from the latter's tight-knit mobilization of the vote, the DC could also rely on the unconditional backing of the Allies, in particular the United States, which was preoccupied with the effects of a communist victory in Italy on international equilibria.

Although the DC's success derived from its function as a bulwark against the advance of communism and from its conservative but moderate political stance (to its right stood the MSI, the heirs to fascism), its entrenchment as the party of power was based on political consensus built through the political use of the state machinery. By brazenly exploiting the state shareholding system (state-controlled enterprises such as Instituto Ricostruzione Italiana [IRI] and Ente Nazionale Idrocarburi [ENI] or state agencies such as the Cassa del Mezzogiorno) by means of laws that granted incredible privileges to certain groups (state pensions or benefits to citizens or firms) and tax concessions to certain professional sectors, and by the political management of public-sector hiring, the DC created a network of electoral consensus.

Internally, the party was split into numerous *correnti* (factions), each with its own leader. Behind apparent differences of political doctrine, these factions were the means whereby their members obtained posts in the government or jobs in the state-controlled enterprises. Although invariably riven by violent internal controversy, the DC held together in pursuit of its self-interested goals and in its bargaining with the other parties forming the government coalitions.

Given the apparent difficulty of eliminating what was commonly called "il sistema di potere democristiano," the majority of the electorate lapsed into resigned conformism. Intense suspicion of the PCI eased over time. But persisting public qualms about the PCI meant that no practicable alternative to a government led by the DC existed. Although it was well known that clientelism and corruption dominated politics and the management of power, the lack of a viable alternative stabilized the vote at the center of the moderate electorate, just as, on the left, the PCI was able rely on a stable and constant constituency. These factors created a situation of "blocked democracy," in which the second most important party in the country was deprived of any chance of governing by its lack of ideological legitimacy. Considering that the Italian electorate has always been distinguished by its close culturally based identification with political parties, and by the transmission of political attitudes within the family, the political system changed only slowly. Until the 1990s, there was no significant difference in voting patterns between one election and the next. After each round of elections, small increments in consensus for one or other of the parties of the governing majority (or internally to the Christian Democrat factions) led to renegotiation of ministerial posts, with the consequent collapse of the government and the introduction of an executive more in tune with the new equilibria thus established.

Alongside the DC and the PCI, an important role was played by the Socialist Party. Indeed, after 1963 when the PSI formed a government coalition with the DC, it was the latter's principal partner. Although internally divided over the form of political relationship to establish with the PCI, its rival on the left, and although it had to contend with the Social Democratic Party on the right, for many years the PSI constituted the link between the government and the left of the country. Its political weight increased considerably in the 1980s when it acted as the arbiter of Italian politics, even though its political consensus in the mid-years of the decade only amounted to 15 percent. Craxi, the leader of the PSI, forged an alliance with the DC, liquidated the left within his party, and became the principal antagonist of the PCI. He was appointed the first socialist president of the Council of Ministers (prime minister) in 1983 and headed the government until 1987. The distinctive feature of the

Craxi government was its greater political dynamism compared with its Christian Democratic predecessors. More than arrogance, Craxi's so-called *decisionismo* (the making of rapid decisions without seeking compromises with the other parties) seemingly inaugurated a new period of Italian politics by breaking with the DC's policy of never directly tackling problems in the hope that they would eventually solve themselves. The Italians experienced a phase of apparent modernization, economic recovery, and increased consumption, albeit at the cost of further deterioration in the public debt. Abroad, too, Italy's image seemed to improve, not only because of the greater stability of the executive but also because of the greater political assertiveness of Craxi, who proved to be less malleable and submissive than his Christian Democrat predecessors. The new socialist elite was characterized, both nationally and locally, by a "yuppie" lifestyle, which flaunted wealth, power, and status symbols. However, this facade concealed a system of corruption that penetrated every level of public life. The new socialist political elite integrated perfectly with the system of clientelism and spoils division created by the DC and, indeed, made it more efficient by organizing it according to managerial principles. What was called "the cost of politics" (which also included the cost of the luxurious lifestyles led by the "politicians") was illegally financed by a pervasive system of kickbacks in the state agencies and the local administrations. Until the end of the 1980s, even after the demise of the Craxi government, the PSI was taken to symbolize the political system and consequently paid the higher price—its dissolution.

In other parties that had always (or almost always) been part of the government coalitions were those that we previously termed the small lay parties of the center: the Partito Liberale (PLI), the Partito Republicano Italiano (PRI), the Partito Social Democratico Italiano (PSDI). Although these parties had in the past been led by men of outstanding political stature (Malagodi [PLI], Spadolini [PRI], Saragat [PSDI]), they never enjoyed broad electoral consensus, squeezed as they were between the "white whale" (as the DC, the Catholic party, was known) and the culture of the left represented by the PSI and the PCI. Essential for the governability of the country, first with the DC alone and then with the PSI, they were almost uninterruptedly in government for years and became part of the power system described above. When the latter collapsed they were inevitably swept away with it.

The political panorama of the period before 1994 included several other parties that never formed part of a government coalition and enjoyed minor electoral success. On the extreme right since the birth of the republic, the Movimento Sociale Italiano rallied nostalgia for fascism, the most conservative and authoritarian right wing, and an extremist fringe. Always in opposition, it acted as the ideological counter-weight to the extreme left, thereby enabling the center to buttress its power by raising the specter of "opposite extremisms." Numerous other small political parties long littered the Italian political scene, some of them transforming themselves, being reborn and disappearing in the space of a few years: Democrazia Proletaria (DP); Partito Socialista Italiano di Unità Proletaria (PSIUP); Il Manifesto; on the extreme left, the liberal-progressive Partito Radicale, Verdi, and La Rete; regional lists like Unione Valdostana, SVP (the South Tyrol party), Partito Sardo d'Azione; and various Leagues (Lombard, Venetian, etc.).

This was the political landscape of Italy until, at the end of the 1980s, an earthquake hit, radically transforming the political system.

THE STRATEGIC CONTEXT OF THE ELECTION OF 1994

The End of Communism

The Collapse of the Berlin Wall, and with it the end of communism in Eastern Europe, utterly changed the international political situation hitherto based on the antithesis between East and West. The impact in Italy was explosive. The most powerful communist party in Western Europe was the Italian PCI, and the fear of a communist takeover dominated the dynamics of the electoral system. The first major effect of the fall of the communist regime in the Soviet Union and the countries of Eastern Europe was greatly accelerated change in the communist party itself. In truth, the PCI had some time previously emancipated itself from direct Soviet influence and in fact was closer to European social democracy than to the communist regimes. The term "communist" itself began to embarrass some of the party's members and leaders, because it no longer reflected its policies or the features of its electoral base, which had by now lost its "proletarian" character. Yet the PCI was a party with a long and tormented history behind it, and it had deep ideological roots (not by chance was it called "the other Church"). A part of its membership naturally was unwilling to renege on its original identity. But the demise of communism forced the PCI to accelerate internal debate on its transformation, and after much acrimony, which effectively split the party, it assumed the name of Partito Democratico della Sinistra (PDS), thereby announcing its definitive abandonment of communist ideology. The schism within the PCI created a new party, Rifondazione Comunista (RC), which comprised the hard-line minority that refused to renounce its "communist" heritage.

The international collapse of communism also had a direct and violent impact on the government parties. As we have seen, the DC, the small centrist parties, and in the 1980s the PSI as well, had based part of their electoral consensus on the fact that moderate voters saw them as a bulwark against advancing communism. For many years this factor enabled the government parties to live on electoral "rent," but it also contributed to their "moral" deterioration. The DC's exploitation of the fear of communist takeover and its reliance on clientelism and on the support of the Church had bred a certainty that it could still preserve large electoral consensus by virtue of the fact that voting was based on considerations of ideology and not performance. Despite the DC's blatant ineptness in governing the country and despite pervasive corruption, a section of the electorate decided that it was better to "hold its nose" and vote DC, the assumption being that an inefficient and clientelistic regime was better than ending in the embrace of the communists. The sense of impunity felt by the political class in power, which enjoyed electoral consensus without having to earn it, led to further sclerosis of the "party-ocracy" system, where even actions of a blatantly illegal nature were legitimized by the fact that "politics" was a free-for-all in which everything was allowed. And in this political arena-cum-system, the DC's allies, the PSI, and the other centrist parties were entirely at their ease.

With the fall of the Berlin Wall and with the transformation of the PCI into the PDS, the fear of communism abated, thereby removing one of the electoral strategies that the DC and the other anticommunist parties had exploited. This development, together with others discussed below, like the anticorruption investigation launched by the judiciary, the advance of the *Lega*, and the referenda, utterly transformed the Italian political situation in the space of a few years.

From the Leagues to the Lega Nord

In the early 1980s, a number of grassroots movements known as *Leghe* (Leagues) sprang up in certain northern regions of the country (first in Veneto, and then Lombardy, Piedmont, Liguria, Emilia, and Tuscany). Born as movements pitting themselves against the central power of a state deemed inefficient and oppressive, the Leagues claimed autonomy and decision-making power for local communities, indicting the traditional parties for their clientelism and rampant corruption. They also highlighted the inefficiency of the public administration and the collusion of the government parties, the opposition, and trade unions to share the spoils of government. They fiercely attacked the tax system and public investments. But the Leagues based their main assault on two lines of cleavage: the divide between North and South and between native Italian and foreign immigrant. *Leghismo* arose in regions marked by strong industrial development and a deeply Catholic and conservative mentality, where there existed and still exists a tradition of entrepreneurship, and where hard work, thrift, and self-help have always been important values. Raucously but effectively, the Leagues assailed the government's Southern-oriented policy, which they accused of subtracting resources from the productive North and conveying them to a welfare-dependent and parasitical South in exchange for votes. The Leagues drew their support from the petty bourgeois business class and the conservative proletariat, which hitherto had been the traditional electoral base of the DC.

These various Leagues attracted little electoral support until 1989, and as a consequence they were underestimated by the large parties. Given the anti-institutional nature of *leghismo* and its violent and often crude attacks on the South and its inhabitants, as well as against non-European immigrants, the traditional parties thought that they could contain the Leagues with facile accusations of racism and by treating their activities as instances of local folklore.

The first surprise came with the European elections of 1989, when the Lega Lombarda collected 8 percent of the votes in Lombardy (after previously achieving 3 percent in the 1987 elections), and with the subnational elections of 1990 when it increased its electoral share to 18 percent (again in Lombardy). The other Leagues (particularly in Veneto, Piedmont, and Liguria) also substantially increased their electoral support. This significant success at the expense of the government parties dismayed the country's ruling political class, although it was unable to meet the demands raised by the richest and most productive part of the country, for whose discontent the Leagues acted as the catalyst.

The main Leagues then united themselves under a single symbol and thus turned themselves formally into a political party called the Lega Nord, which brandished the banner of federalism and threatened the secession of Northern Italy from the rest of the country. The Lega targeted its attacks on the state and the South, and also on foreign immigrants. It argued that Northern Italy had been culturally colonized and economically exploited by the South via the Southern-born politicians who wielded hegemony over the government, Parliament, and the political parties.[2]

The parties of the government coalition, already having difficulties after their defeat in the referendum on the single-preference system—

voters would henceforth vote for only a single candidate—were dealt a further blow by the Lega Nord in 1992, when it won 23.6 percent of the vote in Lombardy, 25.5 percent in Veneto, 16.3 percent in Piedmont, and 14.3 percent in Liguria. Although it only operated in the north and center of Italy, the Lega Nord garnered 8.6 percent of votes on a national basis and thus became the fourth largest party in the country. In the North, indeed, it had become the only non-left alternative to the DC and the other government parties now subject to mounting public hostility. The Lega Nord therefore also acquired the votes of many moderate centrists who, although they did not subscribe to its extremist views, used it to express their dissent with the political management of the country without opting for the left. The themes harped on by the Lega, like "federalism," were appropriated after some revision by the other parties as well, in order to win back an electorate that had discovered voting mobility. The success of the Lega stabilized between 1992 and 1994, when another earthquake shook the center of the political system: the DC was dissolved and other political parties arose in its stead. As we shall see, the Lega campaigned for the political elections of 1994 together with a new party, Forza Italia (FI), and then joined the government, although it would withdraw after seven months.

Judicial Inquiries

The investigations into corruption conducted by the judiciary were a decisive factor in the breakup of the traditional party system. After 1992, when the Milan judges arrested a minor PSI functionary for corruption, the system of illegality that had long dominated the activities of the parties in power was laid bare. Within a short space of time, clear evidence emerged of the direct involvement of party secretaries, ministers and ex–prime ministers, bureaucrats tied to the parties, private industrialists, and public-sector executives in the system of corruption and illegal financing of the political parties. An unstoppable avalanche followed, astonishing even those who had been aware of the illegal financing of the parties but had failed to realize the enormous scale of the phenomenon. Political leaders who had ruled the country only shortly before (Craxi, Forlani, Andreotti, De Michelis, De Lorenzo, and many others) found themselves under investigation by the judiciary, scorned by a public incensed at the country's political class, and deserted by their supporters who felt betrayed or who, more cynically, abandoned the sinking ship. In spite of pressure, attacks, and attempts at delegitimation, the Milanese judges of the so-called Clean Hands anticorruption pool continued inquiries that are today still far from complete. The judiciary thus dealt a decisive blow to the old party political system. They not only indicted corrupt politicians but focused public opinion on the moral degradation of Italian politics and restored faith in the system of justice. The moral decay of Italian politics had long existed, but it had not previously come to light due to the reluctance of many judges to pit themselves against political power. Those courageous few who tried to do so found themselves removed from the inquiry or transferred to another district. Many of the inquiries launched against politicians were systematically "sandbagged" or shelved by a compliant *procura* (prosecutor's office). The *procura* of Rome, which had jurisdiction over many of the investigations against politicians, was known as the "foggy harbor": here the investigations ran aground and then faded into nothing. That the Milanese judges were able to take action and to persist in their inquiries was certainly due to their ability and courage; but it was also because conditions had now changed to such an extent that their investigations were not abruptly cut short. Even before *tangentopoli* ("Bribesville," as the anticorruption inquiry was dubbed), the traditional political system had shown signs of weakness and flagging consensus, although it was still strong enough to survive. The "Clean Hands" investigation was its coup de grâce.

From the Referendum to the Electoral Reform

The referendum on the electoral system held in 1991 was another turning point for Italian politics, not only with regard to the content of the referendum, although important, but because it was the first revolt by the electorate against the decisions imposed on them by the governing political class. Mario Segni—a prestigious DC politician (his father had been president of the republic in the 1960s) but largely isolated within his own party—founded a referendum movement in order to abolish multiple preferences on the ballot sheet. This multiple preference system had given rise to a vote-swap market that underpinned the clientelistic management of Italian politics. If successful, the referendum (which was "abrogative" in the sense that it repealed a previous law) would have introduced a single-preference system, with consequent profound changes to electoral procedure that would make it impossible to check on voters' behavior (previously done by examining "combinations" of preferences).

The proposal was supported by the PDS, the leftist parties, and the reformist wing of the Catholics. Craxi, leader of the Socialist Party, was openly hostile. Forlani, the party secretary of the DC, did not publicly take an official position, but privately he was confident that the number of votes necessary to validate the referendum would not be reached. The single-preference system would have demolished one of the pillars on which the power of the DC and the government parties rested. However, instead of taking Craxi's advice "to go to the seaside,"[3] more than 60 percent of voters went to the polling stations and 95.6 percent of them voted in favor of the single-preference system. Such an overwhelming majority, higher than anyone expected, was a heavy defeat for the government and demonstrated the electorate's new determination to act independently of party instructions. The victory of the 1991 referendum paved the way for reform of the electoral system, while the Constitutional Court admitted two further referenda that would have effectively introduced a majoritarian system. A bicameral committee for electoral reform was set up in April 1992. In March, Parliament approved the reform with regard to local elections, introducing a two-ballot system for the direct election of the mayor. After long and exhausting bargaining, in August 1993 the electoral procedure for the Senate and the Chamber of Deputies was changed, with 75 percent of members being elected with the majoritarian system and 25 percent with the proportional system. Subsequent events have shown that this new system has not resolved the problem of governability because it is unable to ensure stable majorities. The so-called second republic may not yet have assumed its final form. Negotiations are in progress to introduce further reform of the electoral system.

The Dissolution of the DC

In the elections of 1992, the DC lost around 5 percent of its electoral support (which was still approximately 30 percent, however), while the PSI, as expected, did not make any substantial gains. As mentioned, the Lega Nord considerably increased its share of the votes. The socialist Giuliano Amato was asked to form a government, given that the DC did not look kindly on another government led by Bettino Craxi. But 1992 was also the year in which the Milan judges uncovered the illegal system of party financing and the complex web of kickbacks and corruption associated with it. The first notices of indictment were issued for ex-ministers and the administrative secretary of the DC, and the Italian public came increasingly to realize that these were not isolated cases but symptoms of an illegal system that had dominated politics for years. The DC and the PSI, together with the leaders of the lay centrist parties in the government coalition, were dealt a mortal blow by the activities of the Milan judiciary. Mario Segni, the Catholic leader who had promoted the 1991 referendum, left the DC in order to found a new party. The new secretary of the DC, Mino Martinazzoli, tried to reconstitute the party, but internal cleavages and power struggles prevented him from doing so without irredeemably splitting the party. In the end, the DC was forced to disband. From its ruins arose four new political formations: the Partito Popolare Italiano (PPI), led by Martinazzoli; the Patto Segni led by Mario Segni and allied with the PPI; the Centro Cristiano Democratico (CCD), headed by Pierferdinando Casini and Clemente Mastella, which allied with Forza Italia in the 1994 elections; and the Cristiani Sociali led by Pierre Carniti, the former leader of the Catholic trade union.

The Birth of Forza Italia

The birth of Forza Italia in January 1994, and the electoral success it achieved within the space of only a few months, is undoubtedly one of the most astonishing episodes in Italian political history. The year 1993 was marked by the dissolution of the DC, the PSI, and the lay parties of the center, as we have noted. The DC was desperately in search of some way to avert its collapse, the PSI was buffeted by scandal and now in its death throes, and the small centrist parties were also caught up by the storm of *tangentopoli*. In this climate of crisis of the party system, Silvio Berlusconi made his entrance onto the political scene. A wealthy Milanese businessman, Berlusconi had made his fortune in the 1980s as a television entrepreneur. In only a few years he had gained control of the main commercial television stations in Italy while simultaneously expanding his interests in publishing as well as numerous other commercial and financial activities. His link with the government parties was obviously of great importance in gaining the necessary political protection for his business activities. Berlusconi was especially close to Bettino Craxi, with whom he boasted personal friendship when the PSI dominated Italian politics. It was because of Craxi's protection, in fact, that for years every attempt to regulate the Italian television sector was blocked and Berlusconi was able to build a financial empire based on the mass media. And it was Craxi, when prime minister in 1984, who issued the decree, known as the *decreto Berlusconi*, that enabled Fininvest (Berlusconi's company that ran commercial television) to continue its operations even though the judiciary had ruled Berlusconi's private television system to be unlawful. The Milanese entrepreneur was also well known to the public because he was the owner of one of the country's most successful soccer clubs, AC Milan, which had and still has an army of supporters in every part of the country. Given the popularity of soccer in Italy, this guaranteed Berlusconi visibility and prestige.

Despite his close links with politics, and although his companies were under investigation for the illegal financing of the parties and for corruption, Berlusconi had never engaged directly in politics. However, the crisis of the parties that had given him protection, the realization that they would not be able to survive the scandals now threatening to overwhelm them, and the fear that the left might take over government of the country persuaded Berlusconi to enter the political arena. Within a few months, using the football supporters' clubs, his company organizations and resources, and his television network and newspapers, Berlusconi launched a campaign to market his newly founded party, Forza Italia. By ably exploiting the mass media he directly controlled, he inaugurated a new style of "show-business politics," making ample use of opinion polls and presenting himself as the "new" in an exhausted political system. Forza Italia drew its support from the center-right electorate disoriented by the collapse of the old political system. Waving the banner of anticommunism, a slogan still able to attract the more traditional electors, silencing his leftist political adversaries by branding them as "illiberal," Berlusconi made his preparations for the new round of elections, the first to be held under the recently introduced majoritarian system. Since Forza Italia was a new political formation—indeed, it had been hastily put together by co-opting managers and consultants working for Berlusconi's companies to be its executive (it was called, in fact, "the party-company")—it had no links with local realities, apart from the football supporters' clubs, and the outcome of the elections was consequently difficult to predict. With a skillful maneuver, given that the new electoral law forced the parties to form alliances if they were to have a chance of winning the majority share of the vote, Berlusconi allied with the Lega in North Italy, and in the South with Alleanza Nazionale (AN), the right-wing party previously known as the MSI, which had changed its name in order to dispel its image as the postfascist party. Together with the Lega (flushed with its success in the 1992 elections), CCD (born from the breakup of the DC), and UD (Unione di Centro, formed out of fragments of the small lay parties, now disbanded), Forza Italia presented itself in the northern regions of the country as a coalition called "*Polo della Libertà*" (the Freedom Pole), while in the South, where the Lega Nord was obviously absent, and Alleanza Nazionale enjoyed considerable support, the "*Polo del Buon Governo*" coalition (the Good Government Pole) combined the AN, Forza Italia, CCD, and UD.

The Elections of 1994 and Berlusconi's Victory

After a vindictive election campaign marked by violent personal attacks and in which the mass media played a crucial role (the term "videocracy" was coined to stress the part played by television in particular), the coalitions led by Berlusconi won the majority of seats in Parliament.

The left had campaigned for the elections by forming a coalition named *Progressisti* (Progressives), which comprised the PDS, RC, the *Verdi* (Greens), La Rete (another small Catholic party), the Partito Socialista, and the Cristiani Sociali (part of the ex–DC). Campaigning under the name of *Patto per l'Italia* (Pact for Italy) were two parties that had arisen from the breakup of the DC: the PPI and Il Patto Segni. The 25 percent proportional quota in the electoral system, for which the parties presented themselves on an independent basis, highlighted both the fragmentation of the political situation by enabling the small parties to survive and demonstrated the effects of the political earthquake in Italy. The PSI's vote fell from 13.6 percent in 1992 to 2.2 percent in 1994. The four parties born from the ruins of the DC gained half the votes that they had obtained as a single party, Forza Italia won 21 percent of votes, and Alleanza Nazionale won 13.5 percent, more than twice that achieved by its predecessor, the MSI. On the left, gains were made by the PDS, but the Progressista coalition did not achieve the success that it had hoped for.

The survey of ethnic prejudice began its fieldwork just after the elections of 1994, while negotiations for the formation of the new government were in progress. This was to be a center-right government headed by Silvio Berlusconi and also including the Lega Nord, even though the latter had declared its incompatibility with FI and AN and had initially only entered an electoral, not political, alliance. The government only lasted a few months, however, because the Lega Nord shifted its allegiance. The result: a new parliamentary majority on behalf of a "technical" (nonpartisan) government supported by the left. New elections held in 1996 were won by a center-left coalition with Forza Italia, Lega Nord, Alleanza Nazionale, and CCD in opposition.

This, briefly, is the history of the party system immediately following the 1994 elections. With this historical scaffolding in place, we propose to explore the role that hostility toward outsiders played in affecting the choice that Italians made from among the choices on offer in the general election of 1994.

THE GENERAL ELECTION OF 1994:
A PARADOX OF CHANGE AND CONTINUITY

With the established party system swept away, the choices in political parties running up to the general election of 1994 were nearly entirely new. Given the recency of the emergence of the new set of political parties, it seems more appropriate to speak of partisan sympathies than of party identification, and by way of mapping these sympathies, all of our respondents were asked: "What party or political movement do you feel

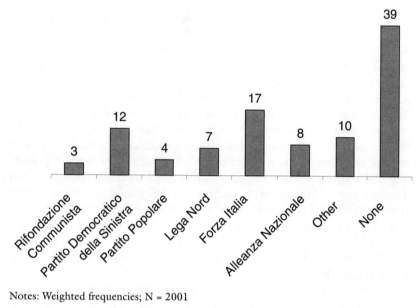

Notes: Weighted frequencies; N = 2001

Fig. 4.1 Distribution of Partisan Sympathies (Percentage)

closest to—the National Alliance, Democratic Party of the Left, the League, Communist Refoundation, Forza Italia, the Popular Party, or some other?"

Figure 4.1 graphically summarizes the distribution of partisan sympathies in the aftermath of the 1994 election. As a moment's inspection will make plain, fragmentation is the outstanding feature of the new political landscape. The principal parties—Partito Democratico della Sinistra (PDS), Forza Italia, Alleanza Nazionale (AN), and the Lega Nord—stand out by virtue of their comparative, not their absolute, size. Forza Italia heads the pack, with roughly one in every six choosing it. The PDS takes second place, with about one in every eight selecting it. The militant parties of the right, by contrast, the Lega Nord and Alleanza Nazionale, trail several steps behind, with less than one in every ten selecting each.

This quartet of political parties easily outnumbers the rest, corralling over two-thirds of those who feel close to any party at all. But even taken together they do not come close to dominating the electoral landscape. Just under one half of Italians, or approximately 40 percent, either say they do not feel close to any party or decline to say anything at all. In absolute terms, then, almost as many Italians did not declare an attachment to any political party as those who feel close to the four principal parties all rolled together. Moreover, the remainder of the public, a sizeable 17 percent, are scattered over the partisan landscape, dispersed among at least another eleven parties, each managing (with the exception of the Partito Popolare and Rifondazione Communista) to attract the support of only 1 or 2 percent. Fragmentation is thus a defining feature in the new party system: less than a majority feel close to the new parties that are at the center of the second republic, while the largest number either do not feel close to any party whatever or feel close to a party that is marginal to the new parties of Italy.

Just because of this fragmentation at the level of parties, the electoral alternatives were organized for the general election of 1994 at the level of coalitional blocs. As we have noted, in the North, Berlusconi's Forza Italia made an alliance with the Lega Nord, running as the Pole of Liberty; in the South, Forza Italia joined forces with the Alleanza Nazionale, running as the Pole of Good Government. With Forza Italia as a common linchpin, the two Poles formed a common bloc, defining the right. The Progressives defined the left. Segni's Pact for Italy, independent of and falling between the blocs of the right and the left, defined the center.

Since the electoral alternatives took the form of coalitional blocs competing head to head for seats in the lower chamber, we asked all respondents:

> Could you tell us what group you voted for in the last election for the Chamber of Deputies, on the ballot for the representative from your district?
> Was it the Pole of Liberty, the Pole of Good Government, the Pact for Italy, or the Progressives?

Table 4.1 compares the electoral choices reported by our respondents and recorded in official statistics. The survey results parallel the actual record of voting choices with remarkable fidelity. The Progressives were the single largest party, officially harvesting 38 percent of the votes (as compared to 36 percent in our survey).[4] The Pole of Liberty was right on their heels, collecting 34 percent of the votes cast (and 33 percent in our survey). The Pact for Italy and the Pole of Good Government picked up nearly equal portions, with 13 percent voting for the former and 11 percent for the latter (12 and 13 in our sample, respectively). The right, on the strength of the combination of the Pole of Liberty and the Pole of Good Government, was clearly the dominant bloc and accordingly formed the government.

To what extent did hostility toward immigrants help carry the right to victory? This would be, except for our special interest in prejudice, a curious question to ask. The volcanic eruption of the *tangentopoli* scandal shook the political system to its foundations. With corruption

TABLE 4.1
Reported and Actual Vote Choice

Political Group	Survey Results	Actual 1994 Election Results
Pole of Liberty	33	34
Pole of Good Government	13	11
Pact for Italy	12	13
Progressives	36	38
Other	5	4

Notes: Unweighted N = 1364; excludes refusals and those not voting; weighted frequencies

dominating public and private discussion of politics, with a half century of political leaders and coalitions swept aside and a whole new system of parties and leaders and electoral rules put in their place, who could possibly suppose that the issue of immigrants would play a major role in determining the voting choices of Italians? Yet, perversely, because the general election of 1994 was exceptional, it provides a truly demanding test of the potential impact of prejudice on politics. For if prejudice can have an impact in an election dominated by the transformation of the electoral system itself, it surely can develop a head of steam when the politics of exclusion is at the center of the campaign.

Did prejudice help the right to victory in the election of 1994? Table 4.2 sets out two models of voting. For transparency, we estimated the models through ordinary least squares (OLS) with the parties scored from right (lowest) to left (highest), though for assurance we replicated the analyses taking advantage of both ordered probit and multinomial logit. The first model focuses on long-term factors, in particular, occupational status, education, age, and personality. As table 4.2 makes plain, although the influence of several of these long-term factors is significant statistically, the impact of prejudice is significant nonetheless. The second model includes additional factors more immediately relevant to the act of voting. Two are familiar from the "Two Flavors" model, economic insecurity and mistrust; the third, ideological self-identification, is a standard element in the analysis of electoral choice.[5] It is to be expected that taking account of a factor that is immediately relevant to the voting decision, such as ideological identification, will attenuate the direct influence of a factor that is much farther removed in the causal chain, such as prejudice. Even so, as table 4.2 shows, hostility to immigrants continues to be a significant factor boosting support for the parties of the right.[6]

TABLE 4.2
Models of Vote Choice

Dependent Variable: Vote	Model 1	Model 2
Immigrant hostility	−0.071**	−0.029**
	(−5.38)	(−2.86)
Personality	0.147*	0.009
	(0.85)	(0.11)
Age	−0.001	−0.002*
	(−0.42)	(−1.54)
Occupational status	0.039**	0.015
	(2.02)	(1.04)
Education	0.033**	0.011*
	(2.89)	(1.36)
Mistrust		0.026
		(0.80)
Economic		−0.034
insecurity		(−1.21)
Ideological		−0.460**
self-identification		(−33.95)
Constant	1.662	3.298
n	1194	970
R^2	0.06	0.58

* $p < 0.10$ (one-tailed)   ** $p < 0.05$ (one-tailed)
   Notes: Numbers in parentheses are t-statistics
   Vote is coded as follows: 1—Pole of Liberty OR Pole of Good Government, 2—Pact for Italy, 3—Progressives; ideological self-identification is coded from 1 (Left) to 5 (Right).
   Ranges of variables: hostility—0 to 10; mistrust—1 to 3; economic insecurity—1 to 3; personality—1 to 2; age—18 to 69; education—1 to 12; occupational status—1 to 7.

It is striking that prejudice still is a significant factor because the impact of ideological self-identification on vote choice is, quite simply, enormous. The zero-order correlation between ideological self-image and voting behavior is .75. At this level of association, the voting decision, for those who see themselves as having an ideological commitment, reduces for all practical purposes to their ideological self-image: voters classifying themselves on the left overwhelmingly voted, in the general election of 1994, for the progressive bloc; those classifying themselves on the right, equally overwhelmingly, voted for the bloc of the right.

By way of underlining the extraordinary strength of the connection between ideological self-conception and electoral choice in Italy,[7] we

TABLE 4.3
Correlation Between Vote Choice and
Ideological Self-Identification

Education Level	1992 (US) National Election Study (N)	Italian National Survey (N)
Pre–high school	0.28 (150)	0.65 (763)
High school	0.37 (419)	0.75 (398)
Post–high school	0.59 (721)	0.77 (148)

Notes: Weighted correlations; unweighted N

have arranged a comparison. It is a standard result from the study of American political behavior that the less politically sophisticated or well educated citizens are, the less the influence of ideological self-identification on electoral choice.[8] The first column of table 4.3 illustrates this garden variety result, reporting the correlation between ideological self-identification and the 1992 presidential vote in the United States as a function of level of education.[9] As a moment's glance at the figures will make plain, the connection between the two is steeply graded. For voters who have graduated from college, the connection between ideological self-classification and electoral choice is quite tight, the correlation between the two being .59. But the less schooling voters have had, the looser the connection between ideological identification and the vote becomes; indeed, so much so that for voters with an eighth-grade education or less, it is only .28. The second column of table 4.3 presents the equivalent calculations for the Italian case. In Italy, by contrast, the impact of ideological identification on the vote for each and every tier of education is enormous. For the (comparatively) small proportion of Italians who are highly educated, the correlation between the two is .77. But more impressive still, for the overwhelming portion of the public who have only an elementary or a vocational educational background—more than one half have less than a high school education—the correlation between vote and ideological self-identification is .65.

Making the connection between ideological self-conception and electoral choice, these results make plain, does not indispensably hinge on political sophistication. In Italy, ideological self-images are woven deeply into everyday life through social practice and symbolism. Less obviously, the continuation of the tie between the two in the face of the collapse of the cold war regime suggests that left and right are natural categories of liberal democracy. The Italian political landscape, defined since the Second World War by the politics of the cold war, was flattened by the collapse of communism. And with the eclipse of the Marxist left came the suggestion that the categories of left and right had themselves been eclipsed. But as our results make plain, having lost their familiar external landmarks, Italians relied on their habitual internal signposts precisely in order to pick out the features of the new landscape that corresponded to the old. And in complementary fashion, the party system reproduced itself in the election of 1994: the left and right of the first republic vanished; the left and right of the second took their place, each propelled by the need to capitalize on persisting public constituencies. The continuity of individuals thus rewarded, and was rewarded by, the continuity of institutions.

IDEOLOGICAL ASYMMETRIES AND THE VULNERABILITY OF THE LEFT

Our results should take some of the wind out of the sails of fashionable arguments that ideology has lost its hold on the political imagination. In determining how they will cast their votes, far and away the most central determinant is voters' ideological self-conception. Prejudice is only a peripheral factor. But a fuller reckoning of the comparative standing of the two hinges on the answers to two questions. First, what is the relation, if any, between intolerance and ideological self-conceptions? Second, what exactly should be made of citizens' conceptions of ideological self-conceptions?

Ideology, we want to suggest, consists in two distinguishable components. There are the values that historically have made up the constitutive commitments of the left and right; and there is also a person's own sense of him- or herself as a part of the left or right. The first we take to be a person's ideological commitments; the second, his or her ideological self-conception.

Just because ideological self-conceptions and ideological commitments are distinguishable, is it necessary to ask what the connection is between the two? When does what people think that they think mirror what they actually think? When what they believe they believe does not correspond to what they really believe, what form does the distortion take? And so far as their ideological self-conceptions and their ideological commitments diverge, which will matter more in the longer run? The trajectory of the politics of exclusion, we shall suggest, depends on this dialectic of ideological self-conceptions and ideological commitments. As we have just seen, ideology—conceived in terms of what people think that they think—dominates the direct influence of prejudice on politics. But as we shall now show, viewed in terms of what people actually think, the left is deeply vulnerable to the right.

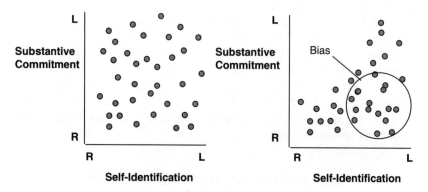

Fig. 4.2 Two Possible Patterns of Deviations in Ideological
Self-Identification and Substantive Ideological Commitments

Consider two versions of what it means to say that the political orientation that people ascribe to themselves and the political values that they actually hold do not correspond. In the first, or weak, version, the lack of correspondence is random; in the second, or strong, version, it is systematic.

The weak and the strong versions carry different implications for politics. To illustrate why, figure 4.2 provides hypothetical depictions of both versions of a mismatch hypothesis. The first version of the mismatch hypothesis, shown on the left side, presumes that the lack of correspondence between citizens' ideological self-conceptions and their ideological commitments is random. In this version, the odds that a person who ought to be on the right, given his actual ideological commitments, will locate himself on the left are the same as the odds that a person who ought to be on the left, given his actual ideological commitments, will locate himself on the right. The political consequences of mismatches thus cancel out just so far as the ideological blocs are of approximately equal size.[10]

To matter politically, a mismatch between what people think they think and what they actually think must be asymmetric. In the hypothetical illustration, shown in the right panel of figure 4.2, people on the left on the basis of their ideological self-images are disproportionately likely to be, in terms of their actual ideological commitments, on the right. So long as their behavior is contingent on their ideological self-conception, the left (in our hypothetical illustration) will not pay a price. But just so far as people's actual ideological commitments come into play, the left is vulnerable to the right. In the strong version of the mismatch hypothesis, then, just so far as one ideological alternative is advantaged, the other is disadvantaged.

We believe that there is a crucial asymmetry to the politics of resentment: the left is vulnerable to the right; the right is not vulnerable to the left. This one-sided vulnerability, we shall show, is rooted in the appeal of a core value of the right to a substantial fraction of the left; an appeal, we suspect, that is likely to increase with time. These two considerations form a natural pair. The first is static, depicting things as they now are; the second dynamic, suggesting how they are likely to be. They point, if both are right, to a potentially decisive asymmetry in Italian politics—and, we suspect, in European politics more broadly. With respect to at least one component of ideological commitment, the position of the right has a strong appeal to those on the left who least well understand the values of the left, but the position of the left does not have a similar appeal to those on the right whether they are well equipped to understand the values of the right or not. And just so far as this asymmetry holds, the right is advantaged. If and as issues of immigration move to the center of political argument, the animating values of the right resonate not only with its own adherents but also with a very large portion of the adherents of the left.

IDEOLOGICAL IDENTIFICATION AND COMPONENTS OF IDEOLOGICAL COMMITMENT

Given the focus of our study, we shall concentrate on the classically central component of political ideology—the cleavage between left and right. In fixing attention on the distinction between left and right, we are not suggesting that other dimensions—postmaterialism, for example, or environmentalism or feminism—are not relevant for other purposes.[11] Nor are we suggesting that the dimensions of left and right we concentrate on are the only ones conceivable.[12] Nonetheless, a growing body of studies in Europe has pointed particularly to two dimensions.[13] One is equalitarianism. Accepting that equalitarianism will take different specific expressions depending on time and place, we can nevertheless say that it characteristically centers on a pair of sometimes complementary, sometimes conflicting objectives: reducing the disparity in the opportunities and conditions of life separating those who are worst-off and those who are best-off and—what is not quite the same thing—seeing that those who are worst-off become markedly better-off.[14] The second dimension (again following the lead of contemporary European research) that distinguishes the political right from the left is a cluster of values centered on authority and order.[15] Again recognizing that its specific expression varies with time and place, this second dimension centers on commitment to a cluster of values: a belief in the indispensability, for individuals and societies alike, of strictness and discipline; of sacrifice and self-denial; and the aggressive enforcement of order and the assurance of stability.

These definitions, though clear in the abstract, hover too far above the actual clash of politics. What do these two dimensions mean concretely, and how can we tell operationally whether, and how far, citizens commit themselves to either or both?

Equalitarianism presents a special case because of the special standing of equality in democratic politics. A century ago, conservatives spoke openly in favor of hierarchy. But as de Tocqueville foresaw, equality has been intertwined with liberty. And just so far as the two together are now the constitutive values of democratic polities, it is difficult directly to challenge equality as a value. But if equality can no longer be frontally assaulted, it is contestable on the same ground that every other value, including liberty, is contestable. Democratic politics requires that choices be made between competing values and—still more important—provides incentives to see that these choices are publicly debated. Hence the pseudo-paradox that left and right simultaneously agree—and disagree—on core values. Because the right favors social order and personal security, it does not follow that the left prefers social chaos and personal vulnerability. Because the left favors those who are badly-off becoming better-off, it does not follow that the right believes that it is better that they remain badly-off. But it does follow, given the normative priorities of both left and right, that when they find themselves required to choose between competing values, as in politics inevitably they must from time to time, they systematically and predictably differ in the choices they make. The left will, for example, distinguish itself by the importance it attaches to equality; the right by the importance it attaches to order.

Value conflict, so understood, consists in clashes over the importance to attach to a particular value *relative to other core values*. The commitment of citizens to core values, it follows, cannot be understood by observing the importance that they attach to each in isolation from the others. We must instead observe how they choose when they actually must choose between them, not because these values on each and every occasion collide, but because the litmus test of commitment is the choice that people make when they do collide. Thus, it will not do to ask citizens how much importance they attach to equality as a value considered by itself. It is necessary to see how they would choose, if they were forced to choose, between equality and other values. But which values? A set of four—liberty, equality, economic security, and social order—are fundamental. Each is a core value, in the sense that it is taken to be of uncommon importance in its own right, and all are competing values, in the sense that obtaining more of one is understood to require obtaining less of another. And just so far as obtaining more of one sometimes requires settling for less of another, people are under pressure to endorse each at the expense of the others.

Taking advantage of these trade-offs between values, we have developed the "forced choice, paired comparison" method to assess the *comparative* importance of equality. The method proceeds in two steps. First, each value is briefly defined, to ensure that everyone understands every term the same way.[16] Then, proceeding two values at a time through all possible pairs, everyone is asked to choose which is the more important value. The "forced choice, paired comparison" procedure thus has a pair of distinctive properties. Everyone must choose between competing values rather than consider each in isolation. Still more important, the choices they make must take account of all possible pairs of competing values. So assessed, the measure that we employ of the importance that people attach to the value of equality is the number of times that they actually choose it rather than a competitive core value.

If it is hard to forswear equalitarian sympathies expressly, given that equality now is a constitutive value of democratic politics, the second dimension distinguishing left and right is directly contestable. Indeed, we have attached the label "authority values" to it precisely in order to underline its distinctively combative admixture of personal values and societal concerns. In thinking of those who exemplify this orientation we have in mind a familiar figure, one who is preoccupied with the threat of disintegration and disorder; who subscribes to the redemptive value, for the individual and for the larger society alike, of self-discipline, self-sacrifice, and self-reliance; who stresses the exigency of law and order. These diverse concerns, intuitively, make up a coherent pattern interweaving two contrasting themes: on the one side, a lack of sympathy with the tender-minded values of compassion and empathy; on the other, an insistence on the values of strictness, sacrifice, and authority. Accordingly, we classify people as committed to the values of authority, order, and discipline to the degree that they agree that "It is better to live in a society in which the laws are vigorously enforced than to give people too much freedom"; "Only the elderly, children, and handicapped should receive public assistance"; and "Whenever a private or public employer finds it necessary to reduce the number of employees, the first to be let go should be women who have a husband who is working."

Equalitarianism and authority values are integral elements of the ideological left and right. But as a generation of public opinion studies has made plain, the specific beliefs of ordinary citizens reflect the abstract categories of political thought only very approximately, and often very inaccurately. What we manifestly must do, then, is to explore to what degree, and in what ways, Italians' conception of themselves ideologically corresponds to their actual ideological commitments.

We take, as our starting point, an axiom in the analysis of public opinion. The public, rather than being an undifferentiated whole, consists in a number of different layers, or strata. These strata correspond to people's level of political awareness or sophistication.[17] Broadly, two propositions about political awareness in mass publics are now agreed. First, the level of political awareness and the density of strata go together: the higher the level of political sophistication, the fewer proportionately the number of citizens who possess it. Second, just so far as an understanding of what ideological orientations entail is a function of people's level of political awareness and sophistication, the lower the stratum, the more the connection between ideological self-conceptions and ideological commitments should be subject to distortion.

Both propositions are uncontroversial and have been at the core of our own work over the last decade.[18] But what we did not realize, and what others possibly have not noticed, is a tacit premise of symmetry. It is standardly supposed that the distortion introduced by a lack of political sophistication is equivalent for left and right, as though both sides pay an approximately equal price in the misunderstanding of their core values among their less politically aware adherents. But is this necessarily so? Is there not at least a possibility of an asymmetry in mismatches between ideological self-images and ideological commitments?

The more we thought about the wide appeal of the values of authority, order, and discipline, the more we thought it possible that there may be a strong asymmetry in mismatches between what people think they think politically and what they actually think. Authority values should have a wide appeal to the less-educated and less politically aware strata generally. And just so far as it does, it follows that a significant portion of the left will share some of the ideological commitments of the right. Correspondingly, it is easy to imagine dire economic circumstances under which equalitarianism reaches across the political spectrum and appeals to a large number on the right, particularly if they lack the education or sophistication to understand the viewpoint of the right. Given the run of prosperity in Italy over the last years, it seems to us that this latter form of asymmetrical mismatch is likely to be modest, if it appears at all.

Of the two substantive dimensions of ideological commitment, we first examine equalitarianism. By way of marking the strata of political sophistication, we rely on level of formal education, distinguishing three

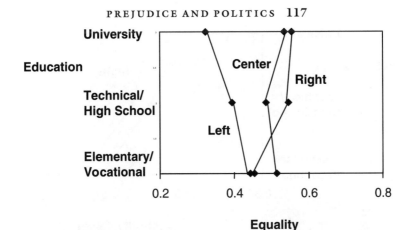

Notes: Authority values scaled to 0-1; Higher score means more value placed on authority. Values are mean authority values scores for each group.

Fig. 4.3 Asymmetric Commitment: Equality, Education, and Ideological Self-Identification

layers: elementary and vocational educations, technical and high school, and university. Figure 4.3 accordingly maps the level of support for equality as a function of ideological self-identification and level of education.

The first point to observe is that the more politically sophisticated Italians are, the closer the correspondence between what they think they think and what they actually think. Those on the left are accordingly more likely to move to the left pole, the better educated they are; those on the right similarly are more likely to move to the right pole, the better educated they are. So we see in figure 4.3 that the positions of those identified with opposing ideological poles increasingly diverge with increasing levels of education. This pattern of increasing divergence conditional on political sophistication we think of as an accentuation effect. This effect, previous work suggests, is a natural feature of engaged political reasoning.[19] It is a mark of political sophistication, according to this line of argument, to accentuate partisan and ideological differences. Graphically, the result is an increasing distance between the mean positions of those on the left and on the right the more politically aware and sophisticated their adherents are. Those who are most engaged by politics, who best understand the logic of their ideological allegiances, who see most clearly how much is at stake in the clash of positions of the left and the right, are the most likely "to spread the alternatives." This impulse to accentuate the difference between ideological alternatives, to emphasize rather than minimize the divergence

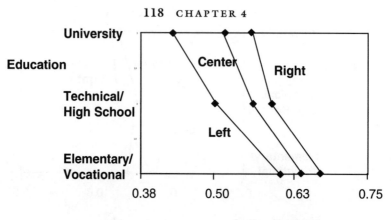

Notes: Authority values scaled to 0-1; Higher score means more value placed on authority. Values are mean authority values scores for each group.

Fig. 4.4 Asymmetric Commitment: Authority Values, Education, and Ideological Self-Identification

between left and right, does not well up from the bottom. Rather, as Converse and McClosky urged a generation ago, ideological alternatives come to life and are clarified in the upper layers of the politically aware and sophisticated. So, with respect to equality as a value, the better educated spread the ideological alternatives, and neither side scoops a markedly disproportionate share of the less-educated stratum of the other side.

What does the politics of order look like? Figure 4.4 maps the locations of those who classify themselves on the left and on the right as a function of their level of education. Again we see a marked accentuation effect conditional on educational level. The more education that citizens have had, the greater the distance between those who see themselves as belonging to the right and those who see themselves as belonging to the left. But comparing figures 4.3 and 4.4, one sees a striking difference. It is as though the less education Italians have had, the more the positions that they take with respect to the values of authority and order are distorted by a force field pulling them to the right. So those with only an elementary education who see themselves as on the right take a position furthest to the right—further even than that of the well educated. But those with an elementary education who see themselves as on the left take a position manifestly on the right—not as far to the right as the least educated who identify with the right but just as far as the most educated. This result points, we believe, to two of the distinctive features of the politics of order.

The first observation concerns the politics of the educated right. The usual rule, we have observed, is that the more politically sophisticated citizens are, the more unconditionally they commit themselves to the ideological tenets of the political side that they favor. But on the dimension of authority values, although the educated right is to the right of the educated left, as figure 4.4 shows, it also is to the left of the uneducated right. The educated left is, in a word, more unconditional in its rejection of authority values than the educated right is in its acceptance of it. Obviously, segments of the leadership of the right are more than willing to commit themselves to an ideology of order, authority, and discipline. But it is nonetheless a mark of the prevailing climate of opinion that the educated right in the public at large is reluctant, just so far as they are broadly and well educated, to commit themselves unconditionally to an ideology of discipline and order.

The second thing to note is still more important. In terms of the importance they attach to authority and order, those with only an elementary education converge even though they ostensibly adhere to opposing poles. They do not completely converge—those on the right are slightly more supportive of authority values than those on the left. But the difference between the two, though statistically significant, is politically irrelevant. More important, as figure 4.4 shows, the distinction between the uneducated left and the educated right is also much smaller than that between the educated and uneducated left. The fundamental cleavage over the values of order and authority is thus not between the left and the right, but within the left itself. Those best able to understand the values of the left, because best educated, reject authority values. But far and away the largest stratum of the Italian public is not highly educated, and within this stratum, those who classify themselves as on the left belong, in terms of their views about authority and order, to the political right.

If and as the issue of immigration moves to the center of public argument, public debate will be framed in terms that advantage the political right, with considerations of order, tradition, and national integrity coming to the fore. And just so far as the larger complex of values centering on respect for authority, order, and discipline become central, the left is vulnerable to the right. Political activists on the right have a free hand to rally their base of support by appealing to authority values, even if they themselves have some reservations about them. But it is not only their own side that is disposed to listen. As we have seen, the importance attached to the values of authority and order by those on the left with only a minimal amount of education is indistinguishable for all practical purposes from those on the right, whether well or poorly educated. The isolation of position of the educated left, by contrast, is striking. They, and they alone, predominantly reject the values of order, discipline, and authority.

Formal education crucially defines the fault line that runs through the left. Democratic politics is ultimately a contest of numbers—and in Italy the poorly educated make up the big battalions. On the left, for example, one out of every two people has had only an elementary or vocational education, while only one out of every ten has had higher education. And for a cluster of values—order, discipline, hierarchy—the leadership of the right enjoys the support of nearly all on the right and that of the largest number on the left. The mismatch hypothesis thus holds—and holds, moreover, not in its weak but in its strong version. It is not merely that those who see themselves on the left fail to support the values of their side; in fact, they adhere to the values of the other.

This misalliance is, we suspect, not peculiar to Italian politics. The politics of mass publics in liberal democracies tends to be marked by a systematic mismatch between ideological self-conceptions and ideological commitments. On at least one fundamental dimension of contemporary politics, a large portion of those who classify themselves as on the left in fact are committed to the values of the right. But what exactly, one surely must ask, follows from this? In the case of the Italian general election of 1994 specifically, we have seen that what counted was not what Italians thought, but what they thought that they thought. And even supposing that in other circumstances what citizens actually think matters more, what is the relation, if any, between favoring authority values and prejudice? It is just these questions we now propose to address.

THE POLITICS OF PREJUDICE: THE "RIGHT SHOCK" MODEL

However much it matters now, the politics of exclusion matters still more because it has the potential to reshape the politics of European democracies over the next decade. Italy, with its separatist movement in the North and its neo-fascist party in the South, is not an outlier. Belgium is threatening to tear itself in two over the politics of identity, and extremist parties of the right have become a feature of the electoral landscape in Austria, France, Germany, and the Netherlands, as well as Norway and Denmark.[20] It is, accordingly, not enough to describe things as they are now at this particular moment. It is necessary to see if it is possible, by examining how things are now, to catch sight of how they are likely to turn out in the immediate future. Accordingly, it is the interplay of politics and prejudice that we must now explore.

Our initial account had the virtue of integrating lines of explanation that had been taken to be mutually exclusive, demonstrating how these seemingly separate explanatory factors influence, and are influenced by, each other. Yet it has the limitation of not providing for the play of expressly political considerations. There are great advantages to analytical economy. But we think the gain in coverage from including expressly political considerations overbalances the loss in parsimony, since the unintended but inevitable effect of omitting political factors is to favor a comparatively static account of prejudice.[21] And the history of the last two decades makes plain the potential for the dynamic interplay of prejudice and politics. Only a few years ago class conflict was considered to be the central dynamic of Western European politics. Ethnic conflict was a peripheral consideration, where it was a consideration at all. But the balance between the two has shifted from the former to the latter. And the politics of exclusion, far from having exhausted itself at the present moment, seems capable of gathering still more strength in the immediate future. Therefore, we want to try to understand the interplay of prejudice and politics.

The first step is obvious. It is clear that changes in the level of prejudice track changes in conditions in the larger society, and it is, moreover, clear what some of these societal conditions are. Peer Scheepers and his colleagues, for example, have shown that changes in the levels of hostility toward immigrants over time track changes in the actual intake levels of immigration.[22] A sharp increase in the number of immigrants evokes an increase in prejudice against them. Similarly, Lincoln Quillian has demonstrated that variations in cross-national levels of public hostility toward immigrants track variations in cross-national economic conditions.[23] Strictly, Quillian aims to account for differences in levels of prejudice across countries rather than over time, but it seems a fair inference from his findings that economic downturns correspond to upsurges in prejudice. Both of these forms of change in societal conditions—a change in immigration or a downturn in the economy—represent external shocks. External shocks can take other forms, but the specific nature of the shock, for the purposes of our model, does not matter. We assume only that spikes in the levels of prejudice over time can be modeled as a function of exogenous shocks. These shocks, acting directly on prejudice, are treated as "external" only because they represent dynamics in a static model—indeed, their specific point of entry could be through any of the mediators in the model.

But granted that spikes in intolerance can be a consequence of external shocks, what in turn are the consequences of these spikes in prejudice? Taking our initial account as a starting point, there is a striking omission. For all the factors the "Two Flavors" model includes, it excludes political values. It should be uncontroversial that a properly rounded account of the interplay of prejudice and politics must take account of the role of values. But which values, and why?

The most obvious candidate, if you attend to the rhetoric of politics on the right, is the complex of authority values. They form a clear chord in the efforts of politicians on the right to exploit popular indignation against outsiders, variously defined. Those on the left, to be sure, can play the same game. But whatever may be true at another time or in other circumstances, we are aware of no commentator on European affairs who believes that the current wave of resentment and anger at foreigners is being stoked by values of the left. On the contrary, it is agreed on all sides that it is being driven by those of the right. It is, therefore, a safe bet that whatever strengthens the appeal of the values of order, discipline, and authority strengthens intolerance.

But this is, we want to suggest, only one view of the phenomenon, and a partial one at that. If it is important to ask what are the habits of thought that bring prejudice in their wake, it is necessary also to ask what are the habits of thought that being prejudiced brings in *its* wake. Prejudice involves deeply charged beliefs, and it is difficult to believe that their influence will not spill over into other domains of individuals' belief systems. In particular, a conviction that there are groups in society that are parasitic, untrustworthy, and dangerous fits naturally with an emphasis on discipline, on the dangers of sentimental compassion, and on the value of order and authority. Supposing this to be true, what follows? According to our first line of argument, authority values are the cause and intolerance the consequence. But according to the second, prejudice, whether it is a consequence of authority values or not, can be a cause of them. If both lines of argument are true, then the causal relation between political values and prejudice is reciprocal: each can be a cause and consequence of the other.

We have, then, a pair of intuitions: first, that external shocks can spike levels of prejudice, and second, that causal connections can be reciprocal rather than just one way. Combining both intuitions yields the "Right Shock" model. Figure 4.5 illustrates the structure of the model. The key idea, by contrast with our initial account, is to show how an increase in prejudice occasioned by some external shock pushing to the right can feed back into politics. If prejudice spikes to new levels in response to an external shock in the form, for example, of an economic downturn, the incentive for political entrepreneurs to capitalize on it should be stronger. But this is, if the intuition behind the model is correct, only a part of the problem. Following the logic of the causal arrows, an increase in the level of prejudice should lead to a corresponding increase in the appeal of authority values. But what exactly is the mechanism by which a greater emphasis on authority values leads to a higher level of

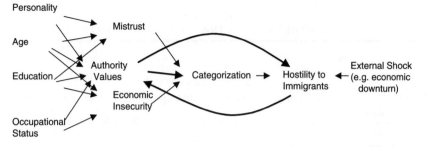

Fig. 4.5 "Right Shock" Model of Hostility Toward Immigrants

prejudice? Figure 4.5 suggests there are possibly direct and indirect effects via the readiness to categorize others as belonging to a group other than one's own. It is worth noting that this suggestion of both direct and indirect effects betrays a lack of confidence in our own theoretical argument. Just so far as group categorization is the central mechanism underlying hostility to immigrants, the impact of authority values on intolerance should be indirect rather than direct.

This model thus formalizes an intuition of how the dynamics of prejudice can reshape the ideological equilibrium of European politics. Formally, the values of authority are rooted in the political right. Yet they have a strong appeal to very large numbers on the left, particularly in the lower strata of education and political sophistication, as we have seen. It surely seems reasonable to suppose that the more that authority values come to the fore in the political reasoning of citizens, the more the political right will benefit. The model thus implies that if the external shocks are large enough and the connection between prejudice and authority values is tight enough, an increase in intolerance should in itself strengthen the platform for right-wing politics.

Taking advantage of the two-stage least squares (2SLS) instrumental variables method, we estimate the full model. Since the new variable added to the model is authority values, we focus on it, taking as a point of departure the third column in table 4.4. As one would expect, age and the values of authority are related: the older a person is the more inclined he is to favor the value cluster associated with authority values. What one would not necessarily expect is the thinness of other sources of authority values: the only other *direct* source is intolerance, suggesting that a disposition to favor authority values is a result in the largest measure of the same forces that lie behind prejudice.[24]

Reversing perspective and asking what are the consequences rather than causes of authority values throws new light on the sources of intolerance of outsiders. In our initial account, categorization was the linchpin variable. Every factor of consequence increasing prejudice against immigrants did so by virtue of increasing readiness to engage in

TABLE 4.4
"Right Shock" Model of Hostility Toward Immigrants

Independent Variable Dependent Variable:	Mistrust	Economic Insecurity	Authority Values	Categorization (1)	Categorization (2)	Hostility (1)	Hostility (2)	Hostility (3)	Hostility (4)
Personality	−0.859**		0.075			−1.309**	−1.916**	−1.146**	−1.146**
	(−18.10)		(0.44)			(−3.36)	(−2.01)	(−5.25)	(−4.70)
Age	−0.006**	0.007**	0.004**	0.017**	0.007	0.005	0.018		
	(−6.22)	(5.64)	(2.00)	(7.89)	(0.96)	(0.49)	(0.83)		
Education	−0.020**	−0.047**	0.011	−0.061**	−0.245	−0.123**	−0.177**	−0.107**	−0.106**
	(−4.03)	(−6.94)	(0.59)	(−6.26)	(−0.93)	(−2.55)	(−1.85)	(−3.86)	(−3.80)
Occupational status		0.025**	0.010			0.032	0.076		
		(1.96)	(0.54)			(0.71)	(0.97)		
Mistrust				0.508**	0.109				
				(5.19)	(0.37)				
Economic insecurity				0.507**	0.489**				
				(3.85)	(3.75)				
Authority values					0.812*		−1.245		0.072
					(1.49)		(−0.71)		(0.09)
Categorization						0.961**	0.948*	1.225**	1.185**
						(1.76)	(1.55)	(6.21)	(2.45)
Hostility			0.286**						
			(3.45)						
Constant	3.992	1.578	3.700	−0.016	−0.774	3.871	7.348	3.236	3.159
n	1982	1969	1769	1700	1694	1735	1731	1735	1731

* p < 0.1 (one-tailed)   ** p < 0.05 (one-tailed)

Notes: t-statistics in parentheses

Estimation technique is two-stage least squares.

Ranges of variables: hostility—0 to 10; categorization—1 to 4; mistrust—1 to 3; economic insecurity—1 to 3; personality—1 to 2; age—18 to 69; education—1 to 12; occupational status—1 to 7; authority values—1 to 4.

categorization. And just so far as factors of quite different sorts—expressive and instrumental—converged on the same point of impact, the "Two Flavors" model offered an integrated account of the sources of prejudice. Given that categorization is a pivotal factor in our account of intolerance, does introducing authority values into the model help us get a better grip on categorization?

As the fifth column in table 4.4 shows, authority values are a pivotal factor in accounting for the readiness of people to engage in categorization. Adding them into the explanation of categorization washes out the (direct) effects of age, education, and mistrust. Adding authority values thus yields an explanatory gain over our initial account in at least two respects. First, it is, in its own right, a significant predictor of categorization, helping considerably in getting a grip on why some people attach special importance to others being like them. Second, its addition to the model eliminates two forms of causal leakage. In our initial model, both age and education have direct effects on categorization; in the extended model, their direct effects are eliminated. Adding authority values thus yields a gain in both explanatory power and parsimony. But every gain exacts a price, and taking account of authority values is no exception. In particular, by adding it to the basic model, we take the starch out of the direct effect of mistrust on categorization. It seems to us that an avowal of fallibilism is in order on several counts. The assessment of mistrust of people, in a culture in which cynicism is itself a norm, is a hard business.[25] Then, too, it is extremely difficult to arrive at a nonarbitrary ordering of "within-the-head" causal factors as a general proposition, and this generic difficulty is further compounded by the requirements of instrumental variables in a two-stage least squares (2SLS) approach. So we should like to underline the limits of our estimation rather than paper them over.

The heart of the matter, however, is the claim of reciprocal causality. Consider, then, the final four columns of table 4.4, which summarize the analysis of intolerance of immigrants. In the original model, intolerance was rooted in three sources—personality, education, and, above all, categorization. In the extended model the three again prove to be significant predictors. The added factor, authority values, does little to explain prejudice directly. The mechanism of reciprocal causality works via categorization, striking support for the central premise of our theoretical account, derived from Tajfel, that the readiness to categorize others as belonging to a group other than one's own is a linchpin of prejudice. Taking account of the model as a whole, we have a circle (dare we say spiral) of causation in which increases in prejudice increase authority values, which in turn increase categorization and, thereby, prejudice.

REPRISE

The ironies of research are not always appreciated. When we first began consideration of this study, the extreme right was on the move in a variety of forms, including the Alleanza in the South and the Lega in the North. Hostility toward and resentment of immigrants was unmistakable. An election was on the horizon. Italy seemed an ideal site to study the impact of prejudice on politics.

Then, catching everyone off guard (very much including us), *tangentopoli* exploded. A year later, the party system that had been unshakable for a half century was collapsing, its most prominent leaders under investigation or in jail, and the electoral rules themselves in the process of revision. The next election would define the shape of a new party system. It made no sense, in these transformed circumstances, to suppose that prejudice would be a factor of primary importance driving the vote choices of Italians. There were too many other more immediate and more pressing issues that would be at the forefront of their attention. But we had committed ourselves to undertake the study, and there were in any event deeply rooted questions to explore as to the nature and sources of prejudice.

It is, we think, remarkable that the hostility many Italians feel toward immigrants proved to be a factor at all in their voting decisions in these exceptional circumstances—remarkable and ironic, for just because the circumstances were exceptional, the hypothesis that prejudice matters politically was put to a far stronger test than we had originally envisioned. If prejudice can assist the right even in a modest way when other quite unrelated issues are at the center of consideration, we fear that it can give a far stronger boost when the issue of immigration is itself at center stage.

The irony of our findings, however, goes deeper. When we undertook our study, it was widely argued that with the collapse of the ideology of communism, the left as traditionally conceived had lost its relevance in Italy. Then, with the collapse of the party system, it was argued that Italians had to find a new compass if they were to find their way in a new political landscape. But as we saw, even though they had lost their familiar external landmarks, they relied on their habitual internal signposts. So change at the level of institutions was accompanied by continuity at the level of individuals. Moreover, we also saw that it was precisely the persisting power of people's ideological identities that restricted the electoral impact of intolerance. It thus appears that the classical ideological categories of left and right, so far from being at odds with an incremental and pluralist style of politics, may in fact be a precondition of it.

There is nothing assured about any of these ironies. Much depends on the political agenda of the next decade. If immigration moves toward the top of publicly debated concerns, the vulnerability of the left will be exposed. But how large a part immigration plays in public debate will depend as much on the individual ambitions and skills of political elites as on the objective conditions of European economies.

CHAPTER 5

Conclusion: Intolerance and Democracy

IT IS TIME to consider the seductions of intolerance in contemporary liberal democracies.

TOCQUEVILLE'S HYPOTHESIS

By the start of our study it had become obvious that distinctions between ingroup and outgroup can be evoked on almost an indefinite number of bases. Some are familiar and have an obvious potential for invidiousness—differences of religion, for example, or ethnicity and nationality. Other grounds of distinction seem bizarre because they transparently are of no consequence and, indeed, may be completely adventitious—for example, putative differences between people in their ability to count dots. But whether the grounds on which distinctions between people are drawn are historically rooted or spontaneously evoked, integral to individuals' conceptions of themselves or peripheral, a frighteningly large number of people are prepared to perceive others as different and, believing them to be different, are ready on that ground alone to be biased against them.

Yet, granting that a plethora of distinctions is possible, some surely cut deeper than others. It is chastening that a spurious distinction between "overcounters" and "undercounters" of dots, evoked in the controlled conditions of a laboratory experiment for a moment only, can elicit a systematic bias in favor of the ingroup at the expense of the outgroup. If so superficial and contrived a distinction can elicit invidious differences, it is only possible to imagine the destructive power of deeper and societally reinforced bases of distinction.

Religion, historically, has been a murderous basis of division in countries otherwise as different as Ireland and India. Nationality patently surged forward after the eighteenth century, and for all the talk of globalism and the transcendence of the nation-state, religion remains a killing ground. Without underplaying the continuing power of either religion or nationality, however, race has assumed a special centrality at the end of the twentieth century. Race, it now is agreed as a matter of science, is a social construction. But it is a social construction that, outside of the context of science, is understood to be a fact of nature. And a—perhaps the—defining marker of race has come to be the color of a person's skin. Color can be variously graded, but there is a grotesque surplus of evidence that darker-colored skin is, certainly in the eyes of those with lighter-colored skin, more demeaning than lighter-colored skin.

Race now is widely agreed to be specially stigmatizing. Certainly it seemed to us that blacks, by virtue of being black, bear a special burden of bias. This surely remains so in many places, but to our surprise it turned out not to be so for the problem of immigration in Italy. There, it is the attribution of difference, and not the form of it, that principally sets immigrants apart. It is not that race does not matter. Italians, for example, are significantly more likely to judge African than Eastern European immigrants to be "inferior by nature"; and it would be foolish to frame the issue in categorical terms, as though it were a matter either of a difference or no difference whatever. The differences that obtain notwithstanding, the main thrust of our results is as unmistakable as it was unexpected. Hostility to blacks by virtue of their black being is overshadowed by hostility to immigrants whatever their race.

Our ideas about prejudice have been principally formed in the American context. But our results have forced us to consider the possibility that intolerance may have a different character in Europe—that it may be still more threatening there, not because Europeans, if they see others as different, are more likely than Americans to be intolerant, but by virtue of being Europeans, they are more likely to see others, even if they are fellow Europeans, as different, as outsiders.

In *Democracy in America* Alexis de Tocqueville presents a comparative theory of prejudice. In most towns or cities in the America of the mid-nineteenth century, he observes, many, perhaps even most, of the people have been strangers. They may have been born in the eastern United States and moved to the Middle West, or have been born in the Middle West and moved to the far West, or very nearly as likely, been born outside the United States altogether and immigrated to it. This flux, Tocqueville believed, gave American society a special character. When so many came from so many places and differed, in consequence, in so many ways, it was difficult to draw definite and fixed lines between strangers and neighbors, between outsiders and insiders. And when differences of ethnicity, religion, and nationality do not pick out who belongs from who does not, skin color becomes the one marker that unambiguously identifies the outsider as an outsider. So in America, Tocqueville contended, there is a focusing of intolerance on race.

And what is the natural contrast to America, to the new world? Tocqueville speaks of Quebec but he has in mind France. And the mark of the old world is that people are fixed in place. They are born, grow up, live their lives, die in the same ambit. They share in consequence the same customs, manners, beliefs, and experiences that mark them as one—and mark off everyone else. And against a background of fixity, any point of difference picks others out as outsiders. What matters is not the particular way they differ, but the fact that they differ.

It is possible that our results apply to Italy uniquely, not to Europe generally, since Italy, until only a few years ago, had only a minimal experience of immigration. But we think Tocqueville's hypothesis applies beyond Italy's borders. Both our findings and the theory underpinning them suggest that the absence of a tradition of immigration, the fixity of social and cultural boundaries, and the presumption of commonality within them all should increase the likelihood that any point of difference can mark a person as an outsider. If so, the decisive difference between America and Europe may lie not in the level but instead in the scope of prejudice: in the former it is more narrowly focused; in the latter, more enveloping.

THE VULNERABILITY OF THE LEFT

It is easy, all too easy, to wind up supposing that understanding prejudice consists, at the deepest level, of understanding how the stream of people's experiences and perceptions come to be transformed within their minds into intolerance. But the roots of prejudice also are embedded in the external world of society and the economy, and the periodic surges in intolerance cannot be understood in isolation from the periodic changes in the objective conditions of life.

Given the limits of data and design, there are great difficulties in pinning down the impact of changes in external conditions. These difficulties notwithstanding, it is useful to think of a class of social and economic changes in terms of external shocks—sudden, jarring, threatening. Shocks come in a number of different forms. Two established by previous research are a slump in the economy and a jump in the numbers of immigrants entering a country. And in either case the effect of the shock is to precipitate a sharp increase in the level of intolerance.

It is necessary, we believe, to acknowledge the periodic impact of external shocks. The design of our own study does not allow us to get hold of them directly, but it does allow us to suggest how they can reverberate politically. Our focal point is a cluster of values making up a core part of the ideological furniture of the political right. This cluster encompasses an array of concerns, among them, the indispensability of respect for authority; the exigency, for individuals and societies alike, of strictness and discipline and of sacrifice and self-denial; and the necessity for aggressive enforcement of order and assurance of social stability. The cluster as a whole we labeled authority values.

It has long been recognized that authority values are tied to intolerance. The thick paste of charges of contaminating the purity of national traditions and values and of exploiting public resources and assistance appeals particularly to the taste of those who insist on the veneration of authority, custom, and the exclusiveness of national identity. But to appreciate the potency of the connection between intolerance and authority values, it was necessary, we came to believe, to understand that the causal traffic between them is a two-way street. The values of authority are a spur to intolerance, but intolerance also is a spur to the values of authority. Each can boost, as well as be boosted by, the other.

This hypothesis of reciprocal causation underpins the "Right Shock" model, and as the estimation of the model has shown, political values can underwrite prejudice while prejudice simultaneously can underwrite political values. The reciprocity of the causal connection between the two throws new light, we believe, on the channels by which prejudice can spill over into politics. Suppose that, a few years from now, the European economy suffers a sharp downturn. One consequence, following the logic of the "Right Shock" model, would be an increase in the level of hostility toward immigrants. But this increase in prejudice, as important as it is in its own right, would not be the most important repercussion politically of economic bad times, because one consequence of a spike in the level of hostility toward immigrants would be a spike in the appeal of the values of authority. And this has, if the full line of our reasoning is correct, potentially large political implications.

The key is the exceptional radius of authority values in the larger ideological landscape. Both in provenance and manifest character, the values of authority, order, and discipline belong to the ideological right. But true as this is as a matter of political history and theory, it misses a deeper-lying truth about the reach of authority and order as a value in the contemporary politics of Italy and, we believe, of Western Europe generally. The constituency for authority values is very far from confined to the right. On the contrary, it reaches over into the left. Indeed, among those with only a limited measure of education, who still form the bulk of the electorate in Italy, the values of order and authority have very nearly as strong an appeal on the ideological left as on the right.

If and as issues of immigration push to the fore, parties of the right have a striking advantage because their position has the support of those on both the right and, in a very large measure, the left. But our findings also point to a constraint that is at once paradoxical and ironic. The right must turn latent sympathies into actual votes. This depends, most obviously, on the resources of parties and the skills of leaders. It also depends, less obviously, on the astonishing hold of past ideological allegiances on the current voting decisions of ordinary citizens. We say astonishing partly because the power of ideology often is said to have evaporated, partly because of the extraordinary circumstances that marked the election that we examined. New parties pushed aside old; new leadership, both in new and old parties, supplanted the old; and new electoral rules adopted in the face of the opposition of established partisan leaders broke the stranglehold of the old parties over candidate nomination. The constraints of a half century of history and habit, of political leaders and political parties, were swept away. And what did voters do with their new freedom? As we saw, voters who saw themselves as belonging to the left sought out the new bloc of the left and overwhelmingly gave it their support, while voters who saw themselves as belonging to the right similarly sought out the bloc coalition of the right and overwhelmingly gave *it* their support. Hence the paradoxical combination of institutional transformation and electoral continuity.

And if this was the paradox of the general election of 1994, where did the irony lie? The politics of the cold war had fixed the politics of Italy in place for a half century. But the collapse of communism meant the end of the political rationale of an electoral system committed to Christian Democratic hegemony because it was dedicated to the exclusion of the communist left. So, fashionable arguments ran, with the end of communism came the end of the meaning of the categories of left and right, opening up the possibility of a more consensual, gradualist style of governance. Our findings suggest a different story. So far from having lost their meaning, the classic categories of ideology, the conceptions that Italians have of themselves as belonging to the political left or right, are far and away the most powerful constraints on their voting behavior. So those on the left, seeing themselves as belonging to the left, are loyal to it. And they give proof of their loyalty in the coin that counts most in electoral politics—by giving it their vote. And so long as people vote on the basis of what they believe that they believe politically, rather than what they actually believe, it is hard for the right to exploit the vulnerability of the left.

There is no shortage of irony here. Ideology once was the paradigm of political rationality, the form of political reasoning of the most engaged and reflective citizens. But what anchors electoral choices is not ideology in the form of a substantive conception of the goals of political action. It is voters' images of themselves ideologically, their conception of themselves as part of the political left or right. The primary bulwark against the irrationality of intolerance may thus turn out to be the tenacity of tradition, custom, and habit.

THE COMPLEMENTARITY OF COMPETING EXPLANATIONS

Research on prejudice has long been marked by an adversarial style, emphasizing points of difference between alternative approaches instead of highlighting common ground. There are times when a combative style pays off. Theoretical constructs are sharpened, the logical consequences of competing hypotheses exposed, and the weaknesses of their evidentiary foundations dissected. But there are also times when a different approach is in order, when more is to be gained by demonstrating how seemingly conflicting explanations, if put into a larger framework, can be shown to capture complementary aspects of a complex process. In this study we have taken the latter, not the former, route.

Our point of departure was to question the lopping off of one of the principal explanatory branches of prejudice. When systematic research on intolerance got underway a generation ago, the spotlight focused first on the psychological sources of prejudice. The classic study, *The Authoritarian Personality*, set out an elaborate scaffolding of theory on the role of parents in shaping the psychological makeup of children and inducing thereby a vulnerability to intolerance. But it was less the innovation in theory than the introduction of a measure of a "basic" personality characteristic, the famous F-scale, which was electrifying.

With the development of the F-scale, the scientific study of both the psychological and social sources of prejudice appeared feasible. Personality characteristics, along with social circumstances, could be measured for representative samples of the public as a whole. In a stroke it became possible to estimate with a previously unimaginable degree of precision the impact of personality on prejudice—and, what is more, systematically take into account the influence as well of an array of social and political factors. But almost from the start there were voices of warning.[1] And with time the pendulum of intellectual fashion swung decisively—and, it seemed—irreversibly. Personality factors, according to the new consensus, are of marginal significance in understanding prejudice as a social problem.

Many arguments underpinned the new consensus. Some scholars, following a social cognition approach, held that personality, though possibly of use in explaining individuals at the extremes of either tolerance or prejudice, was otherwise irrelevant analytically as well as empirically to

the understanding of an inherently "group" phenomenon. Others, following a realistic conflict approach, argued that personality, though perhaps accounting for the behavior of deviant individuals, missed the fact
that the conflict of groups is fundamentally rooted in the clash of their
interests. But whatever the particular line of argument, personality,
which in the 1950s had appeared to be at the heart of an understanding
of prejudice, became by the 1970s a factor of minor importance, and
with the rise of rational choice in political science, it virtually disap-
peared as a factor relevant to the systematic analysis of political behavior.

If truth be told, the arguments against personality had genuine force.
The methodological critique of the F-scale was decisive in a way few
research programs ever are, and the analytical arguments against a personality-oriented approach to prejudice also had weight. Certainly, the
need to attend to factors at the level of groups, and not merely at the
level of individuals, represented a profound extension in the understanding of prejudice and discrimination. For that matter, the focus over
the last several decades on cognitive processes (as distinct from expressive or emotional factors) has indisputably opened new windows on the
processes of judgment implicated in prejudice.

Yet, we found a number of aspects of the new consensus troubling.
The first was the root-and-branch character of the argument against the
utility of personality-based approaches. It was not a question of suggesting that personality mattered less than some other factor, say, social
class, or counted for less under some circumstances, say, an era of economic prosperity, than under others. It amounted instead to a claim that
personality factors counted for little except under extraordinary historical circumstances or in the case of exceptionally aberrant individuals.
Moreover, the arguments that won the day had a worryingly scholastic
flavor. They were, virtually without exception, conceptual and methodological rather than empirical. And a number of them are, in strictly logical terms, overdrawn. For although the criticisms are intended specifically to impeach personality as a wellspring of prejudice, as they are
drawn up they apply to nearly any factor at the individual level, such as
education, that can be deployed to account for why some individuals are
more susceptible to prejudice than others. More generally, the validity
of explanatory approaches to prejudice at the group and individual levels
are not mutually exclusive. Intolerance can be evoked by attachments to
groups; but then, too, in the same set of circumstances some people can
be more susceptible than others to intolerance. Whether personality is
an important factor in accounting for differences between individuals in
their susceptibility to prejudice can only be settled by an empirical demonstration. But on the evidence at hand at the start of our study, it

seemed to us necessary to acknowledge that the burden of proof rested with those who would argue for the centrality of personality factors in the understanding of prejudice.

Two hurdles had to be jumped if the value of personality-based explanations of prejudice were to be established. The first has to do with measurement. How is it possible to gauge a basic characteristic of individuals' personality in a public opinion interview? It is surely very far from obvious that one can grasp deep-lying aspects of people's fundamental makeup—of which they themselves frequently are only imperfectly, and intermittently, aware—by putting questions to them over the telephone. The second hurdle is conceptual. Even supposing that basic personality characteristics can be measured in a public opinion survey and shown to be related to prejudice, it does not follow that the relation observed between the two is genuine. As has frequently been argued, a personality characteristic (for example, authoritarianism) may appear to be a cause of prejudice only because both it and prejudice are caused by yet another factor (for example, social class). And even if the finding of a personality basis of prejudice in our study is not spurious, it may be idiosyncratic, applying to the case of Italy but not to any other.

With only a handful of exceptions, the study of personality and prejudice has been the study of authoritarianism. But the measure of authoritarianism, the F-scale, carries no credibility except for those immunized to any question about its credibility. Over the past years exceptional efforts have been made to salvage the measurement of authoritarianism,[2] but the layers of criticism of both operationalization and interpretation are now so thick that the whole concept no longer has the power to persuade. It was necessary, we reasoned, to stop equating personality with the concept of authoritarianism, its controversial measure, and the no-less-controversial nimbus of psychoanalytic theory.

Acting on the counsel of our colleagues at the Institute for Personality Assessment and Social Research, we selected a measure developed to tap the psychological roots of intolerance. We have detailed a number of its properties. Here we want to remark only that it is one element in one of the most widely used, and most systematically validated, measures of personality. Rather than having to divine what our measure of personality assesses by means of conjectures based on the manifest content of the questions that make it up, we have been able to draw on a virtually unique library of studies carried out over many decades. These studies take advantage of an exceptionally wide array of methods, running from standard self-report studies through assessment by both experts and intimates through studies of actual behavior. And since the facet of personality on which we focus is only one element in an extensive inventory of personality attributes, it is possible to establish, in a way that no single study could, the location of psychological tolerance in a nomological network of personological concepts.

And with this measure of personality in hand, what is it possible to discover about the sources of prejudice? The core of the problem of prejudice, it was widely agreed when we began our study, is social and economic. It follows, if this is true, that psychological factors, particularly in the form of personality characteristics, come into play only under exceptional circumstances or in the case of individuals under the control of manifestly deviant impulses. The reality is quite different. A fundamental source of hostility toward immigrants, our findings indicate, is grounded in the psychological makeup of individuals.

We do not wish to suggest a measure of precision and certitude that our data do not permit. Invoking the concept of personality may call up in a reader's mind tracing in close detail the intricate and layered history of an individual's inner biography. We have instead fixed on only one aspect of people's psychological makeup and assessed only gross points of variation between individuals: it is as though we compare college graduates with high school graduates, and both with elementary school dropouts. Yet the contribution of personality factors, measured by any substantive or statistical standard that we can apply, is comparable to that of the most fundamental social-structural factors, such as education or social class—and this is so whether personality's role is examined in isolation or in conjunction with any or all of the array of other relevant factors.

Much is to be gained if it can be shown that a hypothesis, which could have been false, is true. But even more is to be gained, we have become persuaded, if it can be shown that a set of hypotheses, the truth of one of which is supposed to entail the falsity of the others, in fact are mutually complementary. We have become persuaded of the value of conciliation as things stand now in the study of prejudice and group conflict. In contrast to the seminal work of a figure like Gordon Allport, who had aimed at an encompassing, if eclectic, account, contemporary research programs have aimed at deepening the level of their analysis by differentiating ever more sharply their approach from that of others. This impression of mutually exclusive explanatory alternatives is most obvious in the root-and-branch arguments advanced against personality-based explanations on the part of both those subscribing to social categorization and to realistic group conflict approaches. But if these two approaches joined forces in arguing for the irrelevance of personality, their alliance was only tactical. A social categorization approach construes prejudice and group hostility as contextual and situational. In this view, people characteristically are more disposed to be biased against members of outgroups when, because of circumstances of the moment, their identity as members of another group becomes salient. A rational choice or realistic conflict approach also construes prejudice as contextual and situational, but the very last thing it has in mind by this is people's notions of social identity. On the contrary, in a realistic conflict approach, the root source of outgroup hostility and ingroup identification is a fixed set of external goods (e.g., income, social status, security), divisible only on a zero-sum basis, but assignable such that a gain for a group (and not just an individual) entails a loss for another group (and not just another individual).

The social categorization and realistic conflict approaches have developed independently of one other and in some aspects can provide competing explanatory perspectives. But there is no through-and-through contradiction between the two approaches such that if one is right, the other necessarily is wrong. Nor, for that matter, is there a logical conflict between the two of them and a personality-oriented approach, such that if either of them is true, then a personality-oriented approach is necessarily false. It therefore seemed to us worth the effort of attempting to pull all three together.

But what would and should this entail? It is worth bearing in mind two different senses, the first weak and the second strong, in which explanatory approaches can be brought together. They can be pulled together in the weak sense by a more comprehensive analysis, one that takes account of a wider range of explanatory factors, each capturing some aspect of importance to a particular conceptual approach. There is much to recommend this. But the gain is a limited one. There is something inherently incomplete in assembling a large number of explanatory factors, each separate from the others, running parallel like railway tracks, never intersecting at any point in the causal process. Hence we wanted not merely to take account of, but actually to unify, alternative explanatory approaches; to show how these seemingly different approaches are, if viewed from a more encompassing perspective, interlinked parts of a unified account of prejudice and group conflict.

The central insight that we have built on we owe to Tajfel and his colleagues. At one level their whole approach, with its emphasis on the contextual, is at odds with ours, with its emphasis on the dispositional. But we believe that they have made a compelling case that the willingness to categorize others as belonging to a different group is a causal linchpin of prejudice. Building on this insight, we developed the "Two Flavors" model. A wide range of exogenous factors—a lack of education, for example, or occupational status—manifestly can promote prejudice. The trick is to devise an economical way of explaining how so many different factors come to have a common effect. The intuition behind the "Two Flavors" model is that a hierarchical account is necessary because basic social and psychological factors have to be linked to prejudice via common mechanisms. Our strategy has been to draw these mechanisms from seemingly disparate explanatory approaches. First, taking advantage of the work of Tajfel and his colleagues, we have made categorization the pivotal mechanism of our model, proposing that any factor that increases the likelihood of an individual's categorizing others as different and belonging to a group other than his own increases the likelihood of prejudice. Second, drawing on realistic conflict and personality-oriented explanations for intermediate mechanisms, we have proposed that every factor that increases the likelihood of categorization does so as a result of either instrumental, self-interested concerns or expressive, emotional sentiments. The first mechanism has the flavor of a rational choice account; the second, the flavor of a psychologically oriented account. Hence the designation, the "Two Flavors" model.

The model is only a rough, first approximation, judged on measurement grounds. There is leakage, however calculated. The "Two Flavors" model gives a substantial, but not complete, account of how exogenous factors such as education and personality promote susceptibility to prejudice. The statistical limits of the account follow partly from the limitations of the measurement of the intervening mediators of instrumental concerns and expressive sentiments, partly from the tenuousness of the instruments we use to distinguish endogenous and exogenous effects. As we have emphasized, our empirical results rely, necessarily, on measures and methods that inherently generate concerns about robustness and that call expressly for independent validation. That said, we think that the "Two Flavors" model gets right the structure of a proper account of the sources of hostility toward immigrants in contemporary Europe.

The "Two Flavors" model offers, in particular, a useful baseline for throwing light on the social and psychological sources of prejudice. It is these deeper-lying factors—class, education, personality—that have been at the center of accounts of prejudice and group conflict, and properly so. But the problem of prejudice and group conflict has a dynamic character. It fluctuates in severity with time, and as serious as it now is, it can in short order become far more so. To catch sight of its potential trajectory over time, it is necessary to take account in particular of the interplay of politics and prejudice. Hence our second account, the "Right Shock" model.

In a comparatively close election, a small advantage can make all the difference, and in Italy's general election of 1994, parties of the right benefited from hostility to immigrants. From our perspective, the connection between the two matters, not because of what it reveals about the politics of the moment, but by virtue of what it may portend for the politics of the future.

It is the power of prejudice potentially to reshape the ideological equilibrium that we have wished to explore. In the standard view, intolerance has the advantage of a built-in political constituency. It naturally appeals to those who subscribe to the values of the right—not necessarily to the intellectual core of the right but rather to a cluster of values associated with it. These values include a belief in the indispensability, for individuals and societies alike, of strictness and discipline; of sacrifice and self-denial; and the aggressive enforcement of order and the assurance of stability. Taken both one by one and together, they are distinctively associated with the political right. But—and this is pivotal—their appeal is very far from confined to the right. They have, as we have seen, a large constituency on the left, particularly among the less educated, which makes up the bulk of the left in Europe.

Accordingly, the connection between authoritarian values and prejudice is potentially pivotal politically, and to see the larger role that prejudice can play in shaping the politics over even a middle run, we have underlined two ideas. The first concerns the connection between intolerance and shocks in the real world. An increase in immigration rates or a decrease in employment rates can cause prejudice to spike. The second concerns the consequences of a spike in prejudice in response to an external shock. Prejudice, we have suggested, not only benefits from authoritarian values, but also, and no less important, authoritarian values benefit from prejudice. An increase in the latter swells support for the former no less—and perhaps more—than an increase in the former drives up the latter. Both ideas we have formalized in the "Right Shock" model. All that we would observe here is the core implication of this model. Because hostility to immigrants has the power to swell the appeal of authoritarian values as well as be bolstered by them, it has the potential to transform the ideological equilibrium of Western Europe, undercutting the electoral base of the left to the advantage of the right.

QUALIFICATION

There is an ironic dialectic to research. So far as a study truly succeeds, it does itself in. You begin with ideas marking off what you believe to be true that have not yet been shown to be so. To demonstrate that at least some of your hypotheses are indeed true is ordinarily the measure of success. To manage this may be a necessary condition of progress. But it is not a sufficient condition. Just to show that what you thought to be so at the outset of a study is in fact so is not an adequate return for an investment of many years. To have truly succeeded you must by the end be able to conceive of possibilities you could not have imagined at the start. Yet if you do achieve this, you will at the end be left with the feeling of being as unsure of whether things are as you believe them to be as you were at the start.

So it is with us. And on no other point is there a more vivid sense of what now must be done than on the development of an integrated account of the interplay of prejudice and politics. At the start we, like most others, had conceived the task to be to test the comparative merits of competing lines of explanation. We were ourselves of more than one mind. Recognizing that no one approach was sufficient, some of us favored a more social-psychological or even economic emphasis, others a more psychological one. But our differences as to which was the best approach only underlined our agreement that one was better, closer to the center of understanding the dynamics of prejudice, than the others. We did not see the possibility of pulling them together.

And because we did not anticipate an integrated account, we did not plan for it. The "Two Flavors" and the "Right Shock" models have been operationally assembled taking advantage of spare parts, particularly in the form of various questionnaire items, originally incorporated in the study either for quite different reasons or for no reason other than curiosity. The models make a case, persuasively we hope, that instead of either having to choose from an array of explanatory alternatives differing in kind or allowing them to run on parallel tracks without ever intersecting, it is possible to tie at least some of them together in a common account.

Each model is open to challenge on a number of grounds. We have emphasized the limits of measurement, but at least two other fronts deserve mention. One is the role of political values. The "Two Flavors" model provides analytic traction by interpreting the impact of deeperlying factors in terms of two kinds of explanatory mediators, instrumental and expressive. The two gather up a nice array of exogenous factors, from personality to social class. But it is not clear, as things stand, exactly where political values fit in this scheme. We have taken a stab at a specification with our measure of authoritarian social values, but there is more than one plausible possibility involving values. Until studies are done canvassing a far larger number of values than we have, it will not be possible to advance further on this.

The second question is generalizability. At a number of points we have expressed surprise, acknowledging that the results took a turn that we did not expect. The element of speculation in both our models should not be minimized. There is an upside to seeing things for the first

time. But there is also a downside. Until they are seen again, the claim
that they have been seen at all is necessarily provisional. Findings, to be
authorized as findings, require replication.[3] Moreover, there are historical grounds to question whether they should be generalized to other
countries. The "Switch" experiment, for example, illuminated the interchangeability of Eastern Europeans and Africans as outsiders in Italy.
But Italy stands out among Western European countries in the recency
of its experience with immigration. How likely is it that countries with
a more extensive experience would be inclined to categorize immigrants of different races similarly, as outsiders? We shall have to wait and
see.

Third, there are a number of issues that we recognized as important,
but lacked the means to address in this particular study. Perhaps the
most important of these is the question of religion. The place of Muslim
practices, particularly in public institutions like schools, has become a
major source of friction arguably different in kind than resentment over
other forms of difference. It is different in kind because, to take France
as an example, a normative consensus on tolerance may itself be at odds
with the public expression of religious practice. Religion may divide
more deeply because it stands as a marker not merely of different beliefs
but of opposing ways of life.

There is, finally, the relation of realistic conflict and prejudice. Conceptually, the boundaries between the two are distinct; in practice, they
blur. The reason is partly analytical. Which do we mean to claim—
conflicts of interest spur group conflict, or that in order to spur conflict,
conflicts of interest must be recognized? The problem is partly operational. How is it possible to measure a judgment that your group is
threatened by another without simultaneously measuring a disposition
to respond negatively to it—that is, to be prejudiced against it? In our
account, realistic conflict is recognized as a source of prejudice, but the
recognition of its role is, we fear, partial and blurred. To get a fuller and
more focused picture it will be necessary to subject the analysis of realistic conflict to the discipline of experimental manipulation.

Weighing these points all in all, we think it is clear why the expression
is not "trial and truth" but "trial and error."

PLURALISTIC INTOLERANCE

What are the broader implications of our findings for the character and
operation of democratic politics?

We begin with the concept of pluralistic intolerance. How is it possible, Sullivan, Piereson, and Marcus asked in a classic study, for contem-

porary democracies to cope with intolerance?[4] For the outline of an answer they turned to James Madison. In Federalist 10, Madison discussed the problem of factions in democratic polities. Historically, republics had always succumbed. Sooner or later, the majority had overridden the minority, with the majority itself in the process falling under the thumb of an oligarch or despot. How, then, was it possible to build in protection against the tyranny of the majority?

By exploiting the paradox of scale, Madison argued. It had always been supposed that republics must be small if they were to be genuine republics. Madison, by contrast, insisted that they must be large if they were to remain republics. Size brought diversity. Whether size refers to physical dimensions or populations, the larger the country, the greater "the multiplicity of interests." In turn, since groups organized around interests, the larger the number of interests, the greater the number of factions. And the greater the number of factions, Madison contended, the smaller the likelihood that any one of them would be in a position to dominate all the others. There was thus a perfect parallel between the protection of civil rights and of religious rights. In societies where one religion had the support of the largest number, whether it enjoyed the official support of the government or not, any other was in jeopardy. So, too, in any country where one faction formed a majority, every other was at risk. As Madison put it:

> In a free government, the security for civil rights must be the same as for religious rights. It consists in the one case in the multiplicity of interests, and in the other, in the multiplicity of sects; and this may be presumed to depend on the extent of the country and number of people comprehended under the same government.

Madison's argument is comparative, contrasting the politics of large and small polities. How does it apply to a single country? The same country, Sullivan and his colleagues contend, can vary even over relatively short periods of time in the degree of its consensus on which groups it most dislikes. At one pole, an overwhelming majority can converge on the same group; at the other, the majority can splinter into many small factions, each picking its own target of intolerance. In the 1950s, their argument runs, in the face of an external threat and under the spur of political demagogues, Americans were mobilized against communists, and the witch-hunt of the McCarthy years was launched. By the 1970s, however, the extraordinary concentration of attention on the threat of communist subversion had eased, and instead of agreeing overwhelmingly on the left as the principal threat, Americans splintered into many different factions, each picking a different group as the one they most disliked. And because they splintered there no longer was a majority faction in a position to threaten the rights of the group that it most disliked. Thus, Sullivan and his colleagues conclude: "[T]he *diversity* of the targets of intolerance prevents, for the time being, a concerted effort to eliminate any of these groups."[5]

The concept of pluralistic intolerance offers an original and ingenious resolution to the problem of intolerance in democratic politics. Most obviously, it stands in sharp contrast to the standard presumptions of democratic theory. It abandons the classical assumption that protection of fundamental liberties is to be found in the understanding and commitment of citizens to the value of tolerance. Instead the classical assumption falls away as unnecessary, if not unrealistic. The effective safeguard is not citizens' agreement on tolerance as a value. It is, more modestly but more effectively, their disagreement about whom to be intolerant of.

This shift transforms the terms in which the problem of tolerance in democratic polities is posed. It becomes possible, for the first time, to understand how a society can be tolerant even if the largest number of its citizens are intolerant. It is only necessary that they do not agree on the groups they will not tolerate.

The concept of pluralistic intolerance, if valid, throws important new light on the problem of tolerance in democratic politics. Our findings throw new light on the question of its validity. The linchpin is disagreement about which groups are disliked. This idea is given a specific construction in the research of Sullivan and his colleagues: citizens are asked to pick from a list of groups the one they like the least, and pluralistic intolerance is defined as disagreement as to which group is disliked the most. But remember the most surprising of our findings. The "Switch" experiment showed that it is not possible to tell the difference between, for example, native Italian citizens who evaluate African immigrants through several series of prejudice measures and those who, halfway through, switch to evaluating immigrants from Eastern Europe. The responses to the two, in terms of the consistency of negative evaluations, are virtually interchangeable. What light does this throw on the concept of pluralistic intolerance?

The linchpin claim is that factions that disagree about whom they most dislike are, by virtue of this disagreement, unable or unwilling to make deals with one another. But just what makes conflict of interest a plausible premise for the politics of redistribution renders it an implausible one for the politics of intolerance. It is crucial to understand that people can genuinely dislike more than one group, even if they do not dislike them equally, and they are not barred from acting against any given group they dislike by the fact that they dislike another even more. Consider the logic of the concept of pluralistic intolerance applied to immigrants of very different backgrounds. In principle, one might argue that immigrants have a measure of protection against intolerance just so far as native-born citizens disagree about which group of immigrants they dislike the most. The "Switch" experiment, as it happened, demonstrated the interchangeability of these two groups of immigrants, but a much weaker result would equally have impeached the concept of pluralistic intolerance. Some Italians dislike black immigrants more than white immigrants, and others dislike immigrants from Eastern Europe more than African immigrants. Imagine, then, two neighbors in an Italian town. One dislikes African immigrants even more than he dislikes Eastern European immigrants. The other dislikes Eastern European immigrants even more than he dislikes African immigrants. Now consider a thought experiment. The second person observes the first preparing to go to an extremist rally protesting the presence of African immigrants in Italy and demanding their immediate expulsion. How will he respond? Surely the odds of his objecting and attempting to talk him out of attending the rally are effectively zero. Quite apart from everything else, he, too, genuinely dislikes immigrants from Africa, even though he dislikes Eastern European immigrants even more. It follows that, so far from attempting to thwart his neighbor, he is more likely to approve or even lend his support.

The whole weight of our findings testifies in favor of this thought experiment. The single most striking feature of hostility toward immigrants is the consistency of individuals' evaluative reactions toward different groups of immigrants. We are not at all saying that every group suffers the same level of hostility, nor are we suggesting that people cannot discriminate between outgroups, if directed to do so. What we are saying is that a person who dislikes one group of immigrants is, to a striking degree, likely to dislike other groups of immigrants and is distinctly unlikely to come to the aid of one of these groups even if he dislikes another group more.

There thus may be a fundamental difference between the politics of the toleration of social outgroups and the toleration of expressly political groups of the kind examined by Sullivan and his colleagues. It is at least possible to argue that someone who fixes on a group on the political left as an enemy is constrained from also picking a group on the political right as an enemy.[6] But there is a much larger orbit of groups—racial, religious, ethnic, and sexual minorities, for example—that bear the burden of prejudice and discrimination. And for this larger orbit of groups, there is no conflict of interest, material or ideological, in disliking as many as you wish. Pluralistic intolerance—that is, citizens disagreeing about the particular group they most dislike—affords no protection, because picking any particular group as the one you most dislike puts no constraint on picking any number of others you may also genuinely dislike. On the contrary, to be intolerant of one is to be predisposed toward intolerance of others. Applied to the politics of exclusion, the Madisonian analogy fails.

INSIDERS AND OUTSIDERS

As we have seen, if Italians ascribe any given undesirable personal characteristic to a group of immigrants, they are markedly more likely to ascribe every other such characteristic to the group. If they attribute responsibility for a given societal problem to the group, they are markedly more likely to attribute responsibility for every other societal problem to it. If they believe that one group of immigrants has undesirable personal characteristics, they are markedly more likely to believe that an entirely different group of immigrants is also causing social problems. Consistency is the defining feature of orientations toward the outsider: consistency across the ascription of personal characteristics; across the attribution of responsibility for societal problems; and even across the groups themselves.

This consistency calls to mind the classic concept of ethnocentrism. In William Sumner's classic formulation, ethnocentrism involves a universal disposition to ingroup identification and outgroup hostility, as expressed in a complex of values and sentiments, among them "loyalty to the group, sacrifice for it, hatred and contempt for outsiders, brotherhood within, warlikeness without."[7] The notion of ethnocentrism, so conceived, is expressly double-barreled. It refers, on the one side, to a disposition on the part of those in the ingroup to reject, denigrate, or even aggress against groups to which they either do not belong or with which they do not identify. But equally it refers, on the other side, to a disposition on the part of members of a group to promote, value, and protect the group to which they belong or with which they identify.[8]

From Sumner's point of view, ingroup identification and outgroup hostility are opposite sides of the same coin. As groups sharing common territory or resources struggle for existence, there is pressure for some to draw together and to differentiate themselves from others. The result is a mutually exclusive division into "us" versus "them," we who belong and they who do not, ingroup versus outgroup. From the division into "us" and "them" follows a set of opposing clusters of sentiments: toward the ingroup, loyalty, solidarity, deference, and a willingness to sacrifice for it, identify with it, and honor it; toward the outgroup, suspicion, resentment, disrespect, and hostility. As Sumner says, "Each group thinks its own folkways the only right ones, and if it observes that other groups have other folkways, these excite its scorn."[9]

From the point of view of common experience, this coupling of out-group hostility and ingroup identification seems self-evident.[10] Doesn't an emphasis on dangers external to a group build up loyalty within it? Doesn't the person who evinces contempt for other nationalities tend to glorify his own? Conceived in one way, which centers on the com-monalties in individuals' responses to different circumstances, the an-swers to these questions are straightforward. Conceived in a different way, which centers on the differences in individuals' responses to com-mon circumstances, their answers are anything but straightforward. We want, therefore, to consider in what sense, in democratic politics, hos-tility to the folkways of outgroups entails attachment to folkways of the ingroup.

The idea we want to present is speculative. It is consistent with the results of our study, but not directly demonstrated by them. We have, nonetheless, become persuaded that a paradox at the core of the politics of intolerance deserves attention. Sumner argued that "the most impor-tant fact is that ethnocentrism leads a people to exaggerate and intensify everything in their own folkways which is peculiar and which differenti-ates them from others. It therefore strengthens the folkways."[11] Applied to the folkways of a democratic politics, we believe this to be false. In a democratic society, hostility toward outsiders goes hand in hand, not with identification with the ingroup and its folkways, but with hostility toward them.

The possibility of this inversion of the standard formulation was first suggested by an unexpected result that cropped up in the course of an analysis of the classic cleavage within Italian society, the division be-tween North and South. The standard presumption of ingroup iden-tification going hand in hand with outgroup hostility suggests parallel predictions for Northern and Southern Italians. Other things equal, the more negative Northern Italians' opinion of Southern Italians, the more positive should be their opinion of their own group, fellow Northerners. Equivalently, the more negative Southern Italians' opinion of Northern Italians, the more positive should be their opinion of their own group, fellow Southerners. But rather than it being true that the more they re-ject and disparage the other group, the more they identify with and esteem their own, the very opposite is true. The Northern Italian who disparages Southern Italians also disparages Northern Italians; the Southern Italian who disparages Northern Italians also disparages Southern Italians.[12] For both Northern and Southern Italians, rather than disapproval of members of the outgroup promoting approval of fellow members of the ingroup, consistency in evaluation runs through and through for both.

This result, unanticipated by us, suggested a new line of thought. Ethnocentrism, classically conceived, yokes together outgroup hostility and ingroup identification. Perhaps the two terms should be uncoupled. They ought to be decoupled, we conjectured, not because the one has nothing to do with the other, but because each can bear on the other in quite different ways. In the face of an external threat such as war, hostility toward the outgroup can go together with identification with the ingroup, just as Sumner supposed. But because hostility toward an outgroup can promote identification with the ingroup under some conditions, ought one to conclude that it always, or even usually, does?

And, to raise a quite different consideration, what actually is meant by "ingroup identification?" In our effort to comprehend the hostility toward immigrants now so prominent throughout Western Europe, we have been most struck by its through-and-through character. Whatever distinctions native-born Italians might draw between immigrants from Poland and those from Senegal if directed to do so, they do not draw them spontaneously. White or black, our results show, they are both outsiders to Italians. But the more we have reflected on our results, the more the line between insiders and outsiders has itself seemed a chimera. If consistency is the hallmark of intolerance, then why shouldn't it run through and through? Why should it respect an arbitrary line between insiders and outsiders? And even supposing it did, the notion of insiders lends itself to quite different constructions, and why should it be assumed that it is similarly understood by those who wish to reject outsiders as by those who are prepared to accept them?

Categorization is the pivotal consideration in both of our models of intolerance. As a practical matter, we indexed categorization in terms of a readiness of a person to perceive others as distinct, as belonging to another group, and, more specifically, as failing to conform to the norms of his or her group. They, as the expression goes, should try to be more like us. Categorization thus expresses itself in an insistence on conformity, and it is therefore the connection between conformity as a value and the value of freedom of expression that we want to consider. Freedom of expression, as a norm of democratic politics, depends on conformity understood as a process of socialization. For the norms of a society to persist, each generation must acquire an understanding of and commitment to them. But the process of conformity and the desire for it are not the same. And not only are they different, but in a democratic polity, the one can be at odds with the other.

They can be at odds with one another because, sooner or later, the desire for conformity and actually conforming to the values of a democratic society conflict. Lacking direct evidence, we wish to appeal to an historical example, the radical right in America in the 1950s. One mark of the radical right, as Richard Hofstadter observed in his classic diagnosis,[13] was a pervasive anger and paranoid suspicion of outsiders, which then included foreigners, communists, subversives, and Jews—the last, in some minds, a composite of all the others. Another mark of the radical right was the idealization of America. America was, the far right proclaimed, incomparably superior to any other country. They had entered politics, they insisted, to defend the American way of life—indeed, so much so that they styled themselves as "super-patriots." These two elements, the rejection of conspiratorial outsiders burrowing into American government and the idealization of the American way of life, went hand in hand. The former, the radical right maintained, were threatening the latter. So they presented themselves as true patriots, identifying their very selves with the American way of life, coming to its defense.

But the radical right's protestations of attachment to American values and institutions notwithstanding, its defining feature was precisely its estrangement from them. It was, and saw itself to be, at odds with the leading tendencies of modern American life. It was, and presented itself as being, at war with virtually every dominant political institution—the Supreme Court, the mass media, the State Department, and even (extraordinarily) President Eisenhower were suspect, or worse. The whole thrust of American culture, the far right maintained, had become corrupted. Hostility to established institutions was their raison d'être.

It is tempting to see the eruption of the radical right as an event of the America of the 1950s, a response to social and cultural conditions of the moment, not reproducible at any other time. Yet, acknowledging that aspects of its politics belong to that time and will not be seen in another, we believe that it calls attention to an enduring paradox at the core of the politics of intolerance in democratic societies.

The hallmark of the radical right was its insistence on conformity to the true values of American democracy. In this effort, the radical right presented itself as in service to the values of a democratic society. Its mission was to strengthen them by securing everyone's compliance with them. But the insistence on conformity is rooted, as we have seen, in an aversion capable of indiscriminately attaching itself to those who differ in religion, sexual orientation, or political belief. The flip side of the insistence on conformity is thus the readiness to denounce diversity. But it is diversity—of belief, appearance, background, and, within wide margins, conduct and lifestyle—that the norms of a democratic society are meant not only to protect but to encourage. In a democratic society, those who insist on conformity as a value in and of itself deviate from the values of a democratic society.

There is nothing merely verbal in this paradox. In a democratic society, those who insist on conformity to the values of a society, though they in fact deviate from them, gain strength from their belief that they conform; indeed, they believe that they are the true adherents to the society's values. And since their conception of its values is so narrow, their view of what constitutes deviance from them is correspondingly broad. Wherever they look about them, in politics or in the tendencies of the larger culture, they can see a threat to their way of life. A glitteringly paranoid example was the radical right's representation of Dwight David Eisenhower, supreme commander of the armies liberating France and president of the United States, as a communist dupe. But this is no more than an especially vivid example of a general tendency to believe that those responsible for the institutions of national life must be culpable. How else could the threat, from inside as well as outside, be so imminent? Those at the center of society must be, if not actively subversive of the institutions of national life, negligent in their defense.

The line between insiders and outsiders thus can be not merely erased but inverted. And just so far as the line between insider and outsider can be redrawn, the true stakes of prejudice for a pluralist democracy emerge. The eruption of hostility against immigrants, against outsiders, is of importance in its own right. But our study's last lesson is that outsiders, although the ones most immediately at risk, are not the only ones threatened. As intolerance wells up into public life, "we" can all too easily become "they."

Appendix I

Sampling and Weighting

Sample Design

The Italian Survey on Prejudice was designed to obtain information on the attitudes of the Italian population on the relationship between Northern and Southern Italians and between Italians and immigrants from outside the European Community. Since approximately 90 percent of Italian households now have telephones, it was possible to design the study as a telephone survey, which is more economical than conducting face-to-face interviews. Accordingly, a random sample of residential telephone numbers was selected with the following steps:

1. The database of current residential telephone numbers was divided into separate strata for each of the twenty regions, and each region was divided into five strata based on the population of the town or city. Within each of the resulting strata, a random sample of 1/2,250 of the telephone numbers was drawn. This procedure was carried out by the Milano List Service. The resulting sample contained about 12,200 telephone numbers.

2. The sample received from Milano List Service was divided into random subsamples, to be used as needed to obtain approximately 2,500 interviews. The first subsample of 3,052 telephone numbers was created by systematic random sampling: after a random start, every fourth telephone number in the large sample was selected. This systematic sampling ensured that the stratification by region and size of place would be preserved in the main subsample used for interviewing. A second subsample of 3,052 telephone numbers was drawn from the large sample in the same way; this subsample was then put into a random order, to be used as needed for the fieldwork.

3. Within each selected home, one person aged 18–69 was selected at random for interviewing. Each eligible adult was first listed, and then a computer-generated random number was applied to the list to designate one of the persons as the respondent. No substitutions were allowed, and repeated callbacks were made in order to complete the interview with the selected person. There were 4,558 confirmed households in the sample. Interviews were

completed at 2001 of those households, for a response rate of 43.9 percent.

Weights

Weights were created for each case to compensate for differences in probabilities of selection and to adjust the sample to match certain demographic distributions. These two levels of weights were generated as follows.

1. Sampling Weight

The first weight is the sampling weight, which adjusts for differences in the probabilities of selection among the various respondents. Since only one eligible adult was selected to be interviewed in each household, persons residing in households with more eligible persons were less likely to be selected than persons residing in households with fewer persons.

The relative weight to compensate for this is P, where P is the number of eligible persons in the selected household ($1 - 4$ = actual number, and $5 = 5$ or more). This relative weight was then multiplied by a constant to scale the weight so that the weighted number of cases equals the unweighted number of cases (2001).

2. Poststratification Weight

The second level of weighting is a poststratification adjustment. Since different segments of the Italian population are more likely than others to reside in a household with a telephone and to respond to the interview, certain groups of people are over- or underrepresented in the data file. Therefore, a poststratification weight was used to adjust the distribution of the sample to a reliable standard.

The variables used to poststratify were gender (male/female) and region of the country (7 categories). The criterion distribution was taken from the 1991 census. The 2×7 distribution of gender by region in the sample was weighted (by the sampling weight), and then ratio adjusted to match the census distribution.

The poststratification weight, consequently, incorporates the sampling weight adjustments for unequal probabilities of selection. This weight is also scaled so that the sum of the weighted cases equals the number of unweighted cases. Since this weight implicitly adjusts for noncoverage and differential nonresponse, its use is recommended for most analyses.

Appendix II

Construction of Measures

THIS appendix details the precise codings for all variables that were constructed from the base survey (see appendix VI). All of the transformations and operations listed here were done in CSA 2.4. For a detailed description of the notation consult the CSA webpage http://csa.berkeley.edu. We first list the variables that are computed by operations of other variables. Then we list variables that are recoded from single variables.

Computed from other variables:

categorization = 5 − mean.1(m1, m2)

cpitol (or personality) = mean.3 (r1, r2, r3, r4, r8)

equality = (4 − va1tr) + va4tr + va6tr

imprej = mean.4(k1r, k2, k3r, k4, k5, k6, k7, k8)

imcombo (or hostility toward immigrants) = mean.2(3.3333*(imprej − 1), 2*nprobs)

k1r = 5 − k1

k3r = 5 − k3

minec (or economic security) = (va6tr + va3tr)/4

msouneg = mean.3 (k21, 5 − k22, k23, 5 − k24, 5 − k25, 5 − k26, 5 − k27)

mistrust = mean.2 (q1r, q2r, q3r)

nprobs = mean.2(i1 − 1, i2 − 1, i3 − 1, i4 − 1, i5 − 1)*5

souprob = mean.2(5 − d1, 5 − e2, 5 − e6)

tradval (or authoritarian values) = (5 − c1) + (5 − c2) + (5 − c3) + (5 − c6)

totsou (or hostility toward Southerners) = (msouneg + souprob)

Recoded from a variable:

New	Original	Map (from original variable to new variable)
rocc5(status)	rocc*	3 = 1, 2 = 2, 1 = 4, 4 = 3, 5 = 5, (6, 8) = 7, 7 = 6, md = 4.5
vote	pol3	(1, 2) = 1, 3 = 2, 4 = 3, md = −1
va1tr	va1	2 = 1, 7 = 2, 1 = 3, md = −1
va2tr	va2	2 = 1, 7 = 2, 1 = 3, md = −1
va3tr	va3	2 = 1, 7 = 2, 1 = 3, md = −1
va4tr	va4	2 = 1, 7 = 2, 1 = 3, md = −1
va5tr	va5	2 = 1, 7 = 2, 1 = 3, md = −1
va6tr	va6	2 = 1, 7 = 2, 1 = 3, md = −1

* Spouse's code used if rocc was missing

Missing Data

IN THIS APPENDIX, we analyze the degree and patterns of missing responses to determine if either, or both, introduce bias into the many results we have reported.

We describe the results of our analysis for the items concerning the *attributes* of extracommunitarians (the k1–k8 variables in the survey). In approaching this analysis, we ask three broad questions. First, is the *degree* of missing data abnormally high? Second, is there a systematic pattern of omissions based upon *which group* one is asked about? Third, are certain *types* of respondents more likely to answer than others?

In general, this analysis has yielded four major conclusions. First, the absolute degree of missing data is not abnormal for a survey of this type. Second, response rates do not depend on which group the respondent is asked about. Third, although respondents of different ages and genders differ in their propensities to respond, these differences are not large enough to cause significant biases. Finally, there is a slightly greater chance that "bigoted" people will not respond to attribute questions than "nonbigots," although, again, the difference is not significant enough to compromise any summary measures.

Overview: The Degree of Missing Data

The degree of missing data in the attribute series is not unusual. Figure A3.1 shows the proportion of respondents by number of missing responses. Over 90 percent replied to at least five of the eight items, and nearly three-quarters answered at least all but one. Similarly, on any given question, roughly five-sixths of the respondents replied to the question asked. By comparison, in the *1991 National Race Study*, the response rates on a similar set of questions was approximately ninety-four percent.[1] Although the rates in the Italian study are slightly lower, they are not enough to cause alarm.

Patterns of Missing Data Internal to the Series

Despite the prima facie evidence that the degree of missing responses in the survey is not abnormal, due to the potential for bias, it is worthwhile to look further. Systematic patterns of unresponsiveness might occur in

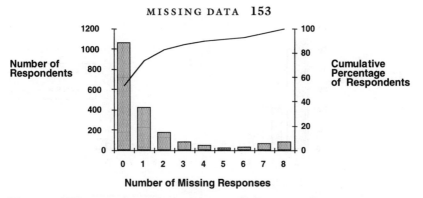

Number of Respondents

Cumulative Percentage of Respondents

Number of Missing Responses

Notes: n = 2001

Fig. A3.1 Number and Proportion of Missing Responses to the Attribute Series

two forms: first, if missing responses are more likely to occur when a respondent is asked about a particular group (either Africans or Eastern Europeans); second, if certain types of people are less responsive than others.

One of the techniques used to evaluate prejudice was to ask respondents *randomly* about either Africans or Europeans. Although randomization increases the power of comparative results, it also introduces a potential hazard: if respondents asked about one group are more likely to refuse to answer, the true attitudes toward that group, particularly relative to other groups in Italy, might remain submerged. Fortunately, this is not the case. As can be seen in figure A3.2, survey respondents are divided into those who were asked about Africans and those who were asked about Eastern Europeans. For both groups, the likelihood of a missing response is roughly equal.[2]

Patterns of Missing Data Based on Characteristics of the Respondent

We are also interested in seeing if certain types of respondents are more or less likely to be unresponsive. Here the analysis can be divided into two categories based on *demographic* characteristics and *attitudinal* ones. In particular, we examined the pattern of missing responses based on gender, age, education, and region of origin on the one hand, and based on a measure of prejudice on the other.

As the results summarized in table A3.1 indicate, there *are* some biases based on demographic characteristics. Although two types of demographic characteristics appear to have minimal effect on the propensity to respond—whether a person is from the North or from the South, on

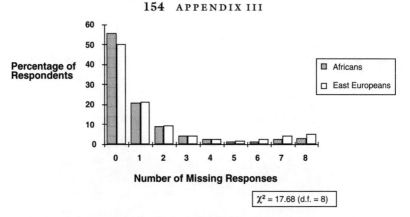

Number of Missing Responses

$\chi^2 = 17.68$ (d.f. = 8)

Notes: Number of respondents asked about Africans: 1007
Number of respondents asked about Eastern Europeans: 994

Fig. A3.2 Missing Responses by Extracommunitarian Group

TABLE A3.1
Differences in Propensity for Missing Data by
Demographic Characteristics

Characteristic	Chi-Square Value	Degrees of Freedom	Significant (5%)
Male-Female	44.76	8	yes
North-South	9.90	8	no
Education	18.71	16	no
Age	98.64	16	yes

Notes: North-South based on region of birth and region of father's birth.
Education groups respondents in three categories: those without high school education, those with high school education or vocational training, and those with post-secondary education.
Age divided into three categories: 18–29, 30–54, 55+.
n = 2001

the one hand, and a respondent's level of education on the other—women are less likely to respond than men, and, similarly, older Italians are less likely to respond than younger Italians. The degree to which these differences influence the analytical results is minor, however, since in both the case of age and of gender, although differences do exist, most of those occur between individuals who respond to all questions and those who will not respond to one. In other words, despite an occasional missing response, the vast majority of respondents responded to most of the questions, irrespective of age and gender. For example, as shown in table A3.2, more than three-quarters of the respondents in

TABLE A3.2
Degree of Unresponsiveness by Age and Gender

Characteristic	Category	Percent Answering at Least 75% of Items	Chi-Square	Significant (5%)
Age	18–29	89.2		
	30–54	82.5	5.137	no
	55+	75.3		
Gender	Male	87.2		
	Female	79.7	3.315	no

every category answered at least six of the eight questions. Further, these proportions are roughly equivalent. The implication, therefore, is that although respondents might not answer a particular question, they will answer enough such that a collapsed measure incorporating a number of the variables will still be robust.

In addition to demographic biases, it is important to consider attitudinal ones. Here the question is, "Do people who are prejudiced have a different pattern of response than those who are not prejudiced?" To find the answer, we divide the respondents into three groups based on the degree of their average negativity toward extracommunitarians. Each group comprises roughly one-third of the total sample.[3] The distribution of missing responses is shown in Figure A3.3. This data has two striking features.

First, there is a significant difference between the propensity of less and more prejudiced people to respond to questions about the attributes of extracommunitarians: *"bigots" are less likely to respond.* A propensity to refuse to answer among bigots raises concerns since it means that the group we are most interested in is potentially underrepresented in the sample. The situation is not as dire as might at first be assumed, however, since as with the demographic variables, this fact is tempered by another. Again, although relatively more prejudiced persons will tend to opt out of responding to items, this generally occurs only for a few questions. Indeed, over 85 percent of the most prejudiced answered at least six of the eight questions (table A3.3). When classified, in this manner, there is *no difference* between a bigot's tendency to respond to most questions and one who is not so bigoted. Thus, while there might be some potential for bias in a question-by-question analysis, this risk is drastically reduced by the use of summary measures that incorporate responses to all of the answered questions.

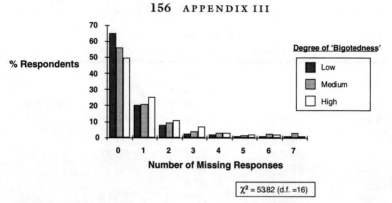

$\chi^2 = 53.82$ (d.f. =16)

Notes: n = 1885
Excludes totally unresponsive individuals
Roughly one-third in each group
Classification based on average negativity towards extracommunitarians

Fig. A3.3 Missing Responses by Degree of "Bigotedness"

TABLE A3.3
Degree of Unresponsiveness by "Bigotedness"

Degree of Prejudice	Percent Answering at Least 75% of Items	Chi-Square	Significant Difference (5%)
Low	89.2		
Medium	86.2	0.546	no
High	85.5		

Appendix IV

Instrumental Variables

THE instrumental variables requiring justification are set out in the far right column of table A4.1. Each row of that table contains, first, the variable to be predicted, then the endogenous predictor, then the instrumental variables. The justification for the instruments follows directly from the theoretical arguments set out in chapter 3 for the "Two Flavors" model, as modified and extended in chapter 4 for the "Right Shock" model.

Judgments of economic well-being fall under an instrumental, realistic conflict theoretical account rather than affective, personality-centered perspective on prejudice, and the focus under realistic conflict theories is on appraisal of temporally proximate threats. The argument is necessarily that group conflict is exacerbated by judgments taking the form that if "they" are better-off, I shall shortly (or immediately) be worse-off. Appraisal of a potential threat over an extended (or indefinite) horizon cannot qualify as a direct spur to group conflict: the appraisal of realistic conflict, extended over an indefinite time horizon, degenerates into paranoia. On the other side, one reason people may become apprehensive about the prospects in front of them is that they are apprehensive over their longer-run prospects. It follows that judgments of economic dissatisfaction over an extended time span (b2) will not be connected either to an increased readiness to categorize others as belonging to groups as different (conformity) or to hostility to immigrants (imcombo) except insofar as these judgments influence contemporaneous judgments of economic security.

The fundamental point of distinction between the basic form of our account, in terms of the "Two Flavors" model, and the extended form, in terms of the "Right Shock" model, is that the latter, but not the former, expressly incorporates political values. In principle, a forbidding amount of territory could be roped in under the heading of ideology, and so we have expressly set out, in chapter 5, the reasons, both theoretical and normative, for favoring a two-component conception. Of the two dimensions—equalitarianism and authoritarian values—there is a theoretical justification for a relation between only the latter and prejudice. The instruments va1r and va2r index (which are just va1 and va2 reversed in direction), by contrast, shards of political values of relevance

TABLE A4.1

Instrumental Variables Used for Estimation of "Two-Flavors"
and "Right Shock" Models

Dependent Variable	Endogenous Variables	Instruments
Categorization	Mistrust	b2
	Economic insecurity	va1r
		va2r
Categorization	Mistrust	b2
	Economic insecurity	va1r
	Authority values	va2r
Hostility toward immigrants	Mistrust	va1r
	Economic insecurity	va2r
	Categorization	
Hostility toward immigrants	Mistrust	va1r
	Economic insecurity	va2r
	Categorization	
	Authority values	
Authority values	Hostility toward im-migrants	h1
Hostility toward southerners	Categorization	none

Notes: Exogenous variables also used as instruments. Instruments not related to
specific endogenous variables.

to intermediate elements in our models of prejudice. Aspects of liberalism are tied to images of man—and particularly a view of other men as trustworthy and dependable—as they are also tied to judgments of comparative well-being; it follows that va1r, which indexes a preference for liberty over equality, is connected to a readiness to categorize others as different (conformity) or prejudice itself (imcombo) only so far as it is connected to judgments of others, in the form of trust, or a sense of economic well-being, in the form of economic security. The instrumental role of va2r is straightforward. The heart of the theoretical argument underpinning the "Two Flavors" model is that the role of social and structural factors in evoking prejudice is mediated by a readiness to categorize others as different, and this readiness to categorize others as different in turn is mediated by mistrust of others or apprehension about economic security or both. Va2r indexes a preference for economic security, in preference to social order. Va2r, it follows, can bear on prejudice or conformity just so far as it bears on judgments of economic security.

The final instrument is h1, which indexes whether respondents have had occasion to meet, speak with, or get to know non–EEC immigrants. The theoretical argument here is also straightforward. On the one side there is a long-standing recognition in the study of prejudice that contact and prejudice can be connected. As Allport and others have demonstrated, being exposed to others in general (though not in all specific circumstances) tends to promote a more positive, tolerant response to them. On the other side, there is no theoretical connection whatever between placing a high value on order, authority, or tradition and the actual contingency of being exposed, in the course of ordinary life, to an immigrant. It follows that h1 has no direct connection to authoritarian values and, so far as it may empirically be associated with those values, it is so only insofar as it is related to prejudice.

Accounting for Measurement Error:
An Alternative Estimation of the "Two Flavors" and "Right Shock" Models

The Problem and a Solution

This appendix tests the models laid out in chapters 3 and 4 with an alternative estimation technique in order to determine the extent to which unidentified measurement error biases or clouds the results presented thus far. In the classical regression model, one of the basic assumptions is that the explanatory variables are uncorrelated with the error term. If this assumption is violated, then ordinary least squares (OLS) estimates will not be consistent (asymptotically unbiased). In hierarchical or multistage models, such as the "Two Flavors" model presented in chapter 3 and the "Right Shock" model presented in chapter 4, this assumption is commonly violated for three reasons: omitted variables or unobserved heterogeneity, simultaneous causation, and measurement error. The first two of these problems we deal with in the estimation methods presented in chapters 3 and 4. When these conditions are present, instrumental variable estimation, such as the two-stage least squares (2SLS) estimator we use, gives us accurate estimates provided we can find suitable instruments.[1] These methods do not, however, necessarily filter out all of the measurement error. Unfortunately, as we note in chapter 2, the constructs with which we are concerned here are notoriously difficult to measure and our measures are no exception.[2] The third problem—measurement error—therefore requires additional treatment to solve in this case.

An attractive solution to this problem is to use structural equation modeling (also known as LISREL) techniques, which specify both latent and observed variables in the model and are therefore able to incorporate measurement error explicitly. LISREL models are generally estimated with a maximum likelihood (MLE) fitting function. However, like OLS for the standard econometric method, MLE will give asymptotically biased estimates for simultaneous models. More appropriate are the set of 2SLS estimators that have been adapted for structural equation models (Jöreskog and Sörbom, 1993; Bollen 1996). Below, we estimate the "Two Flavors" and "Right Shock" models with Bollen's 2SLS method (the more advanced and well documented of the 2SLS LISREL estimators).

Bollen's 2SLS Estimator for Latent Variable Equations

In this subsection we summarize the key aspects of Bollen's method. Following convention, the general structural equation model can be written as:

$$\eta = \alpha + B\eta + \Gamma\xi + \zeta \qquad (A5.1)$$

where η is an $m \times 1$ vector of latent endogenous variables, B is an $m \times m$ matrix of coefficients of the effect of the η's on each other, ξ is an $n \times 1$ vector of latent exogenous variables, Γ is an $m \times n$ matrix of ξ's impact on η, α is an $m \times 1$ vector of intercept terms, and ζ is an $m \times 1$ vector of random disturbances with an expectation of 0 and which are uncorrelated with ξ. Each of the latent constructs (the combination of η's and ξ's) is measured with a set of observed x's and y's, commonly termed indicators. The objective of the analysis is to estimate the parameters of equation A5.1 using the observed indicators.

As in standard LISREL analysis, one of the x's or y's for each latent construct is selected to scale the factor loadings (the loading for the scaled factor is set to 1 and its intercept set to 0). In table A5.1, we describe the variables we chose as scaling variables for our constructs.[3] Following the standard equation for the measurement model in LISREL we can express the scaled variables as:

$$y_1 = \eta + \varepsilon_1$$

and

$$x_1 = \xi + \delta_1.$$

Substituting into the general model in equation A5.1—a substitution that provides the key step in Bollen's insight, we can then write,

$$y_1 = \alpha + By_1 + \Gamma x_1 + u \qquad (A5.2)$$

where $u = \varepsilon_1 - B\varepsilon_1 - \Gamma\delta_1 + \zeta$. Note, therefore, that u, which contains δ_1, will only be uncorrelated with x_1 when it is measured without error. A 2SLS estimator with suitable instrumental variables will give unbiased estimates of this equation.

We need, then, instrumental variables that will be able to predict y_1 and x_1 but will not be correlated with u. As Bollen describes, this means all the nonscaled indicators of the x's and y's on the right side of the equation, any x's and y's that pertain to constructs that are not further down the causal chain, as well as the exogenous variables in the system

TABLE A5.1

Scaling Indicators Used in
Measurement-Error Models

Latent Variable	Scaling Indicator
Personality	r2
Mistrust	q3r
Economic insecurity	va3r
Categorization	m2
Hostility toward immigrants	k6
Authority values	c1

Notes: Scaling variables were chosen based on having the highest intercorrelation with other indicators for the construct.

Scaling variables were reflected in some case to preserve directional meaning of latent construct.

of equations, are valid instruments for equation A5.2. Indicators for constructs that enter the structural model at posterior levels of the model, however, are ruled out since these indicators will have correlated measurement errors with the x's included in equation A5.2.

The "Two Flavors" Model

Specification

Figure A5.1 gives a "path diagram" of the combined measurement and structural relationships in the "Two Flavors" model. Following conventional notation, the ovals represent latent constructs and the squares observed causal variables or observed indicators of constructs. This hierarchy can be written as a system of equations:

$$\eta_1 = \alpha_1 + \gamma_{11}\xi_1 + \gamma_{12}Age + \gamma_{13}Education + \zeta_1$$

$$\eta_2 = \alpha_2 + \gamma_{21}Age + \gamma_{22}Education + \gamma_{23}Occupational\ Status + \zeta_2$$

$$\eta_3 = \alpha_3 + \beta_{31}\eta_1 + \beta_{32}\eta_2 + \gamma_{31}Age + \gamma_{32}Education + \zeta_3$$

$$\eta_4 = \alpha_4 + \beta_{41}\eta_3 + \gamma_{41}\xi_1 + \gamma_{42}Education + \zeta_4$$

where η_1 = mistrust, η_2 = economic insecurity, η_3 = categorization, η_4 = hostility, and ξ_1 = personality. As we note earlier, any variable chosen as a scaling item can be used directly in this system of equations. Substituting the appropriate scaling variables described above minus their respective measurement error for the latent constructs leads to the following specification of the "Two Flavors" model:

$$q3r = \alpha_1 + \gamma_{11}r2 + \gamma_{12}Age + \gamma_{13}Education + \varepsilon_1 + \zeta_1$$

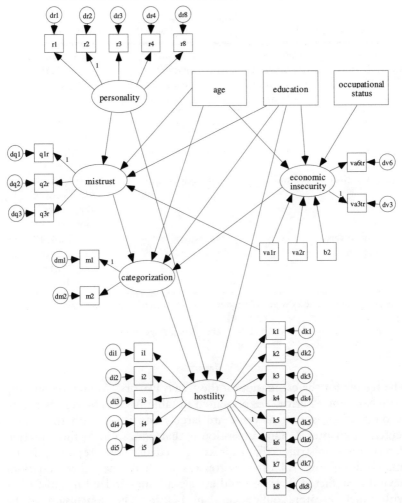

Notes: Circles indicate errors; rectangles indicate exogenously determined variables; squares represent indicators; ovals represent latent variables

Fig. A5.1 Path Diagram of "Two Flavors" Model

$$va3r = \alpha_2 + \gamma_{21}Age + \gamma_{22}Education + \gamma_{23}Occupational\ Status + \varepsilon_2 + \zeta_2$$

$$m2 = \alpha_3 + \beta_{31}q3r + \beta_{32}va3r + \gamma_{31}Age + \gamma_{32}Education + \varepsilon_3 + \zeta_3$$

$$k6 = \alpha_4 + \beta_{41}m2 + \gamma_{41}r2 + \gamma_{42}Education + \varepsilon_4 + \zeta_4$$

Finally, following the general guidelines outlined above for selection of instruments, the appropriate indicators employed for the first-stage equations are provided in table A5.2.[4]

TABLE A5.2
Specification for "Two Flavors" Model with Measurement Error

Dependent Variable from "Two Flavors" Model	Dependent Variable in Measurement Model	Independent Variables in Measurement Model	Instrumental Variables in Measurement Model
Mistrust	q3r	r2, age, educr	r1, r3, r4, r8, age, educr, roccr
Economic insecurity	va3r	age, educr, roccr	r1, r3, r4, r8, age, educr, roccr
Categorization	m2	age, educr, q3r, va3r	r1, r3, r4, r8, age, educr, roccr, q1r, q2r, va1r, va2r, va6r, b2
Hostility toward immigrants	k6	r2, educr, m2	r1, r3, r4, r8, age, educr, roccr, q1r, q2r, va1r, va2r, va6r, b2, m1

Notes: Scaling variables were reflected in some cases to preserve directional meaning of latent construct.

Constant was also included in all first- and second-stage models.

Results

The results for the estimation of the "Two Flavors" model, accounting for measurement error, are presented in table A5.3. The results taking account of measurement error are largely consistent with those presented in chapter 3. One exception is that education in the equation determining mistrust, the expressive mediator of prejudice, is no longer significant. All other regressors in all of the other equations have the predicted direction and are significant—indeed in most cases with much greater confidence than before. The conclusion to be drawn, then, is that although measurement error did induce some noise into the earlier estimation, the substantive results were *unaffected,* providing strong evidence for the robustness of the results presented in chapter 3.

THE "RIGHT SHOCK" MODEL

Specification

Figure A5.2 gives a "path diagram" of the combined measurement and structural relationships in the "Right Shock" model. The representation of the model is analogous to that presented for the "Two Flavors"

TABLE A5.3

Estimation of "Two Flavors" Model with Measurement Error

Independent Variable Dependent Variable	Mistrust	Economic Insecurity	Categorization	Hostility
Personality	−1.681**			−0.883**
	(−10.41)			(−3.35)
Age	−0.007**	0.003**	0.022**	
	(−3.60)	(2.05)	(10.15)	
Education	0.007	−0.058**	−0.074**	−0.036**
	(0.71)	(−6.50)	(−6.76)	(−3.35)
Occupational status		0.029**		
		(1.80)		
Mistrust			0.503**	
			(5.99)	
Economic insecurity			0.357**	
			(5.06)	
Categorization				0.099**
				(3.67)
Constant	5.117	1.711	0.277	3.527
n	1732	1762	1511	1244

* $p < 0.1$ ** $p < 0.05$

Notes: t-statistics in parentheses

Estimation technique is two-staged least squares with measurement error (per Bollen 1996).

Latent variables represented by their scaled indicators as in table A5.1.

model in the previous section. Again, we can represent the model as a system of equations:

$$\eta_1 = \alpha_1 + \gamma_{11}\xi_1 + \gamma_{12}Age + \gamma_{13}Education + \zeta_1$$

$$\eta_2 = \alpha_2 + \gamma_{21}Age + \gamma_{22}Education + \gamma_{23}Occupational\ Status + \zeta_2$$

$$\eta_3 = \alpha_3 + \beta_{31}\eta_1 + \beta_{32}\eta_2 + \beta_{33}\eta_5 + \gamma_{31}Age + \gamma_{32}Education + \zeta_3$$

$$\eta_4 = \alpha_4 + \beta_{41}\eta_3 + \beta_{42}\eta_5 + \gamma_{41}\xi_1 + \gamma_{42}Education + \zeta_4$$

$$\eta_5 = \alpha_5 + \beta_{51}\eta_4 + \gamma_{11}\xi_1 + \gamma_{52}Age + \gamma_{53}Education$$
$$+ \gamma_{54}Occupational\ Status + \zeta_5$$

where η_1 = mistrust, η_2 = economic insecurity, η_3 = categorization, η_4 = hostility, η_5 = authority values, and ξ_1 = personality. Again, substituting the appropriate scaling variables described above, we can rewrite the "Right Shock" model to include measurement error as:

$$q3r = \alpha_1 + \gamma_{11}r2 + \gamma_{12}Age + \gamma_{13}Education + \varepsilon_1 + \zeta_1$$

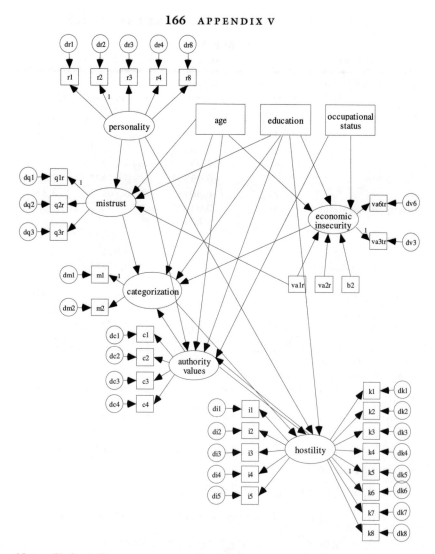

Notes: Circles indicate errors; rectangles indicate exogenously determined variables; squares represent indicators; ovals represent latent variables

Fig. A5.2 Path Diagram of "Right Shock" Model

$$va3r = \alpha_2 + \gamma_{21}Age + \gamma_{22}Education + \gamma_{23}Occupational\ Status + \varepsilon_2 + \zeta_2$$
$$m2 = \alpha_3 + \beta_{31}q3r + \beta_{32}va3r + \beta_{33}c1 + \gamma_{31}Age + \gamma_{32}Education + \varepsilon_3 + \zeta_3$$
$$k6 = \alpha_4 + \beta_{41}m2 + \beta_{42}c1 + \gamma_{41}r2 + \gamma_{42}Education + \varepsilon_4 + \zeta_4$$

TABLE A5.4
Specification for "Right Shock" Model with Measurement Error

Dependent Variable from "Right Shock" Model	Dependent Variable in Measurement Model	Independent Variables in Measurement Model	Instrumental Variables in Measurement Model
Mistrust	q3r	r2, age, educr	r1, r3, r4, r8, age, educr, roccr
Economic insecurity	va3r	age, educr, roccr	r1, r3, r4, r8, age, educr, roccr
Authority values	c1	r2, age, educr, roccr, k6	r1, r3, r4, r8, age, educr, roccr, q1r, q2r, va1r, va2r, va6r, b2
Categorization	m2	age, educr, q3r, va3r, c1	r1, r3, r4, r8, age, educr, roccr, q1r, q2r, va1r, va2r, va6r, b2
Hostility toward immigrants	k6	r2, educr, m2, c1	r1, r3, r4, r8, age, educr, roccr, q1r, q2r, va1r, va2r, va6r, b2

Notes: Scaling variables were reflected in some cases to preserve directional meaning of latent construct.

Constant was also included in all first- and second- stage models.

$$c1 = \alpha_5 + \beta_{51}k6 + \gamma_{51}r2 + \gamma_{52}Age + \gamma_{53}Education$$
$$+ \gamma_{54}Occupational\ Status + \varepsilon_5 + \zeta_5$$

Using Bollen's guidelines, the appropriate indicators employed for the first-stage equations are provided in table A5.4.[5]

Results

The results for the estimation of the "Right Shock" model, again accounting for measurement error, are presented in table A5.5. As with the earlier results, the model provides results consistent with those presented in both chapters 3 and 4. In the first instance, adding authority values to the model does not change any of the basic results seen in table A5.3: except for the lack of significance of education in determining mistrust, which we commented on in the previous section, and also the lack of its direct effect on prejudice, all the results are consistent from

TABLE A5.5
Estimation of "Right Shock" Model with Measurement Error

Independent Variable Dependent Variable	Mistrust	Economic Insecurity	Authority Values	Categorization	Hostility
Personality	−1.681** (−10.41)		0.107 (0.30)		−0.614** (−2.96)
Age	−0.007** (−3.60)	0.003** (2.05)	0.012** (3.38)	0.015** (3.79)	
Education	0.007 (0.71)	−0.058** (−6.50)	−0.033** (−1.91)	−0.044** (−2.44)	−0.007 (−0.49)
Occupational status		0.029** (1.80)	0.017 (0.59)		
Mistrust				0.383** (5.25)	
Economic insecurity				0.261** (2.92)	
Authority values				0.502** (2.10)	0.074 (0.39)
Categorization					0.332** (2.27)
Hostility toward immigrants			0.474* (1.43)		
Constant	5.117	1.711	0.805	−0.592	2.246
n	1732	1762	1247	1488	1228

* $p < 0.1$ ** $p < 0.05$

Notes: t-statistics in parentheses

Estimation technique is two-staged least squares with measurement error (per Bollen 1996).

Latent variables represented by their scaled indicators as in table A5.1.

the "Two Flavors" model to the "Right Shock" model. In the second instance, comparing the results presented here to those presented in chapter 4 (see table 4.4), accounting for measurement error actually *solves* some of the puzzles presented by the analysis in chapter 4: effects that were predicted theoretically but did not materialize with the earlier estimation procedure now appear as expected. In particular, when no measurement error was accounted for, inclusion of authority values "washed out" the effects of age, education, and, perhaps most important, mistrust in determining categorization. In this estimation procedure, once we have accounted for measurement error, all of those variables have the expected effects outlined in the theoretical developments of chapters 3 and 4. The one exception to the strengthening of the evidence is that here, in the authority values equation in the third column of table A5.5, the reciprocal effect of hostility to immigrants is attenuated, attracting less significant an effect than previously, although still strong enough to draw the conclusion about the appropriateness of the theoretical expectation. Combined with the results above for the "Two Flavors" model, this analysis indicates that the results presented previously are robust against measurement error.

The Survey Questionnaire

THIS is a condensed English version of the questionnaire used for computer-assisted telephone interviewing for the 1994 Survey on Regional and Ethnic Prejudice in Italy. Administrative and computer-oriented material is excluded, but all of the substantive material is contained here.

The translation is intended to be a very literal one, not a polished English version that would be used as is in the United States. The original Italian version can be viewed in the Italian codebook currently online on the following website: http://sda.berkeley.edu

Many questions in this interview had two or more randomized versions. Depending on the value of a random number generated for each such question for each respondent, the computer-assisted interviewing system (CASES) would display the appropriate wording of the question to be read by the interviewer to the respondent. The values of the random numbers were then used to determine which version of a question each respondent answered.

Background Variables—Part 1

sex: Sex of the respondent.
    (CODE OR ASK AS NEEDED)

age: Can you tell me how old you were on your last birthday?

educ: What is the highest school diploma you have received?
    (IF R IS A STUDENT, INDICATE THE LATEST DIPLOMA OBTAINED.)

a4: Can you tell me in which REGION you were born?

a5: In what region was your FATHER born?

a6: In what region was your MOTHER born?

region (The region of residence was determined from the sampled telephone number.)

cstr (The size of the town in which the respondent resides was coded at the time the sample was drawn.)

Economic Satisfaction

b1: Could you tell me whether you are very, somewhat, a little, or not at all satisfied with the economic situation of your family?

b2: Try to think about your family five years from now. Do you think that the economic situation of your family will be better than now, remain the same, or become worse?

Social Justice Issues

c1: Now I will read some statements about problems that are often talked about today. For each of these statements, please tell me if you agree strongly, agree somewhat, disagree somewhat, or disagree strongly with each statement.

Whenever a private or public employer finds it necessary to reduce the number of employees, the first to be let go should be women who have a husband who is working.

c2: Only the elderly, children, and handicapped should receive public assistance.

c3: It is better to live in a society in which the laws are vigorously enforced than to give people too much freedom.

c4: It is right that people who are more competent and talented be economically rewarded at a higher level than people who are less competent and talented.

c5: In a just society, everybody should start out with equal opportunities.

c6: In general women are less suitable than men to fill jobs that entail a certain amount of responsibility.

c7: Because of the discrimination existing in Italy, it is difficult for women to reach professional levels that match their talents and training.

c8: These days most people with economic problems are that way through their own fault.

Problems of the South

d1: I will mention now some of the reasons that are usually given to explain why the economic situation and the quality of life are better in the North than in the South.

For each of the following statements can you tell me whether you agree strongly, agree somewhat, disagree somewhat or disagree strongly?

People of the North have a greater commitment to work than people of the South.

d4: The culture and way of life prevalent in the South do not encourage economic development as, on the other hand, they do in the North.

e1: The problems of the South come from the fact that all of the industries have been created in the North of Italy, to the detriment of the Southern economy.

e2: Too much government money has been spent and is still being spent for the South.

e3: The North of Italy wants to impose on the South its own way of living and producing.

e4: The presence of the Mafia and the Camorra is one of the principal causes of the problems of the South.

e6: A great part of the hostility of the North toward the South is due to the fact that most government jobs are filled by Southerners.

North/South Experiments—Part 1

Depending on the value of the random number variable "resp," approximately half of the respondents were asked "esp2" and "esp3." The other half were asked "esp4" and "esp5." Each of these questions has two versions. The wording of each question depends on the random number variable corresponding to that question.

esp2: Now I will present a series of situations, and I would like to ask for your opinion about them.

(CHANGE RANDOMLY THE CITY: MILAN/NAPLES)

Mr. Bianchi would like to have a permit to drive into the restricted downtown area of [CITY] even though he is not entitled to one. He goes to a relative who works in the city permits office to see if he can get a permit.

What chance do you think Mr. Bianchi has of getting a permit even though he is not entitled to one? Does he have a good chance, some chance, or no chance?

esp3: (CHANGE RANDOMLY THE REGION: LOMBARDY/CALABRIA)

There is a contest for a position in the regional government of [REGION]. Mr. Rossi goes to the test, completes the assignment excellently, but has not been recommended by anyone.

What chance do you think Mr. Rossi has of winning the job in the regional government of [REGION]? Does he have a good chance, some chance, or no chance?

esp4: (The following two questions are asked if "resp" equals 2.)

Now I will present a series of situations, and I would like to ask for your opinion about them.

(CHANGE RANDOMLY THE CITY: MILAN/NAPLES)

Mr. Bianchi is a builder who has constructed some apartments in [CITY] which do not conform to the building codes, for example the height of ceilings, the insulation, size, etc. However, Mr. Bianchi has many contacts with local politicians, and he goes to see them to resolve the problem.

What chance do you think that Mr. Bianchi has of getting a permit for the apartments in [CITY] without their being in compliance with the law? Does he have a good chance, some chance, or no chance?

esp5: (CHANGE RANDOMLY THE REGION: LOMBARDY/CALABRIA)

Mr. Rossi takes his car to a repair shop to be fixed. The mechanic who takes care of his car is a person from [REGION] who has worked there for a long time.

What do you think are the chances that the mechanic will do a good job and carry out the repairs in a serious and professional manner? Is there a good chance, some chance, or no chance?

Attitudes about Social Problems

hs1: I will now read another group of statements. For each one please tell me if you agree strongly, agree somewhat, neither agree nor disagree, disagree somewhat, or disagree strongly.

Ordinary people receive their due part of the nation's wealth.

hs2: There is one law for the rich and another for the poor.

hs3: There is no need for strong unions to protect the working conditions and the salaries of workers.

hs4: It is the government's task to guarantee a job to everyone who needs one.

hs5: The best way to solve Italy's economic problems is through private entrepreneurship.

hs6: The main public services should be owned and run by the government.

North/South Experiments—Part 2

The questions "esp6" and "esp7" each have four versions. The wording of each question depends on the random number variables corresponding to that question.

esp6: I will now present another series of situations.

(CHANGE RANDOMLY GENDER: MR./MS., AND THE CITY: VENICE/COSENZA)

[MR./MS.] Verdi is a teacher from [CITY] in a middle school in Florence. For Easter s/he goes to visit his/her relatives in [CITY] and wants to spend a few extra days there after the vacation ends.

What do you think are the chances that [MR./MS.] Verdi will arrange to get a medical statement in order to extend his/her vacation? Is there a good chance, some chance, or no chance?

esp7: (CHANGE RANDOMLY THE PLACE: THE SOUTH/THE NORTH/ AFRICA/EASTERN EUROPE)

Now imagine a situation that could affect you personally.

Let us suppose that you have an apartment to rent. A man from [PLACE] applies who has a steady job, has no problem paying a good rent, and is married with one child. How willing would you be to rent him the apartment?

Would you be very willing, quite willing, not very willing, or not at all willing?

Facts About Immigrants

f1: Now let's talk about some general issues.

How many people do you think live in Italy?

(CODE ANSWER IN MILLIONS)

f2: Do you think that most immigrants from outside the European Community in our country come from African countries or from Eastern Europe?

f3: How many non–EEC legal or illegal immigrants do you think are in Italy today?

esp1:

Immigrant Neighbor Experiment

The wording of the question "esp1" is based on the values of three random number variables. To reconstruct the description of the person asked about, use the text corresponding to the code value of each random number.

ORIGIN, WORK, AND BEHAVIOR ARE CHANGED AT RANDOM:

ORIGIN: AFRICA/EASTERN EUROPE

WORK: IS WORKING ON A REGULAR BASIS/IS UNEMPLOYED OR WORKS AS A STREET PEDDLER

BEHAVIOR: BEHAVES LIKE A GOOD NEIGHBOR/DOES NOT BEHAVE LIKE A GOOD NEIGHBOR

If an immigrant from [ORIGIN] moved next door who [WORK] and who [BEHAVIOR], would you be very happy, somewhat happy, indifferent, somewhat unhappy, or extremely unhappy?

Contact with Immigrants

h1: Have you ever had occasion to meet, speak with, or get to know non–EEC immigrants?

(IF NEVER, SKIP TO QUESTION "j1")

h2: Have you only met non–EEC immigrants on the street, or have you had more direct and meaningful contacts with them?

(IF ONLY ON THE STREET, SKIP TO QUESTION "j1")

h3: Do any non–EEC immigrants live near you?

h4: Does your group of friends include any non–EEC immigrants?

h5: Do any non–EEC immigrants work (or go to school) with you?

h6: Is a non–EEC immigrant a member of your family?

h7: (IF A MEMBER OF FAMILY, ASK:)
Is he (or she) your spouse, your adoptive child, or some other relative?

Policies Concerning Immigrants

j1: Now I will ask you a few questions about how to deal with the issue of immigration into Italy of persons from countries outside the EEC.

What do you think about having them come to Italy?

Do you think it should be made easier than it is now (to emigrate to Italy), or should it be made more difficult than it is now?

j2: (CHANGE AT RANDOM: LEGALLY/NOT LEGALLY)

As for the non–EEC immigrants now in Italy [Legally/Not Legally], should the government provide them with assistance, or should it get them to go back to the countries they came from?

(SKIP TO QUESTION "i1" IF THE RESPONDENT DOES NOT WANT THE GOVERNMENT TO PROVIDE ASSISTANCE.)

Housing Counterarguments

After answering "j3," respondents were presented with a counterargument. For those in favor of providing public housing, the counterargument was "j4." For those not in favor, the counterargument was "j5."

j3: Are you favorable to the fact that public housing can be provided for needy immigrants residing LEGALLY IN ITALY, on the same basis as for Italians?

j4: (IF IN FAVOR, ASK:)

Are you still in favor even taking into account that many Italians would have to wait longer to get public housing, or would this make you change your mind?

j5: (IF NOT IN FAVOR, ASK:)

Are you still against it, even taking into account that many of them would be forced to live in difficult and unhealthy conditions, or would this make you change your mind?

Conflicts with Immigrants

The immigrant group asked about in questions "i1" through "i5" was either African or Eastern European, depending on the value of a random number variable.

i1: (FOR THE NEXT SERIES OF QUESTIONS ON CONFLICTS, CHANGE AT RANDOM THE GROUP: AFRICANS/EASTERN EUROPEANS)

Some people think that the presence of [GROUP] in our country has made worse some problems that already existed.

Do you think that the presence of [GROUP] in our country has made crime rates go up?

i2: Do you think that the presence of [GROUP] in our country has increased unemployment for Italians?

i3: Do you think that the presence of [GROUP] makes it even more difficult for Italians to find a place to live?

i4: Do you think that the presence of [GROUP] creates health problems, in the sense that they carry new diseases?

i5: Do you think that the presence of [GROUP] will involve an increase in taxes, inasmuch as the demand for public services will increase?

Stereotypes of Africans or East Europeans

The group asked about in questions "k1" through "k9" was determined by the random number variable "rk." Approximately half of the respondents were asked about Eastern Europeans; the other half were asked about Africans, randomly described either as North Africans or as Central Africans.

k1: Now we'll talk about different groups of people living in our country. For each of the characteristics that I mention, can you tell me whether you agree or not that it applies to the majority of persons belonging to that group.

(CHANGE RANDOMLY THE DESCRIPTION OF THE FIRST GROUP:)

Version 1: North Africans, like Moroccans, Tunisians, or Algerians

Version 2: Africans from the regions of Central Africa, like Senegal and Somalia

Version 3: Eastern Europeans, like Poles, Albanians, or Slavs

Let's begin by talking about [GROUP]

Do you agree that most of them are HONEST?
(they behave honestly and properly toward others)

Do you agree strongly, agree somewhat, disagree somewhat, or disagree strongly with this description?

k2: Still referring to [North Africans / Central Africans / Eastern Europeans,

do you agree that most of them are SELFISH?
(they think only of themselves, without concerning themselves very much about others)

Do you agree strongly, agree somewhat, disagree somewhat, or disagree strongly with this description?

k3: Do you agree that most of them are LAW-ABIDING?
(they behave like good citizens, observing the regulations and laws of the government)

k4: INTRUSIVE?
(they press themselves on you in an annoying and insistent way)

k5: SLACKERS?
(they try to avoid working or at any rate to do tiring and heavy work)

k6: VIOLENT?
(they often use physical force, or threaten to use it, in order to impose their will on others)

k7: COMPLAINERS?
(they try to make others feel sorry for them)

k8: Do you agree that most of them are BY NATURE INFERIOR to Italians?

Sterotypes of Northern Italians

k11: Now, on the other hand, let's talk about Italians living in the regions of the North, like people from Lombardy, Veneto, and Piemonte.

Do you agree that most of them are HONEST?
(they behave honestly and properly toward others)

Do you agree strongly, agree somewhat, disagree somewhat, or disagree strongly with this description?

k12: Still referring to Northern Italians, do you agree that most of them are SELFISH?
(they think only of themselves, without concerning themselves very much about others)

Do you agree strongly, agree somewhat, disagree somewhat, or disagree strongly with this description?

k13: LAW-ABIDING?
(they behave like good citizens, observing the regulations and laws of the government)

k14: INTRUSIVE?
(they press themselves on you in an annoying and insistent way)

k15: SLACKERS?
(they try to avoid working or at any rate to do tiring and heavy work)

k16: VIOLENT?
(they often use physical force, or threaten to use it, in order to impose their will on others)

k17: COMPLAINERS?

(they try to make others feel sorry for them)

Stereotypes of Southern Italians

k21: Let's talk now about Italians who live in the regions of the South, like people from Sicily, Puglia, and Campania (Naples).

Do you agree that most of them are HONEST?
(they behave honestly and properly toward others)

Do you agree strongly, agree somewhat, disagree somewhat, or disagree strongly with this description?

k22: Still referring to Southern Italians, do you agree that most of them are SELFISH?
(they think only of themselves, without concerning themselves very much about others)

Do you agree strongly, agree somewhat, disagree somewhat, or disagree strongly with this description?

k23: LAW-ABIDING?
(they behave like good citizens, observing the regulations and laws of the government)

k24: INTRUSIVE?
(they press themselves on you in an annoying and insistent way)

k25: SLACKERS?
(they try to avoid working or at any rate to do tiring and heavy work)

k26: VIOLENT?
(they often use physical force, or threaten to use it, in order to impose their will on others)

k27: COMPLAINERS?
(they try to make others feel sorry for them)

Political Values—Paired Comparisons

va1: Now I would like to talk about things that are important for our society like LIBERTY, EQUALITY, ECONOMIC SECURITY, and SO-CIAL ORDER.

To avoid any misunderstanding, I would first like to define what we mean by each of these concepts. Then I will ask which ones, in your opinion, are most important.

By LIBERTY we mean being able to act and think as one believes best.

By EQUALITY we mean narrowing the gap in wealth and power between the rich and the poor.

By ECONOMIC SECURITY we mean the guarantee of a steady job and a decent income.

By SOCIAL ORDER we mean being able to live in an orderly and peaceful society, where the laws are respected and enforced.

All these things are important for our society, but sometimes we have to choose between what is more important and what is less important.

In your opinion, which is more important for our country?

LIBERTY
(understood as being able to act and think as one believes best)
OR
EQUALITY
(understood as narrowing the gap in wealth and power between the rich and the poor)

va2: If you had to decide, which do you believe is more important?

ECONOMIC SECURITY
(understood as the guarantee of a steady job and a decent income)
OR
SOCIAL ORDER
(understood as being able to live in an orderly and peaceful society, where the laws are respected and enforced)

va3:
LIBERTY
(understood as being able to act and think as one believes best)
OR

ECONOMIC SECURITY
(understood as the guarantee of a steady job and a decent income)

va4:

EQUALITY
(understood as narrowing the gap in wealth and power between the rich and the poor)
OR
SOCIAL ORDER
(understood as being able to live in an orderly and peaceful society, where the laws are respected and enforced)

va5:

LIBERTY
(understood as being able to act and think as one believes best)
OR
SOCIAL ORDER
(understood as being able to live in an orderly and peaceful society, where the laws are respected and enforced)

va6:

EQUALITY
(understood as narrowing the gap in wealth and power between the rich and the poor)
OR
ECONOMIC SECURITY
(understood as the guarantee of a steady job and a decent income)

Personal Values—Paired Comparisons

va7: Up to now we talked about what would be more important for our country. Now I would like to ask you to tell us how important, for you personally, are values or goals such as RELIGION, PROFESSIONAL SUCCESS, A GOOD FAMILY LIFE, AND PERSONAL SELF-FUL-FILLMENT.

Here also, to avoid any misunderstanding, I would first like to define what we mean by each of these concepts. Then I will ask which ones, in your opinion, are most important.

By RELIGION we mean believing and having faith in a God.

By PROFESSIONAL SUCCESS we mean being successful in one's work and being rewarded for one's abilities.

By A GOOD FAMILY LIFE we mean living in a family in which the members get along and where you feel loved and protected.

By PERSONAL SELF-FULFILLMENT we mean being able to develop one's own talents and personality to the fullest

All these things are important, but if you had to decide, which is more important to you:

RELIGION
(understood as believing and having faith in a God)
OR
PROFESSIONAL SUCCESS
(understood as being successful in one's work and rewarded for one's abilities)

va8:

A GOOD FAMILY LIFE
(understood as living in a family in which the members get along and where you feel loved and protected)
OR
PERSONAL SELF-FULFILLMENT
(understood as being able to develop one's own talents and personality to the fullest)

va9:

RELIGION
(understood as believing and having faith in a God)
OR
A GOOD FAMILY LIFE
(understood as living in a family in which the members get along and where you feel loved and protected)

va10:

PROFESSIONAL SUCCESS
(understood as being successful in one's work and rewarded for one's abilities)
OR
PERSONAL SELF-FULFILLMENT
(understood as being able to develop one's own talents and personality to the fullest.)

va11:

RELIGION
(understood as believing and having faith in a God)

OR

PERSONAL SELF-FULFILLMENT

(understood as being able to develop one's own talents and personality to the fullest.)

val2:

PROFESSIONAL SUCCESS

(understood as being successful in one's work and rewarded for one's abilities)

OR

A GOOD FAMILY LIFE

(understood as living in a family in which the members get along and where you feel loved and protected)

Conformity and Tolerance

m1: Now I will make another series of statements that reflect different ways of thinking about how to relate to other persons. For each of these statements, could you tell me if you agree strongly, agree somewhat, disagree somewhat, disagree strongly with that statement?

One should distrust those who act differently from most people.

m2: People who come to Italy should try to act like the Italians.

Rights for Disliked Groups

The question "n1" identifies which of four groups or movements the respondent liked the least. That group or movement was then mentioned in questions "n2" and "n3." If a respondent volunteered the name of some other group or movement in answering "n1," the pronoun "they" was used in questions "n2" and "n3."

n1: Now I will name some groups or movements that appear often in the news of our country.

Which of these groups OR movements do you like the least: extreme right-wing, extreme left-wing, feminists, or homosexuals?

n2: Do you think that [MOST DISLIKED GROUP] should or should not have the right to hold public rallies?

n3: Do you think that [MOST DISLIKED GROUP] should or should not have the right to spread their ideas on television?

Anti-Semitism

o1: Now I am going to read you some statements concerning various attitudes that people have about Jews. For each of these statements, could you tell me if you agree strongly, agree somewhat, disagree somewhat, or disagree strongly with that statement?

Most Jews are very ambitious and work very hard to succeed in life.

o2: Most Jews are more likely than other people to use improper practices to succeed in life.

o3: Most Jews believe that they are better than other people.

o4: Most Jews do not care about the problems of other people who are not Jewish.

Trust in Others

q1: Now let's go back and talk about general issues.

In your opinion, can most people be trusted, or do you have to be very cautious when it comes to dealing with people?

q2: Do you believe that most people are willing to help others, or do you think on the other hand that most people think only about themselves?

q3: Do you believe that most people would take advantage of you if they had the chance, or do you think on the other hand that they would do their best to act properly?

Personality Items

r1: Now I'm going to make a few more statements. For each one can you tell me whether, in your opinion, the statement is true or false?

Most people are honest primarily because they are afraid of being caught.

r2: Most people, deep down, do not like putting themselves out to help others.

r3: Considering how things are going, it is very difficult to keep up the hope of becoming someone in life.

r4: Most people make friends in the hope that they may be useful.

r5: I sometimes feel satisfied when I can break the rules and do things that nobody would expect me to do.

r6: I find it difficult to start a conversation with strangers.

r7: I sometimes pretend to know more than I really do.

r8: I have the feeling that I have often been punished without cause.

r9: I certainly don't have enough self-confidence.

r10: I have strong doubts about my ability to be a good boss.

Criteria for Deciding about Autonomy

Depending on the value of the random number variable "rsa," approximately a third of the respondents were asked the questions "s1" and "s2." Another third were asked the same two questions in reverse order. The other third were not asked those questions at all.

s1: There is a lot of discussion in Italy these days about autonomy for the regions and about the role that the central government should play.

To decide whether regional autonomy is or is not the way to go, how important do you think the goal is of improving the economic situation?

Is it very important, somewhat important, not very important, or not important at all?

s2: To decide whether regional autonomy is or is not the way to go, how important do you think the fact is that taxes collected in one region are spent in other regions?

Is it very important, somewhat important, not very important, or not important at all?

Autonomy Counterarguments

After answering "s5," respondents were presented with a counterargument. For those in favor of greater autonomy, the counterargument was either "s6" or "s7," depending on the random number variable "rsb."

For those opposed to greater autonomy, the counterargument was either "s8" or "s9," depending on the value of "rsc." Note that the second counterargument in each set is basically irrelevant.

s5: (There is a lot of discussion in Italy these days about autonomy for the regions and about the role that the central government should play.)

What do you think personally about the possibility of giving greater autonomy to the regions in Italy?
Are you very much in favor, somewhat in favor, somewhat opposed, or completely opposed?

s6: Considering that there would be a risk of increasing government bureaucracy, are you still in favor of greater autonomy for the regions, or would this make you change your mind?

s7: Considering the complexity and the uncertainty of problems in Italy nowadays, are you still in favor of greater autonomy for the regions, or would this make you change your mind?

s8: Considering that with a centralized system public services could become even less efficient than they are now, are you still opposed to greater autonomy for the regions, or would this make you change your mind?

s9: Considering the complexity and the uncertainty of problems in Italy nowadays, are you still opposed to greater autonomy for the regions, or would this make you change your mind?

European Unity Counterarguments

After answering "t1," respondents were presented with a counterargument. For those in favor of European unity, the counterargument was either "t2" or "t3," depending on the random number variable "rta." For those opposed to European unity, the counterargument was either "t4" or "t5," depending on the value of "rtb."

t1: Now let's talk about Europe and its proposed unification. Are you in favor of or opposed to the completion of European unity?

t2: Are you still in favor of European unity, even if Italian agriculture will suffer and some workers will lose their jobs, or would this make you change your mind?

t3: Are you still in favor of European unity, even if a number of Italian industries will suffer and some workers will lose their jobs, or would this make you change your mind?

t4: Are you still opposed, even considering that Italy would be isolated from other European countries and that it would be left on its own, or would this make you change your mind?

t5: Are you still opposed, even if the standard of living of many Italians would get worse, or would this make you change your mind?

Associationism

as1: Some people take part in the activities of associations or groups that carry out leisure, cultural, or sporting activities.

In the last year have you participated REGULARLY in any group or association of a cultural nature?

as2: And in the last year have you participated regularly in any group or association of a religious nature?

as3: In the last year have you participated regularly in any group or association for leisure or sports (either as a player or a fan)?

as4: In the last year have you participated regularly in any group or association that does volunteer work?

as5: In the last year have you participated regularly in any political group?

Background Variables—Part 2

a7: We're almost finished now. I have just a few more questions for statistical purposes.

What is your marital status?

v1: Do you consider yourself a member of a religion or of a church or religious group? If so, which one?

v2: How often do you go to mass or attend religious services?

a8: At present do you have a job that is a principal means of support for yourself or that helps to support your family?

a9: (IF NOT WORKING AT PRESENT, ASK:)
What is your current employment situation? Are you looking for your first job, unemployed, retired, disabled, a student, in military service, a housewife, or in some other situation?

a10: In the past, have you worked continuously for at least six months, or have you done seasonal work for at least two years?

a11: In which year did you stop working?

(CODE LAST 2 DIGITS OF THE YEAR)

a13: Can you briefly describe your present/last job? In other words can you tell me what your normal tasks and responsibilities are/were?

(OPEN-ENDED RESPONSES WERE CODED AFTER THE INTER-VIEW)

a15: Do/did you work full-time, or part-time?

a15a: Are/were you an employee, or self-employed?

a16: Can you tell me what your father's job was when you were four-teen? In other words can you tell me what type of work he did, what tasks and responsibilities he carried out?

(OPEN-ENDED RESPONSES WERE CODED AFTER THE INTER-VIEW)

a17: Can you tell me what your mother's job was when you were 14? In other words can you tell me what type of work she does, what tasks and responsibilities she carried out?

(OPEN-ENDED RESPONSES WERE CODED AFTER THE INTER-VIEW)

a18: (IF MARRIED, ASK:)
What is your husband's/wife's occupation? In other words can you tell me what type of work he/she does, what tasks and responsibilities he/she carries out?

(OPEN-ENDED RESPONSES WERE CODED AFTER THE INTER-
VIEW)

Political Ideology and Party

pol1: Speaking generally about politics, do you consider yourself to be
on the left, center-left, in the center, center-right, or on the right?

pol2: What party or political movement do you feel closest to—National
Alliance, Democratic Party of the Left, The League, Communists Re-
established, Forza Italia, the Popular Party, or some other?

pol3: Could you tell us what group you voted for in the last election for
the House, on the ballot for the representative from your district?

Was it for the Pole of Liberty, the Pole of Good Government, the
Pact for Italy, or the Progressives?

This was the last question. Thank you for your cooperation.

Notes

Chapter One

1. *Corriere Della Serra*, February 21, 1994.
2. See Tajfel, 1981; Brown, 1995. We take up this line of argument in chapter 3.
3. See, for example, the recent encyclopedic review of research on prejudice by Susan Fiske, 1998.
4. See Coenders and Scheepers, 1998.
5. Quillian, 1995.
6. See, for example, Green and Shapiro, 1994, and Friedman, 1996.
7. A wide-ranging and especially reflective collection of work on the role of mechanisms in social theory is offered by Hedström and Swedberg, 1998.
8. The questionnaire is itemized, in an English translation, in appendix VI.
9. Details of the sampling design and response rate are set out in appendix I.
10. Borradori, 1994, p. 63.

Chapter Two

1. See, for example, Rokeach, Smith, and Evans, 1960; Rokeach and Mezei, 1966; and Triandis and Davis, 1965.
2. For two of the most recent and thoughtful reviews of the contemporary research in social psychology, see Fiske, 1998, and Brewer and Brown, 1998. We have also found Duckitt, 1992, uncommonly helpful.
3. Figure 2.1 is based on Duckitt, 1992, p. 10, table 2.1. His work, if we may say again, is empirically the most comprehensive and intellectually the most open-minded review of contemporary research on prejudice, and not merely here but at many points elsewhere we have benefited from it.
4. We follow here, as at many other points, John Duckitt's review of the research literature on prejudice. See Duckitt, 1992, table 2.1, p. 10.
5. Milner, 1975, p. 9.
6. Allport, 1988, p. 9.
7. Jones, 1986, p. 288.
8. We have in mind here particularly the work of Henri Tajfel and his colleagues, which we shall examine in detail in the next chapter.
9. There is a minor ambiguity to the expression "responding negatively to members of a group by virtue of their membership in the group." In the 1970s, capitalizing on this ambiguity, research expanded the meaning of prejudice to include responding negatively to public policies intended to help members of a group. To dislike affirmative action, in this view, was just as directly a sign of prejudice as to derogate blacks. Not the least reason that this more expansive conception has been abandoned is that it renders the relation between prejudice

and policy preferences tautological. See Sniderman and Tetlock, 1986a and 1986b.

10. Hamilton, Stroessner, and Driscoll, 1994 make this point in a particularly compelling, unusually cool manner.

11. Brown, 1986, pp. 587–88.

12. Sniderman and Piazza, 1993.

13. We follow here the account of Hamilton, Stroessner, and Driscoll, 1994.

14. For a recent overview, see ibid.

15. These are the so-called Princeton studies: see Katz and Braly, 1933; Karlins, Coffman, and Walters, 1969; and Gilbert, 1951.

16. In both the original and follow-up studies, it is worth bearing in mind that although the test subjects were drawn from the same population, it is a rather special one—namely, undergraduates at Princeton.

17. Glock and his colleagues (Apostle et al., 1983) advanced the temporal variability of stereotypes as one of the principal considerations persuading them of the need to explore the use of "explanatory modes," alternative types of explanations of group differences, which they considered to operate at a deeper level and therefore to be more time-invariant.

18. The outstanding figure in this field has been Hamilton. He and his colleagues have effected a revolution, reorienting the study of stereotyping on cognitive lines. See Duckitt, 1992, p. 81.

19. Dichotomies, as here between cognitive and affective, can themselves uselessly dichotomize analyses. Those who adhere to a view of stereotyping as a cognitive process at its core recognize also the importance of affect to the analysis of prejudice (e.g., Hamilton, Stroessner, and Driscoll, 1994).

20. It is not contradictory to observe both that stereotypes often are inaccurate and that it often is difficult to demonstrate that they are.

21. It still is customary, for example, to define racism as a belief in the biological inferiority of the group. However useful as a sign of racism this was once, it is no longer.

22. Katz and his colleagues have made a plausible case that in the American context and in the stratum of the young and well educated, ambivalence toward blacks may occur (Katz and Hass, 1988; Katz, Wackenhut, and Hass, 1986). Nor do we have doubts that it occurs elsewhere. What is less obvious to us is the empirical value of the construct of ambivalence in this context. In our studies of race and American politics we sought expressly to assess it and its consequences without profit. It would be flagrantly wrong to conclude that because we did not find anything of significance there is nothing of significance to be found. But we do think that the burden of proof is on those who believe the idea of ambivalence is a useful construct in the context of prejudice to demonstrate its utility.

23. In deriving this list of personal attributes, we followed the thrust of recent measures of prejudice developed in the United States. See, particularly, the measures of racial prejudice developed in the National Race and Politics Study (RAP) and in the General Social Survey (GSS). There are a number of specific points of difference, particularly in response formats. Moreover, the GSS measure, in addition to making use of a semantic differential format (contrasting polar positive and negative descriptors on a single scale), operationally defines

prejudice as the difference in evaluative ratings of groups. Intensive analyses have persuaded us that these and other differences in measurement procedure are not of substantial consequence. See Sniderman and Carmines, 1997, for evidence on the interchangeability of the GSS and the RAP studies.

24. For an analysis of missing data, see appendix III.

25. These differences in the proportion of agreement on these items are significant at the .05 level.

26. Again, the differences in proportions of agreement on these items are significant at the .05 level.

27. The difference, whether calculated between responses to North Africans and Eastern Europeans, or between responses to Central Africans and Eastern Europeans, is statistically significant ($p < .05$).

28. Campbell and Fiske, 1959.

29. Since it was important to vary the response format as well as the item content, in the problem series the questions were asked in a yes-no format as opposed to the modified Likert agree-disagree format in the evaluative characteristic series.

30. In discussing the realistic conflict hypothesis in detail, we shall take up again the specific pattern of attributions of responsibility for social problems to Africans and Eastern Europeans distinctively.

31. For our initial causal analysis, see the "Two Flavors" model in chapter 3 and for the full examination, the "Right Shock" model in chapter 4.

32. As we noted earlier, most methods for determining the dimensionality are necessarily somewhat ad hoc. To ensure that our results are robust, we applied a number of different methods for determining the underlying dimensions of the data, in addition to the analysis of the scree plot and subsequent contribution to explained variance we discussed. An alternative method suggested for recovering the dimensionality of a set of variables suggested originally by a number of psychometricians (Kaiser, 1958; Guttman, 1954; and Harmon, 1967), is to fit up to the number of dimensions that have an eigenvalue greater than unity. In this case, the second dimension for Africans marginally meets this standard (1.07), while for Eastern Europeans it marginally does not (.99). An even stronger test is a chi-square test for additional dimensions (beyond one). In this case, the model fails the test, as we can reject the hypothesis that going from a single to two dimensions does not improve the likelihood ($p = .02$). However, in samples this large, the chi-square test will almost always reject such a hypothesis, making it less useful in this context. Another criterion suggested by Piazza (1980), among others, is that items could be combined only when they have a common explanation. Since we have not fully specified a causal structure of prejudice yet (see chapters 3 and 5), it is not yet possible to do that. However, anticipating that model, we also ran regressions of each individual item on a number of more primitive, causal variables. In this case, we found a great deal of structural stability in common parameters as we changed dependent variables among potential elements of the hostility index. A final set of tests for goodness-of-fit were also examined. Here, there are a number of options, including Akaike's Information Criterion (AIC) and Bozdogan's consistent version of the AIC. These, however, are versions of the chi-squared statistic and provide little

additional insight. Alternatively, a few practical criteria, notably Bentler and Bonnett's Normalized Fit Index (NFI) and Comparative Fit Index (CFI) are conventional measures of fit for a factor model. In general, if these indices are greater than 0.90, the model is deemed an acceptable formulation (Byrne [1994], pp. 55–57; Bentler [1989]; Bentler [1980]). By these criteria, a one-dimensional model for the attribute series is appropriate, as both yield values above .90 in all cases (for Africans, the NFI is .972 and CFI is .978, and for Eastern Europeans, the NFI is .982 and CFI is .974).

33. Krzanowski, 1988; Johnson and Wichern, 1992.

34. Possibly one of the most recent and easily one of the most thoughtful presentations of this view is offered by Cacioppo and Berntson, 1994.

35. There are circumstances in which two "factors" do emerge, one ostensibly positive, the other negative; but in the largest number of these cases, the appearance of separable positive and negative factors is a methodological artifact. See Green and Citrin, 1994.

36. Many (e.g., Green and Citrin, 1994) have observed that in certain contexts there can be directional biases in survey questions: the type of responses will vary systematically when one asks a positively "signed" or negatively "signed" question. Indeed, one of our primary reasons for including both positive and negative evaluations was to avoid a trap of correlated and systematic method error. To determine if this was indeed the case, we estimated a two-factor model with the positive attribution items as indicators of one latent variable and the negative attribution items as indicators of the second. A test, then, of a method error of this form (and bi-dimensionality) is to measure the correlation between these two. In this case, we reject the hypothesis that the two factors are identical—the chi-square statistic of 65.1 with one degree of freedom yields rejection of $p < .01$, indicating some systematic method error, even though the underlying latent variables measured *are* correlated at -0.71. Despite the fact that they are not tapping into statistically identical factors (and indeed because of correlated measurement error) we did include the positive evaluations in our subsequent analysis. In the end, the critical fact is that inclusion or exclusion of these items has little effect on the analysis: the correlation between a measure constructed based on the factor loadings and without them is .97 for both Africans and Eastern Europeans.

37. A chi-square test for a difference in the loadings yields a test statistic of 11.721 with 7 degrees of freedom, indicating that the hypothesis of equivalence is not rejected ($p = 0.11$). However, if both the loadings *and* the errors (following Bollen and Hoyle, 1990) are constrained to be identical, the chi-square statistic is 27.394 with 15 degrees of freedom, signifying that the hypothesis of equivalence should be rejected ($p = .03$) and that the variances are *not* the same across the groups.

38. Indeed, the correlation between a factor-loading weighted linear combination of the measures and a straight average of the item is .95.

39. The specific scoring algorithm is described in appendix II.

40. Here a chi-square test for the hypothesis that the loadings *and* errors are equivalent is not rejected (the chi-square statistic of 0.599 with 9 degrees of

freedom yields a p-value of .99). This indicates that the items load equivalently for the two groups.

41. Again, an alternative would be to use the factor loadings to generate an index. The correlation between our measure (using the average) and such a factor-loadings-weighted measure is .99 for Africans and 1.00 for East Europeans.

42. An alternative way to conduct this analysis would be to combine a measurement and structural analysis in a single analysis. LISREL, for example, could be employed as a means of conducting such a disaggregation. For reasons of both exposition and methodological soundness, however, we are performing the analysis of measurement and structure separately—with the causal analysis to follow in the following chapters. For confirmatory reasons, however, an analysis of a LISREL-style structural model with measurement error was conducted, as detailed in appendix V, with largely the same results.

43. In this case, the first two eigenvalues in both cases are significantly greater than one, while the third is marginally so (1.11 for Africans and 1.04 for Eastern Europeans). The practical criteria, the NFI and CFI, lend additional evidence that a one-factor model is not sufficient but a two-factor model is. In this case, for one-factor models, both the NFI and CFI yield relatively low values (for Africans, the NFI is .794 and CFI is .744, and for Eastern Europeans, the NFI is .761 and CFI is .722). A two-factor model, alternatively, yields sufficiently good fit, with both indices above 0.90 for both groups (for the two-factor model, for Africans, the NFI is .956 and CFI is .962, and for Eastern Europeans, the NFI is .944 and CFI is .927).

44. The Index of Personal Attributes and the Index of Blame for Social Problems, equally weighted, are summed to form the Index of Hostility toward Immigrants. For details of index construction, see appendix II.

45. The "Switch" experiment is thus multimethod, since it takes advantage of a pair of distinct approaches to measurement: multitrait, since each measurement approach makes use of multiple indicators; and multigroup, since all the indicators in both approaches are applied to both African and Eastern European immigrants. The estimation of evaluative consistency in the "Switch" experiment, it also is worth noting, is symmetrical. Nothing hinges on whether the ascription of negative personal characteristics is regressed on the attribution of responsibility for societal problems, or the latter is regressed on the former.

46. The similarity of intercepts between responses to Eastern European and African immigrants on the first prejudice series is the bellwether of equivalence independent of order of presentation.

47. See Campbell, 1967.

48. See Hagendoorn, 1995; Hagendoorn and Linssen, 1994; and Verkuyten, Hagendoorn, and Masson, 1996.

Chapter Three

1. See Sherif and Sherif, 1953; Sherif, White, and Harvey, 1955; and Sherif et al., 1961.

2. We describe here the paradigmatic form of the summer camp experiment.

There were different versions—one, for example, permitting initial contact across groups in the first phase—to test alternative hypotheses.

3. See Turner, 1981.

4. Hoskin, 1991.

5. It is worth observing that realistic group conflict theory holds that real threat expressly increases ethnocentrism. See LeVine and Campbell, 1972, 31–33.

6. Quillian, 1995.

7. See Asch, 1951.

8. The notoriety of his results notwithstanding, Asch himself read the findings in a more conservative fashion, observing that independence from group pressure was the modal response and rejecting conventional assertions of the hegemony of conformity pressures. For a commentary unusual for its shrewdness and conciseness, see Mutz, 1998, pp. 199–201.

9. See, for example, Tajfel, 1981.

10. Classically conceived, the authoritarianism syndrome consists of a large number of aspects—conventionality, authoritarian aggression, authoritarian submission, anti-intraception, superstition and stereotypy, power and toughness, destructiveness and cynicism, projectivity and sex. In the most influential reformulation, developed by Altemeyer, the syndrome centers on the first three. See Altemeyer, 1988.

11. See Adorno et al., 1950, pp. 35–45.

12. For an analysis of Mack uniquely, see Sanford, 1967, pp. 138–67.

13. See, for example, Oakes, Haslam, and Turner, 1994, pp. 83–84.

14. These are the conditions specifically identified by ibid., p. 83.

15. See, for example, Altemeyer, 1996.

16. Our claim is not, it should be observed, that categorization is the sole source of hostility toward immigrants. It could not be, as a moment's reflection will make plain—otherwise the distinction between prejudice and categorization would collapse, since explaining the one would be equivalent to explaining the other. Hence the arrow in figure 3.2 running from ε, the error term, to hostility to immigrants.

17. In invoking expressivism we are relying obviously on one of the classic three functions of opinions identified by Smith, Bruner, and White, 1956.

18. For the classic example of an account of prejudice centered on education and cognitively driven, see Selznick and Steinberg, 1969.

19. Lipset, 1981, offers the classic exposition of working-class authoritarianism.

20. The work of Inglehart affords the paradigmatic example of cohort-value explanatory accounts. He has produced a prodigious body of work. For an illustrative example, see Inglehart, 1990 and 1977.

21. The critical literature is voluminous, but the classic critique is by Hyman and Sheatsley, 1954. There are a number of distinguishable problems, but the one proving most potent over the longer run has been the vulnerability of the standard survey measure of authoritarianism, the F-scale, to acquiescence. There have been valiant efforts to remedy the problem by counterbalancing the F-

scale, with discouraging results. For a recent review, see Duckitt, 1992, pp. 198–99.

22. This general line of argument was inspired by Henri Tajfel and has been pressed home by a number of his students. See, for example, Billig, 1976 and Brown, 1995.

23. See Minard, 1952.

24. Seago, 1947.

25. Sales, 1972.

26. Brown, 1995, p. 18

27. Lipset, 1981.

28. Selznick and Steinberg, 1969.

29. For the most recent report of this innovative research program, see Marcus et al., 1995.

30. It is worth underlining that in speaking of research on personality and group prejudice, we have in mind the vast literature in psychology and social psychology that examines prejudice per se. Studies of political tolerance, notwithstanding the common use of the term tolerance, are targeted at a behaviorally distinct phenomenon, and the relevance of research on political tolerance, if any, to studies of prejudice has yet to be established.

31. We weighed this alternative with special care, given our own studies of personality and political belief. See Sniderman, 1975.

32. Published translated versions with manuals and established norms are available for the United States, France, Great Britain, Italy, and Japan, as well as foreign-language editions used in active research in China (three dialects), Israel, Poland, and Portugal, among many others.

33. The Institute of Personality and Social Research (IPSR) is a unit of the University of California, Berkeley.

34. The approaches to assessment include various personality self-report measures, interviews, observers trait ratings, staff Adjective Check List and California Q-Set descriptions, interviewer checklists, behavior ratings in controlled situations, and objective life-history information.

35. The CPI Tolerance scale was derived from an early Anti-Semitism scale (Gough, 1951a, 1951b, 1951c). The scale was constructed by contrasting groups of students who scored highest and lowest on the Levinson-Sanford Anti-Semitism scale. Minnesota Multi-Phasic items (MMPI) were selected for inclusion on the scale, which discriminated between these two groups. Later, four MMPI items were discarded and replaced with CPI items. In a recent CPI revision, the 32-item To scale was updated by dropping 10 items and replaced these with 10 other CPI items. The correlation between the old and new is .91 for 1,000 males and .93 for 1,000 females. Stability coefficients are in the range of .88 for 1–4 weeks test-retest and .68 for long-term (one-year) test-retest.

36. Five of the thirty-two Tolerance items were chosen, relying on two selection criteria: (1) high item-total correlations, to maximize construct validity; and (2) low inter-item correlations, to maximize comprehensiveness of coverage within the trait domain. The correlation of To5 with the full Tolerance scale is .81 and .83 for males and females respectively. We want to thank Kevin Lanning for carrying out the item-selection analysis.

37. The standard CPI item format is true-false, not agree-disagree. The five items selected are numbers 94, 136, 209, 219, and 294.

38. For a full discussion of the psychological profile of To5 scorers, together with supporting statistical results, see the special report prepared by Pamela Bradley. We want to thank her for her meticulous analysis and specially acknowledge that we rely on her report here to highlight some of their most telling characteristics.

39. Occupational status was then recoded as described in appendix II. A number of such codings were tested, including the use of dummy variables. All led to substantively similar results in the following analyses.

40. Tajfel, 1981, pp. 241–42.

41. The items are selected from a larger set originally advertised by Pettigrew, 1958, as a measure of conformity to societal values. As inspection of the manifest content will make plain, the items do not mention any particular values—for example, individualism, or order, or property rights, or civil rights—and so cannot possibly assess the extent to which individuals conform to the core values, whatever these may be, of the society to which they belong.

42. The largest correlation between the distrust item in the Categorization Index and any of the Mistust of People items is .17.

43. Marilyn Brewer has played a pioneering role in establishing the independence of ingroup identification and outgroup hate. For a recent statement, see Brewer, 1999.

44. See, for example, Mummendey et al., 1992.

45. These are standard measures taken from the American National Elections Studies.

46. Berlin, 1969, is the seminal work. For an exposition of the idea of value pluralism applied to the politics of rights, see Sniderman et al., 1996.

47. By way of scoring the index, a point each was given when a respondent chose economic security in preference either to equality or to liberty. Scores thus range from zero to two.

48. Rosenberg, 1956.

49. Endogeneity makes OLS estimates inconsistent for equations 3.3 and 3.4 only if the errors are correlated with those in the earlier equations. To test whether this is the case, we employ a Durbin-Wu-Hausman (DWH) test for endogeneity. Using the instrumental variables estimator we outlined earlier, we estimate equations 3.3 and 3.4 both by OLS and 2SLS. With no endogeneity (the null hypothesis), both OLS and 2SLS are consistent. With endogeneity (the alternative hypothesis) only 2SLS is consistent. Thus, per the DWH test, the Wald statistic

$$W = (\mathbf{b}_{OLS} - \mathbf{b}_{2SLS})'(\mathbf{V}_{OLS} - \mathbf{V}_{2SLS})^{-1}(\mathbf{b}_{OLS} - \mathbf{b}_{2SLS})$$

is distributed $\chi^2(k)$ where k is the number of parameters, $\mathbf{b}_{OLS}$ is the coefficient vector estimated by OLS, V_{OLS} the variance-covariance matrix estimated by OLS and $\mathbf{b}_{2SLS}$, and $\mathbf{V}_{2SLS}$ analogously defined for 2SLS. These chi-squared statistics are 7.89 for equation 3.3 and 36.69 for equation 3.4, yielding rejection of uncorrelated errors (with p = .09 and p = .01 respectively).

50. Greene, 1993, chapter 17; Davidson and MacKinnon, 1993.

51. The smallest t-statistic in absolute value in these auxiliary regressions is 2.12.

52. Two comments about our presentation of the results bear noting. First, in all of the analysis we estimate the model on the full sample of available respondents. We do this in order to use as much information as possible. This leads to unequal sample sizes in the individual equations we estimate, potentially raising concerns about the effects of missing data. We allay these concerns by two facts. We also estimated all of the models on the intersection of single-equation samples (in other words, estimated all of the models based on the same sample) and obtained identical results. In addition, as we outline in appendix III, we have been unable to find any systematic biases in item-response rates, which tempers concerns about selection bias. Second, we report p-values based on one-tailed tests. This is appropriate since our hypotheses predict not only the significance of effects but also the direction. We also report t-statistics, however, so readers can draw their own inferences about the results.

53. See Altemeyer, 1988.

54. The correlation between education and occupational status for all respondents is .34, and for respondents in the workforce, .59.

55. To examine the relation between status and hostility in more detail, the effects of occupational status were also estimated using "dummy" variables to determine whether the effect of each stratum, considered by itself, is significant or not. Two points in particular stand out. On the one side, those in the agricultural sector appear distinctively susceptible to prejudice; on the other, those in the very highest occupational stratum—entrepreneurs and professionals—are *not* the least vulnerable to prejudice.

56. This result reflects, we believe, the special status of cynicism in Italian culture. It is worth underlining that nothing in the overall argument about the centrality of categorization, and in particular the integration of expressive and instrumental mediators, hinges on this.

57. The apparent causal "leakage," in the form of the direct effects of education and age on categorization, evaporates in the full specification. See table 4.4.

58. To aficionados of symmetry it may seem that if we examine the prejudice of Northerners against Southerners, we should examine that of Southerners against Northerners. There is, however, no comparable institutionalization of prejudice, a state of affairs that betrays itself in our data in the lack of structure of Southerners' evaluative responses to Northerners.

59. Here we define "Northern Italians" as those respondents who were born in Rome or farther north and whose fathers were also born in Rome or farther north. We used alternative, less expansive definitions, without significant difference in results.

60. The measure of hostility toward Southern Italians is built in parallel fashion to that of hostility toward immigrants. It consists of two series of items, equally weighted. The first series involves the personal attributes series, repeated exactly as for immigrants, except for omission of the last descriptor "inferior by nature." The second series consists of three items similar to the social problem series. They are: "People of the North have a greater commitment to work than people of the South" (given as a reason to explain why Southern Italians are

worse-off than Northern Italians: strongly agree, somewhat agree, somewhat disagree, strongly disagree); "Too much government money has been spent and is still being spent for the South" (strongly agree, somewhat agree, somewhat disagree, strongly disagree); and "A great part of the hostility of the North toward the South is due to the fact that most government jobs are filled by Southerners" (strongly agree, somewhat agree, somewhat disagree, strongly disagree).

61. Note here that we report the model for hostility using the second model from table 3.4, as this was both robust and parsimonious. This is one case, however, where there are limits on robustness, since the fully specified model yields less convincing results.

62. Allport, 1988.

Chapter Four

1. See, for example, Gregor, 1969. It would be a pity, we would add, for English readers not to consult the historical studies of Denis Mack Smith—for example, 1982 and 1998.

2. See de Resedo, 1991.

3. The political premise of Craxi's advice was the constitutional requirement for 51 percent of voters to participate for a referendum to be valid.

4. The percentages reported from our survey are based on those respondents who both acknowledged voting and were willing to divulge the party they voted for. In our survey, 22 percent of the respondents refused to answer the question about vote choice, which is not unusual for Italian surveys. An additional 10 percent of respondents said that they had not voted in the election.

5. The exact wording is: "Speaking generally about politics, do you consider yourself to be on the left, center-left, in the center, center-right, or on the right?" Sixty-five percent classified themselves: of these, 29.8 percent classified themselves as left, 14.3 percent center-left, 17.9 in the center, 20.8 percent as center-right, and 17.2 percent as right.

6. The models are estimated by OLS. This imposes a structure on the vote choice that assumes that vote choice is a continuous variable with a particular scaling. Alternative, and perhaps more appropriate albeit less parsimonious, models were also employed: ordered probit and multinomial logit (Greene, 1993). Both of these models treat vote choice as a discrete variable. Estimation by these methods yields substantively identical conclusions.

7. We are not suggesting that the Italian results are exceptional for the European context; only that the contrast with the American context is striking.

8. See, for example, the discussion of the sophistication-interaction hypothesis in Sniderman, Brody, and Tetlock, 1991.

9. Parallel to defining the Pact for Italy as a center choice in the Italian election, support for Ross Perot was defined as a center choice in the 1992 U.S. presidential election. Also to maximize comparability, in both cases ideological self-identification was treated categorically—on the left or liberal, center, on the right or conservative, with those not classifying themselves classified in the center, and education in both countries was divided into the same three strata—those with less than high school, high school graduates, and those with some college or more.

10. Attached to this statement is an "all things equal" clause, obviously, including, among other conditions, equivalence of turnout.

11. See Van Deth and Scarborough, 1995, in our judgment the best single source now available for summarizing research on values and politics.

12. In particular, because our interest is in the politics of prejudice, we pay no direct attention to a conception of the new right, important in other contexts, which emphasizes the importance of the market and involves a reaction to social and sexual liberation (King, 1987). The dimensions we do concentrate on, equalitarianism and authoritarian values, are, we believe, implicated in this "new" right, but to what extent and in exactly what way remains to be determined.

13. Knutsen, 1995.

14. Frankfurt, 1988.

15. In thinking about the components of the left-right cleavage, we have been particularly influenced by Grunberg and Schweisguth, 1990. See also Knutsen, 1995, for a valuable review.

16. The exact measurement procedure for the "forced choice, paired comparison" method is shown in the questionnaire reproduced in appendix VI.

17. V. O. Key, to our knowledge, originally suggested this hypothesis. And it was the heart of the classic papers of McClosky, Hoffman, and O'Hara, 1960, and Converse, 1964. For imaginative recent treatments, see Delli Carpini and Keeter, 1996, and Zaller, 1992.

18. See, for example, the arguments on the sophistication-interaction hypothesis in Sniderman, Brody, and Tetlock, 1991.

19. See ibid., especially chapter 9, "Information and Electoral Choice."

20. For a seminal analysis of the politics of the new right, see Kitschelt, 1995.

21. We say comparatively because the economic apprehension mediator in the "Two Flavors" model provides an obvious conduit for a dynamic account.

22. See Coenders and Scheepers, 1998. We have benefited much from the research of Scheepers, and wish to acknowledge its direction on a number of points.

23. See Quillian, 1995.

24. See appendix IV on the selection of instruments.

25. The highly skewed marginals on at least two of the three trust items—with nearly 80 percent of the sample declaring that "you have to be very cautious when it comes to dealing with people," and 70 percent believing that "most people think only about themselves"—underline the need for caution.

Chapter Five

1. Christie and Jahoda, 1954.

2. We should again like to salute the work of Altemeyer.

3. And if there is a need for replication as a matter of principle, it holds with special force for estimations like two-stage least squares when the instruments were chosen ex post rather than selected ex ante.

4. Sullivan and his colleagues were concerned specifically with political tolerance, but intolerance as a political problem in modern societies manifestly

encompasses a variety of forms of intolerance. See Sullivan, Piereson, and Marcus, 1982.

5. Ibid., p. 262, italics in original.

6. Even this is a matter of debate. For an argument on the consistency of liberalism as a source of political tolerance across the political spectrum, see Sniderman et al., 1989.

7. Quoted by Duckitt, 1992, p. 67.

8. For instructive commentary on features of the concept of ethnocentrism more relevant to analysis from an anthropological perspective, see LeVine and Campbell, 1972.

9. Sumner, 1906, pp. 12–13.

10. Brewer and Kramer, 1985.

11. Sumner, 1906, pp. 12–13.

12. Expressed in terms of the standard product moment coefficient, the correlation between the two measures of negative personal characteristics is .32 and .53 for Northern and Southern Italians, respectively.

13. Hofstadter, 1967.

Appendix III

1. From the 1991 National Race Survey (based on s-series; whites only).

2. The appropriate test statistic for differences in proportions is a chi-square value. In this case, we compare 25.37 to the critical value (at a significance level of .05) of 26.30 and cannot reject the hypothesis that the proportions are the same.

3. Individuals who did not respond to any of the eight questions are excluded.

Appendix V

1. We address the issue of instrument selection in appendix IV.

2. In chapter 2 we undertake an exhaustive analysis of the appropriate way to measure our constructs and to determine the degree of measurement error. That analysis is largely independent of the structural models we present in chapters 3 and 4. In this section, we join these two efforts, by simultaneously estimating a measurement and structural model, in order to ensure that our two-step procedure is robust.

3. We use the notation for the indicators as outlined in appendices II and VI. As the primary scaling variable, we chose the item that had the greatest inter-item correlation. The choice of the scaling variables was tested, and the results were largely very robust against alternative choices.

4. Note that the instruments used here include those "outside of the model," which we use in chapter 3 and discuss in appendix IV. Here we replicate the same structural analysis, but now account for measurement error in our latent variables. This requires the use of the same exogenous instruments as in the earlier estimation.

5. Note that here, some instruments that were valid in the (mis-specified) "Two Flavors" model are no longer valid since now there is a "circle of causal-

ity" among conformity, authority values, and hostility. As we described before, it is invalid to use indicators for constructs that occur at "equivalent or higher" levels of the causal chain as instruments in a particular equation. The inclusion of authority values as a predictor of conformity, therefore, means we can no longer validly use $m1$ as an instrument in the hostility equation. Further, although it might be valid to use $h1$ as an instrument, we omit it in the analysis here, since again it determines a construct at the highest level of the causal chain. However, including it as an instrument does not affect the results.

Bibliography

Ackerman, N., and M. Jahoda. 1950. *Anti-Semitism and Emotional Disorders: A Psycho-analytic Interpretation.* New York: Harper.

Adorno, Theodor, Else Frenkel-Brunswick, Daniel Levinson, and R. Nevitt Sanford. 1950. *The Authoritarian Personality.* New York: Harper.

Allport, Gordon. 1954. *The Nature of Prejudice.* Reading, MA: Addison-Wesley.

———. 1988. *The Nature of Prejudice.* Reading, Mass.: Addison-Wesley.

Altemeyer, Robert. 1981. *Right-Wing Authoritarianism.* Winnipeg: University of Manitoba Press.

———. 1988. *Enemies of Freedom: Understanding Right-Wing Authoritarianism.* San Francisco: Jossey-Bass.

———. 1996. *The Authoritarian Specter.* Cambridge, Mass.: Harvard University Press.

Apostle, Richard A., Charles Y. Glock, Thomas Piazza, and Marijean Suelzle. 1983. *The Anatomy of Racial Attitudes.* Berkeley: University of California Press.

Asch, Solomon E. 1951. "Effects of Group Pressure upon the Modification and Distortion of Judgment." In *Groups, Leadership and Men,* ed. Harold Guetzkow. Pittsburgh: The Carnegie Press.

Bentler, Peter M. 1980. "Multivariate Analysis with Latent Variables: Causal Modeling." *Annual Review of Psychology* 31:419–456.

———. 1989. *EQS Structural Equations Program Manual.* Los Angeles: BMDP Statistical Software.

Berlin, Isaiah. 1969. "Two Concepts of Liberty." In his *Four Essays on Liberty.* Oxford: Oxford University Press. 118–72.

Billig, Michael. 1976. *Social Psychology and Intergroup Relations.* London: Academic Press.

Bollen, Kenneth A. 1993. "Liberal Democracy: Vaidity and Method Factors in Cross-National Measures." *American Journal of Political Science* 37:1207–26.

——— 1996. "An Alternative 2SLS Estimator for Latent Variable Models." *Psychometrika* 61:109–21.

Bollen, Kenneth, and Rick H. Hoyle. 1990. "Perceived Cohesion: A Conceptual and Empirical Examination: Group Members' Perceptions of Their Cohesion to a Particular Group." *Social Forces* 69:479–504.

Bonacich, E. 1972. "A Theory of Ethnic Antagonism: The Split Labor Market." *American Sociological Review* 37: 447–559.

Borradori, Giovanna. 1994. *The American Philospher: Conversations with Quine, Davidson, Putnam, Nozick, Danto, Rorty, Cavell, MacIntyre and Kuhn.* Chicago: University of Chicago Press.

Brewer, Marilynn B. 1999. "The Psychology of Prejudice: Ingroup Love or Outgroup Hate?" *Journal of Social Issues,* forthcoming.

Brewer, Marilynn B., and Rupert J. Brown. 1998. "Intergroup Relations." In *The Handbook of Social Psychology*. Vol. 2. 4yh ed., ed. Daniel T. Gilbert, Susan T. Fiske, and Gardner Lindzey. Boston: McGraw-Hill. 554–94.

Brewer, Marilynn, and Roderick M. Kramer. 1985. "The Psychology of Intergroup Attitudes and Behavior." *Annual Review of Psychology* 36:219–43.

Brown, Roger. 1986. *Social Psychology*. New York: Free Press.

Brown, Rupert. 1995. *Prejudice: Its Social Psychology*. Cambridge, Mass.: Blackwell.

Buss, A. H. 1961. *The Psychology of Aggression*. New York: Wiley.

Byrne, Barbara M. 1994. *Structural Equation Modeling with EQS and EQS/Windows: Basic Concepts, Applications, and Programming*. Thousand Oaks, CA: Sage Publications.

Cacioppo, John T., and Garry G. Berntson, 1994. "Relationship between Attitudes and Evaluative Space: A Critical Review, with Emphasis on the Separability of Positive and Negative Substrates." *Psychological Bulletin* 115:401–23.

Campbell, Donald T. 1967. "Stereotypes and the Perception of Group Differences." *American Psychologist* 22:817–29.

Campbell, Donald T., and Donald W. Fiske. 1959. "Convergent and Discriminant Validation by the Multitrait-Multimethod Matrix." *Psychological Bulletin* 56:81–105.

Christie, Richard, and Marie Jahoda, eds. 1954. *Studies in the Scope and Method of "The Authoritarian Personality."* New York: Free Press.

Coenders, Marcel, and Peer Scheepers. 1998. "Support for Ethnic Discrimination in the Netherlands, 1979–1993: Effects of Period, Cohort, and Individual Characteristics." *European Sociological Review*. 14, no. 4:405–22.

Converse, Philip E. 1964. "The Nature of Belief Systems in Mass Publics." In *Ideology and Discontent*, ed. David E. Apter. New York: Free Press. 206–61.

Davidson, Russell, and James G. MacKinnon. 1993. *Estimation and Inference in Econometrics*. New York: Oxford University Press.

Delli Carpini, Michael X., and Scott Keeter. 1996. *What Americans Know about Politics and Why It Matters*. New Haven: Yale University Press.

de Resedo, Riccardo Fragassi. 1991. *Leghismo*. Sesto Fiorentino, FI: Edizioni Agemina.

DiPalma, Giuseppe, and Herbert McClosky. 1970. "Personality and Conformity: The Learning of Political Attitudes." *American Political Science Review* 64:1054–73.

Duckitt, John. 1992. *The Social Psychology of Prejudice*. New York: Praeger.

Fiske, Susan T. 1998. "Stereotyping, Prejudice, and Discrimination." In *The Handbook of Social Psychology*. Vol. 2. 4th ed., ed. Daniel T. Gilbert, Susan T. Fiske, and Gardner Lindzey. Boston: McGraw-Hill. 357–411.

Forbes, H. D. 1985. *Nationalism, Ethnocentrism, and Personality: Social Science and Critical Theory*. Chicago: University of Chicago Press.

Frankfurt, Harry, G. 1988. *The Importance of What We Care About: Philosophical Essays*. New York: Cambridge University Press.

Friedman, Jeffrey, ed. 1996. *The Rational Choice Controversy: Economic Models of Politics Reconsidered*. New Haven: Yale University Press.

Gilbert, G. M. 1951. "Stereotype Persistence and Change among College Students." *Journal of Abnormal and Social Psychology* 46:245–54.

Gough, Harrison G. 1951a. "Studies of Social Intolerance: II. A Personality Scale for Anti-Semitism." *Journal of Social Psychology* 33:247–55.

_____. 1951b. "Studies of Social Intolerance: III. Relationship of the *Pr* Scale to Other Variables" *Journal of Social Psychology* 33:257–62.

_____. 1951c. "Studies of Social Intolerance: IV. Related Social Attitudes." *Journal of Social Psychology* 33:263–69.

Green, Donald P., and Jack Citrin. 1994. "Measurement Error and the Structure of Attitudes: Are Positive and Negative Judgments Opposites?" *American Journal of Political Science* 38:256–81.

_____. and Ian Shapiro. 1994. *Pathologies of Rational Choice Theory: A Critique of Applications in Political Science*. New Haven: Yale University Press.

Greene, William H. 1993. *Econometric Analysis*. 2d ed. New York: Macmillan.

Gregor, A. James. 1969. *The Ideology of Fascism: The Rationale of Totalitarianism*. Princeton: Princeton University Press.

Grunberg, Gerard, and Etienne Schweisguth. 1990. "Liberalisme Culturel, Liberalisme Economique." In *L'Electeur Français en Questions*, ed. Daniel Boy and Nonna Mayer. Paris: Presses de la Fondation Nationale des Sciences Politiques. 45–64.

Guttman, Louis. 1954. "Some Necessary Conditions for Common Factor Analysis." *Psychmetrika* 19:149.

Hagendoorn, Louk. 1995. "Intergroup Biases in Multiple Group Systems: The Perception of Ethnic Hierarchies." *European Review of Social Psychology* 6:199–228.

Hagendoorn, Louk, and H. Linssen. 1994. "National Characteristics and National Stereotypes: A Seven-Nation Comparative Study." In *Cross-National Perspectives on Nationality, Identity and Ethnicity*, ed. R. Farnen. New Brunswick, N.J.: Transaction. 103–36.

Hamilton, David L., Steven J. Stroessner, and Denise M. Driscoll. 1994. "Social Cognition and the Study of Stereotyping." In *Social Cognition: Impact on Social Psychology*, ed. Patricia G. Devine, David L. Hamilton and Thomas M. Ostrom. New York: Academic Press. 292–323.

Harding, J., H. Proshansky, B. Kutner, and I. Chein. 1969. "Prejudice and Ethnic Relations." In *The Handbook of Social Psychology Vol. 5*, ed. G. Lindzey and E. Arsonon. Reading, MA: Addison-Wesley. 1–76.

Harmon, H. H. 1967. *Modern Factor Analysis*. Chicago: University of Chicago Press.

Hedström, Peter, and Richard Swedberg, eds. 1998. *Social Mechanisms: An Analytical Approach to Social Theory*. Cambridge: Cambridge University Press.

Hofstadter, Richard. 1967. *The Paranoid Style in American Politics*. New York: Vintage Books.

Hoskin, Marilyn. 1991. *New Immigrants and Democratic Society: Minority Integration in Western Democracies*. New York: Praeger.

Hyman, Herbert H., and Paul B. Sheatsley. 1954. "'The Authoritarian Personality'—A Methodological Critique." In *Studies in the Scope and Method of*

"*The Authoritarian Personality*," ed. Richard Christie and Marie Jahoda. New York: Free Press. 35–39.

Inglehart, Ronald. 1977. *The Silent Revolution: Changing Values and Political Styles among Western Publics.* Princeton: Princeton University Press.

———. 1990. *Culture Shift in Advanced Industrial Society.* Princeton: Princeton University Press.

Johnson, Richard A., and Dean W. Wichern. 1992. *Applied Multivariate Statistical Analysis.* 3rd ed. Englewood Cliffs, N.J.: Prentice Hall.

Jones, James M. 1986. "Racism: A Cultural Analysis of the Problem." In *Prejudice, Discrimination, and Racism*, ed. John F. Dovidio and Samuel L. Gartner. New York: Academic Press.

Jöreskog, Karl G., and Dag Sörbom. 1993. *LISREL 8: Structural Equation Modeling with the SIMPLIS Command Language.* Chicago: Scientific Software International.

Kaiser, Henry F. 1958. "The Varimax Criterion for Analytical Rotation in Factor Analysis." *Psychometrika* 23:187–201.

Karlins, Marvin, Thomas L. Coffman, and Gary Walters. 1969. "On the Fading of Social Stereotypes: Studies in Three Generations of College Students." *Journal of Personality and Social Psychology* 13:1–16.

Katz, Daniel, and Kenneth Braly. 1933. "Racial Stereotypes of One Hundred College Students." *Journal of Abnormal and Social Psychology* 28:280–90.

Katz, I., and R. G. Hass. 1988. "Racial Ambivalence and Value Conflict: Correlational and Priming Studies of Dual Cognitive Structures." *Journal of Personality and Social Psychology* 55:893–905.

Katz, I, J. Wackenhut, and R. G. Hass. 1986. "Racial Ambivalence, Value Duality and Behavior." In *Prejudice, Discrimination, and Racism*, ed. J. F. Dovidio and S. L. Gaertner. San Diego: Academic Press. 35–60.

Kelman, H. J., and T. Pettigrew. 1959. "How to Understand Prejudice." *Commentary* 28: 421–36.

King, Desmond S. 1987. *The New Right: Politics, Markets, and Citizenship.* Basingstoke, Eng.: MacMillan Education.

Kitschelt, Herbert. 1995. *The Radical Right in Western Europe: A Comparative Analysis.* Ann Arbor: University of Michigan Press.

Klineberg, O. 1968. "Prejudice: The Concept." In *Encyclopedia of the Social Sciences.* Vol. 12. Ed. D. Sills. New York: MacMillan. 439–48.

Knutsen, Oddjorn. 1995. "Left-Right Materialist Value Orientations." In *The Impact of Values*, ed. Jan W. Van Deth and Elinor Scarbrough. Oxford: Oxford University Press. 160–96.

Krech, D., Crutchfield, R., and E. Ballachey. 1962. *Individual in Society.* New York: McGraw-Hill.

Krzanowski, W. J. 1988. *Principles of Multivariate Analysis: A User's Perspective.* New York: Oxford University Press.

Levitin, Teresa E., and Warren E. Miller. 1979. "Ideological Interpretations of Presidential Elections." *American Political Science Review* 73:751–71.

LeVine, Robert A., and Donald T. Campbell. 1972. *Ethnocentrism: Theories of Conflict, Ethnic Attitudes, and Group Behavior.* New York: Wiley.

Lipset, Seymor Martin. 1981. *Political Man: The Social Bases of Politics.* Baltimore: Johns Hopkins University Press.

Mack Smith, Denis. 1982. *Mussolini.* New York: Knopf.

———. 1998. *History of Italy.* New Haven: Yale University Press.

Marcus, George E., John L. Sullivan, Elizabeth Theiss-Morse, and Sandra L. Wood. 1995. *With Malice toward Some: How People Make Civil Liberties Judgments.* New York: Cambridge University Press.

McClosky, Herbert, Paul J. Hoffman, and Rosemary O'Hara. 1960. "Issue Conflict and Consensus among Party Leaders and Followers." *American Political Science Review* 54:406–27.

Milner, David. 1975. *Children and Race.* Harmondsworth, Eng.: Penguin.

Minard, Ralph D. 1952. "Race Relationships in the Pocahontas Coal Field." *Journal of Social Issues* 8:29–44.

Mummendey, A., B. Simon, C. Dietze, M. Grunert, G. Haeger, S. Kessler, S. Lettgen, and S. Schaferhoff. 1992. "Categorization Is Not Enough: Intergroup Discrimination in Negative Outcome Allocations." *Journal of Experimental Social Psychology* 28:125–44.

Mutz, Diana. 1998. *Impersonal Influence: How Perceptions of Mass Collectives Affect Political Attitudes.* New York: Cambridge University Press.

Oakes, Penelope J., S. Alexander Haslam, and John C. Turner. 1994. *Stereotyping and Social Reality.* Cambridge, Mass.: Blackwell.

Pettigrew, Thomas E. 1958. "Personality and Sociocultural Factors in Intergroup Attitudes: A Cross-National Comparison." *Journal of Conflict Resolution* 2:29–42.

Piazza, Thomas, 1980. "The Analysis of Attitude Items." *American Journal of Sociology* 88:584–603.

Piazza, Thomas, Paul M. Sniderman, and Philip E. Tetlock. 1989. "Analysis of the Dynamics of Political Reasoning: A General Purpose Computer-Assisted Methodology." In *Political Analysis,* Vol. 1. ed. James Stimson. Ann Arbor: University of Michigan Press. 99–120.

Putnam, Robert D. 1993. *Making Democracy Work: Civic Traditions in Modern Italy.* Princeton: Princeton University Press.

Quillian, Lincoln. 1995. "Prejudice as a Response to Perceived Group Threat: Population Composition and Anti-Immigrant and Racial Prejudice in Europe." *American Sociological Review* 60:586–612.

Rokeach, Milton. 1973. *The Nature of Human Values.* New York: Free Press.

———, and L. Mezei. 1966. "Race and Shared Belief as Factors in Social Choice." *Science* 151:167–72.

Rokeach, Milton, P. Smith, and R. Evans, eds. 1960. "Two Kinds of Prejudice or One?" In *The Open and the Closed Mind.* New York: Basic Books. 132–68.

Rose, S. 1951. *The Roots of Prejudice.* Paris: UNESCO.

Rosenberg, Morris. 1956. "Misanthropy and Political Ideology." *American Sociological Review* 21:690–95.

Sales, S. M. 1972. "Economic Threat as a Determinant of Conversion Rates to Authoritarian and Non-Authoritarian Churches." *Journal of Personality and Social Psychology* 23:420–28.

Sanford, Nevitt. 1967. *Self and Society*. New York: Atherton Press.

Seago, Dorothy W. 1947. "Stereotypes: Before Pearl Harbor and After." *Journal of Social Psychology* 23:55–63.

Selznick, Gertrude, and Stephen Steinberg. 1969. *The Tenacity of Prejudice: Anti-Semitism in Contemporary America*. New York: Harper and Row.

Sherif, Muzafer, and Carolyn W. Sherif. 1953. *Groups in Harmony and Tension: An Integration of Studies on Intergroup Relations*. New York: Octagon Books.

Sherif, Muzafer, B. Jack White, and O. J. Harvey. 1955. "Status in Experimentally Produced Groups." *American Journal of Sociology* 60:370–79.

Sherif, Muzafer, O. J. Harvey, B. Jack White, W. R. Hood, and Carolyn W. Sherif. 1961. *Intergroup Conflict and Cooperation: The Robbers Cave Experiment*. Norman: University of Oklahoma Press.

Simpson, G. E., and J. M. Yinger. 1985. *Racial and Cultural Minorities: An Analysis of Prejudice and Discrimination*. 5th ed. New York: Plenum.

Smith, M. Brewster, Jerome S. Bruner, and Robert W. White. 1956. *Opinions and Personality*. New York: Wiley.

Sniderman, Paul M. 1975. *Personality and Democratic Politics*. Berkeley: University of California Press.

———. 1993. "The New Look in Public Opinion Research." In *The State of The Discipline II*, ed. Ada Finifter. Washington, D.C.: The American Political Science Association.

Sniderman, Paul M. and Philip E. Tetlock, eds. 1986a. "Symbolic Racism: Problems of Political Motive Attribution." *Journal of Social Issues* 42:129–50.

———. 1986b. "Reflections on American Racism." *Journal of Social Issues* 42:173–88.

Sniderman, Paul M., and Thomas Piazza. 1993. *The Scar of Race*. Cambridge, Mass.: Harvard University Press.

Sniderman, Paul M., and Douglas Grob. 1996. "Innovations in Experimental Design in General Population Attitude Surveys." *Annual Review of Sociology* 22:377–99.

Sniderman, Paul M., and Edward G. Carmines. 1997. *Reaching beyond Race*. Cambridge, Mass.: Harvard University Press.

Sniderman, Paul M., Joseph F. Fletcher, Peter Russell, and Philip E. Tetlock. 1996. *The Clash of Rights: Liberty, Equality, and Legitimacy in Pluralist Democracy*. New Haven: Yale University Press.

Sniderman, Paul M., Richard A. Brody, and Philip E. Tetlock, eds. 1991. *Reasoning and Choice: Explorations in Political Psychology*. Cambridge: Cambridge University Press.

Sniderman, Paul M., Philip E. Tetlock, James M. Glaser, Donald P. Green, and Michael Hout. 1989. "Principled Tolerance and Mass Publics." *British Journal of Political Science* 19:25–45.

Staiger, Douglas, and James H. Stock. 1997. "Instrumental Variables Regression with Weak Instruments." *Econometrica* 65, no. 3:557–59.

Sullivan, John L., James Piereson, and George E. Marcus. 1982. *Political Tolerance and American Politics*. Chicago: University of Chicago Press.

Sumner, William G. 1906. *Folkways*. New York: Ginn.

Tajfel, Henri. 1981. *Human Groups and Social Categories: Studies in Social Psychology.* Cambridge: Cambridge University Press.

Triandis, H. C., and E. E. Davis. 1965. "Race and Belief as Determinants of Behavioral Intentions." *Journal of Personality and Social Psychology* 2:715–26.

Turner, John C. 1981. "The Experimental Social Psychology of Intergroup Behaviour." In Intergroup Behavior. Vol. 2. Ed. J. Turner and H. Giles. Oxford: Blackwell. 66–101.

Van Deth, Jan W., and Elinor Scarbrough, eds. 1995. *The Impact of Values.* Oxford: Oxford University Press.

Verkuyten, M., L. Hagendoorn, and C. Masson. 1996. "The Ethnic Hierarchy among Majority and Minority Youth in the Netherlands." *Journal of Applied Social Psychology* 26:1104–18.

Young-Bruehl, Elizabeth. 1996. *The Anatomy of Prejudices.* Cambridge, Mass.: Harvard University Press.

Zaller, John R. 1992. *The Nature and Origins of Mass Opinion.* New York: Cambridge University Press.